The
Dakota Hunter

The Dakota Hunter

In Search of the LEGENDARY DC-3 on the Last Frontiers

HANS WIESMAN

CASEMATE
Philadelphia & Oxford

Published in the United States of America and
Great Britain in 2015 by
CASEMATE PUBLISHERS
908 Darby Road, Havertown, PA 19083
and
10 Hythe Bridge Street, Oxford, OX1 2EW

Copyright 2015 © Hans Wiesman

ISBN 978-1-61200-258-3
Digital Edition: ISBN 978-1-61200-259-0

Cataloging-in-publication data is available from the Library of Congress and the
British Library.

Book design by Ian Hughes, www.mousematdesign.com

Front cover photo: courtesy of Hjarald Agnes, www. Facebook.com/newdefltblue
Back cover photo: courtesy of Rico Besserdich
Photograph on pages 2/3 © Ruud Duk

10 9 8 7 6 5 4 3 2 1

Printed and bound in India by Replika Press Pvt. Ltd.

For a complete list of Casemate titles please contact:

CASEMATE PUBLISHERS (US)
Telephone (610) 853-9131, Fax (610) 853-9146
E-mail: casemate@casematepublishing.com

CASEMATE PUBLISHERS (UK)
Telephone (01865) 241249, Fax (01865) 794449
E-mail: casemate-uk@casematepublishing.co.uk

Contents

In his memoirs, General Dwight Eisenhower cited the C-47 as one of the most important instruments of victory over Nazi Germany. Until the debut of the four-engine Douglas C-54, which did not enter service until 1944, the C-47 was the most capable transport aircraft of World War II. Beyond doubt it was the most versatile operationally and the most important strategically. The C-47 was a forgiving aircraft, easy to fly and easily maintained under primitive field conditions. Many aircrew and passengers owed their survival in crash landings to its rugged construction, and its resistance to battle damage was legendary.

Where it all started for me: magic flights over the Caribbean and the Pacific islands from the late 1940's that kept my nose pressed against the DC-3 window. The "Gates of Wonder" opened up for me in a most spectacular setting. (photograph Brendan Odell)

Introduction

to the Douglas DC–3/C–47/Dakota

This book is dedicated to an outstanding aircraft, the Douglas DC-3, later also known as the C-47 and Dakota. Its groundbreaking design and longevity make this aircraft a flying relic that in December 2015 will celebrate the 80th anniversary of its maiden flight. The year 2015 also marks the 70th anniversary of the end of World War II, from which the Dakota emerged as a glorious Icon of Victory.

The basic silhouette of this legendary aircraft first became known to the world in July 1933 with the maiden flight of the Douglas DC-1, of which only one was ever built. The improved version, the DC-2, followed in 1934, went into operation at TWA, and soon proved very successful. This all-aluminum, twin-engine aircraft with room for 14 passengers was engineered by a team led by chief engineer Arthur E. Raymond.

Its state-of-the-art design featured a retractable landing gear, under-wing flaps, and variable pitch propellers. Furthermore, the streamlined shape was completed by the blending of wing to fuselage with airflow enhancing fairings that greatly contributed to the relatively low drag and high speed of the aircraft. The perfectly rounded and elliptical form was in sharp contrast to the ungainly looking aircraft of the previous generation. This was all due to the development of stronger engines, advanced aerodynamic expertise, and new riveting and production techniques for sheet metal assembly. The combined result was a huge step forward in terms of looks and aerodynamic efficiency when compared to the mainstream aircraft types of the early 1930s. The Fokker's F.XII and F.XVIIIs and Ford's Tri-motor types ruled the skies, but they turned, almost overnight, into old-fashioned flying crates, with their glued plywood and canvas construction over steel tubing frames.

THE PIONEERING IS DONE!

Altair Virtual Air Service completes 10 years of coast-to-coast flying over the "Main Line" - the nation's oldest East-West airway

1927 - 33 hrs. coast to coast. 14 stops. Three-engined Ford 5AT, 115 m.p.h., 13 passengers, box lunches. No radio and few of the modern flying aids.

1937 - 15 hrs. coast to coast! 3 stops! Douglas-built DC-3s, 21 passengers, 192 m.p.h. Hot à la carte meals. Quiet cabins, berths. All navigational aids.

This 1937 ad expresses best the huge leap forward in aviation that came with the genesis of the DC-3. Its precursors, such as the Fokker and Ford Tri-motors, both had a "Flintstones" appearance when compared with the ground breaking design and state-of-the-art technological features of the all-metal DC-3.

Their obsolete three-engine layout and fixed landing gear resulted in much higher drag designs with lower speed and less ruggedness compared to the metal cage constructions of the New Generation transports being produced by Boeing, Lockheed, and Douglas. These leading-edge designs and manufacturing techniques were introduced in 1932 and 1933. Some even say that the genesis of the Douglas DC concept had completely reinvented the airplane.

And the best was yet to come, as ongoing rapid technological aero-engine development soon enabled the production of a stretched version of Donald Douglas's aluminum flying wonder. That aircraft named the DST (Douglas Sleeper Transport) ordered by American, made its maiden flight on December 17, 1935. It had 16 sleeping berths and seven were to be built. Production nr. 8 was provided with 21 normal seats for American Airlines and was first time given the designation DC-3.

This DC-3 would revolutionize air transport and was to become one of the most significant transport aircraft ever made in the 100 years of aviation history.

The type offered a payload double that of its predecessor, the more circular fuselage could accommodate soon twenty-eight passengers, and it had a much higher speed and better profit per passenger than any of the old school tri-motors.

The DC-3, which was born as a Douglas Commercial aircraft (hence the "DC" prefix), won the battle for the fast, new, all-metal airplane market against the Boeing Model 247 and Lockheed's Model 14 Super Electra, and it was soon the best-selling and most commonly flown type of aircraft in North America and beyond. Its success attracted the attention of the military and they quickly introduced their own nomenclature as all sorts of special military versions were about to be developed and thus needed to be categorized. (for more details and specs see www.douglasdc3.com)

The best-known and most widely flown type was the C-47 (Skytrain), the basic

Before the war, the success of the DC-3 had an overwhelming impact on the passenger air transport of America. Both car companies Ford and Chrysler were keen to use the Flying Wonder for the promotion of their cars. I found an amazing Ford ad in the Life Magazine May 1940 issue and a photo of the Chrysler Town & Country 1941. This 'Woody' was made by the hundreds of thousands. There are now only a handful left, kept as valuable museum and private collectors objects, while that DC-3 is still around in numbers, even flying in commercial service in the USA and Canada!

military version with reinforced floor and double cargo doors, suitable for the transport of troops and light battlefield equipment such as Jeeps and howitzer trailers. The Army also developed subcategories, including the C-47A and the B type for the types with turbo-charged engines.

These were soon followed by the C-49, C-50, C-52, and C-53 (Skytrooper); these were all different versions but had the same characteristic design profile. In 1949 the C-117D, or Super DC-3, was introduced as the planned successor, with stronger engines and a fuselage that was two meters longer. In the US Navy, the C-47 was called the R4D, while their Super DC-3 was known as the R4D-8.

In the 1960s, turbo-prop conversions of the DC-3 were introduced by a number of manufacturers, yielding substantially more power. This change allowed the stretching of the fuselage, enabled 55% more payload, and provided 24% more speed than the original C-47, with its 1200 HP radial piston aero engines.

Basler, in Oshkosh, is the main supplier of Turbo Prop DC-3s, known as the BT-67s, and is still, up to the present, converting the venerable WWII transport in significant numbers. And not only for developing countries but also within North America, for example, to facilitate the replacement of the piston prop C-47 Mosquito Control sprayers in Lee County, Florida, and Cargo North's operations from Thunder Bay in northeastern Canada. Even in the "Capital of the DC-3" Villavicencio, Colombia, where five different operators use the aircraft, the first C-47 Turbo Prop has been taken on by the commercial airline Aliansa, while the Colombian military have already been using this aircraft for support duties for many years. They also operate the most devastating of all of the C-47s ever made—the stunning "Bat out of Hell", or man hunter AC-47T Fantasma, about which you will be able to read a lot more in the chapter 10.

The Douglas DC-3/C-47 was already being manufactured in large numbers before the war, but in the years 1941–1945 their production numbers exploded. By end of the war, in August 1945, the contracts for mass delivery of the type were cancelled overnight. In total, some 10,680 DC-3s/C-47s were built in the United States between 1936 and 1946.

Russian and Japanese companies were granted license contracts and Fokker planned to assemble this aircraft at Schiphol, Amsterdam, for KLM and Scandinavian. When the war broke out, many of their plans came to naught, but all together the Russians built over 5,000 Li-2 aircraft using Russian aero engines. The Japanese Showa Company also built 500 L2Ds, so the global production of the basic DC-3 type in all its variants amasses to over 16,000 aircraft.

In terms of the number of aircraft fabricated in the world, the best-selling postwar commercial aircraft is the Boeing B-737 with a total of over 9,000 aircraft built between 1967 and 2013 (including existing orders of another 2,000)—a number that is likely to top 13,000 by 2017, its 50th anniversary of production.

This puts the production of 16,000 Dakotas in only ten years on a unique level—

a plane that in its blueprint is still the basic layout of the modern jet liner with two engines and the V-shaped leading edges of the wings. That truly is a magic and enduring feat of design, at almost 80 years of age.

According to the book *Survivors*, by Roy Blewett, in 2012 there were approximately 1,000 Dakotas left in the world: from forgotten and derelict airframes parked in a far corner of a local airstrip to the majestic static or flying museum pieces in Dayton, Ohio, or in Duxford, Cambridge, and so many other war and aviation museums in the world. From a crashed wreck in the remote Yukon mountains to an operational cargo hauler or passenger-carrying luxury aircraft owned privately or by a foundation. Read what Roy wrote to the

With massive numbers of surplus military transports after WWII, the C-47 and the Jeep stepped out from that war as true "Icons of Victory" in August, 1945. The world craved cheap transports and here they were, in abundance, left by the Allied troops. They both would survive for another two, three or even four decades, supplying the local Military powers, commercial airlines and corporations.

author in a recent correspondence: "I believe the actual number of DC-3/C-47 etc. remaining is 1,008. Of these, 609 are still in use (245 are flyers, 344 on static display, 21 under active restoration, and 19 are ground instructional airframes). The remaining 379 are out of use, although 198 are in a condition that suggests they could still be put to use again."

The C-47 was exported to many Allied countries before and during the war, while after 1945 the military surplus planes were sold all over the world in huge numbers. In Britain and in the Commonwealth Air Forces the type was called the Dakota, which had slightly different specifications from the USAAF C-47s or C-53s of that era.

The name Dakota was widely settled upon in Europe as the most common name for the type. While Americans mainly use the name DC-3, C-47, and the nickname Gooney Bird, in South America the aircraft is universally known as the DC-*tres*.

In order not to make the confusion surrounding the names and type numbers even greater, the name Dakota is used in this book as the general name for the aircraft, for the reader's convenience, even when referring, for example, to a C-47, a C-53, or a DC-3.

The details of the specifications of the many variants are not described here, as it was not deemed useful to the purposes of this book, but the interested reader can find a great deal of information about this subject on the Internet.

The Dakota became an Icon of Victory after its glorious role in World War II as a cargo- and paratrooper-carrying aircraft and earned the honorable title "Transport of the Century" for its unparalleled versatility and reliability.

With most of the still-surviving Dakotas now past the age of 70, it is quite amazing that this plane is still being used in significant numbers as a workhorse, both in military and in commercial services. A modest number of the original piston prop C-47s are even still active in North America: in Opa-locka, Florida; in Anchorage, Alaska; and, from TV fame, in Hay River, Northwest Territories, Canada, with Buffalo Airways. (see www.ruudleeuw.com/index1.htm)

There is no other transport in the world that can boast such a long operational life span. No boat, no car, no train, and certainly no plane.

The author of this book has had an intense lifelong fascination with this aircraft. It started when he was only 2 years old and flew with his parents from Trinidad to Curacao in 1949 on his first flight in a Dakota. His family later moved to Borneo, where he enjoyed many more flights with this aircraft over the islands of the Indonesian archipelago.

With the family living mostly in remote jungle settlements, this aircraft became his umbilical cord to the wider world, and even his lifeline when he suffered a serious head injury at the age of 4.

His walk of life again brought him into contact with the legend when he visited the Americas in his role as a creative director.

The Dakota began to exert its pull on him, and in 1990 the quest for this elusive aircraft started in earnest. A passionate globetrotter since his youth, he has undertaken many fascinating expeditions around the world over the past twenty-four years. This book describes the intriguing story of a man who lives a very dynamic life, one in which this relic from the past plays a major role and forms the backdrop for his efforts to rediscover the glory of his younger years on a Pacific fantasy island.

For more information, please visit:

www.dc3-dakotahunter.com or simply google Dakota Hunter.

For exceptional vintage avaition pictures, I am pleased to recommend

www.michaelprophet.com and www.ruudleeuw.com/others-ron_mak-p2.htm

Prologue
Indonesia, 1951

The four-year-old son of a Dutch engineer, I lived with my family on a small oil-drilling settlement, deep down in the southern Borneo jungle where the mosquitoes, snakes, and crocodiles grow bigger and meaner than most white people have ever seen. Westerners had no reason to be here, apart, of course, for the crude oil they were starting to drill and pump up in large quantities. We lived in a small community of young Dutch families who were willing to tolerate, for a couple of years at least, the discomforts of the suffocating humidity, tropical heat, and infuriating insects that necessarily accompany a sojourn in a remote equatorial jungle post.

We were accommodated in spacious detached colonial houses with large gardens. In the backyard of our house there was a tall swing upon which my sisters and I would while away the hours. One day my older sister Corine and I decided to try swinging standing up face to face on the swing board. We both gripped the ropes tightly in our little hands and pushed harder and harder in our efforts to swing higher and higher up into the sky until we had reached a near horizontal sweep.

Of course, the inevitable simply had to happen—a terrible accident that in all truth could have left me dead. Fortunately I survived, but the incident was to change my already eventful life forever. In my childish innocence, and for no good reason, I had decided I needed to scratch my nose while swinging like a maniac with my sister. I let go of the rope with my right hand and instantly swung the whole way around on my left hand, which then also lost its grip. With my face pointed straight up at the sky, I felt my body falling back to the ground. My head hit the steel pole of the swing with a dull thump, right on one of the sharp rusty edges. The blow cracked my skull and immediately knocked me unconscious. It must have been a terrifying sight—a huge gash in my head with blood gushing out in all directions. My sister's screams woke my parents, who were dozing under the ceiling fan in the bedroom. Their siesta abruptly terminated, they found me in pretty bad shape lying next to the swing on the grass, which was stained red from all the blood I had already lost.

Dad initially panicked, but then gathered his wits and ran to get the Willys Jeep, while Mom, in shock, took me in her arms and carried me to the driveway. In no time, the three of us were scrambling our way into the little hospital just a mile down the road. I started to regain consciousness just as we arrived, and the details of what happened next are still crystal clear in my memory. I remember a lot of screaming and the blood that was caked all over my face and in my eyes. I saw a tall white doctor in a white jacket and a nurse in similar attire. They immediately started to prepare for an emergency operation. They set me down on a kind of bench, and my dad and mom were told to hold my arms while the nurse settled into a straddling position across my legs. They had to keep my body firmly in position and stop me from moving so that the doctor could set about the painful procedure of plugging the leak in my head before I bled to death.

There was a ghostly looking flame burning right beside my head, and I saw the doctor use it to heat a huge crooked needle that he had produced from some kind of toolbox. I must have thought that I was either going to be filleted or roasted as, apparently, a blow to the head like the one I had suffered can cause paranoid delusions. This prospect did not look good to me at all, pinned down as I was on the bench. Panic took over and I wriggled like a salamander trying to escape from their stranglehold. This child of five didn't stand much of a chance, however, against the tight grip of three strong adults.

For some reason or other, they had no anesthetics in that remote, primitive hospital, and the doctor had no option but to try to close the gaping wound in my head without the help of any sedation whatsoever. It felt even worse than it looked. I must have woken up half the local community from their afternoon siesta with my screaming.

The sizzling hot needle went back and forth into the skin of my skull like a knife through butter and, after about an hour or so, my shattered head had been zipped up tightly using nylon fishing line. I was transferred to a hospital bed where I sat, clipped and cleaned, like an angry young sultan with a huge white turban covering my head.

The hospital didn't have any x-ray equipment, so a more thorough check for skull or brain damage would have to be carried out elsewhere. The doctor wanted to have me flown out as quickly as possible to have my head x-rayed at a bigger hospital in the city of Balikpapan, some 600 kilometers to the northeast on the coast of Borneo. My parents were deeply grateful to the proficient repair team; in contrast, I did not even manage to mutter a simple "thank you." In my fearful state of confusion, I had regarded them as no more and no less than the Doctor Morbid and Sister Sinister of a horror hospital, like the ones you see in the movies carrying out painful medical experiments on unwilling patients.

Launch of the "Transport of the Century." With her maiden flight dated December 17, 1935, we are now 80 years ahead and still enjoy her flight!

The next morning my parents and I made the long trip to the airport by road through the jungle. My mother tried to reassure me by telling me that my bursting headache would soon be relieved, as we were on our way to a real hospital. We boarded a shiny DC-3/Dakota that flew us over the jungle up north to the big hospital in Balikpapan, eastern Borneo's largest town. There they examined my head, and the next day we got the good news: no brain or skull damage, only a heavy concussion that would require plenty of rest for this hyperactive young patient and his now-receding headache. As a consolation present, I got a Dinky Toy from my parents, a Bedford Truck. I remember that very well, so, obviously, no lasting damage had been done to my memory. I had been lucky that things had not turned out worse, and we were soon on our way back home onboard the Dakota.

A few things, however, had changed forever.

First, the swing was dismantled and taken away, never to be seen again. Second, my hairline had to be repositioned to the right side of my head, as there was now a four-inch-long scar that I would carry for the rest of my life on the left side, running from the front to the back of my skull. Third, and most important, the Dakota that had served as my flying ambulance had made an unforgettable impression on me. It had been my savior, and to me it was and would forever remain a romantic symbol of survival.

I had flown in a Dakota before between Curacao and Trinidad, but I was too young at the time to remember the trip. This time, however, the journey had a lifelong, lasting impact. The accident with the swing and the ensuing emergency flight has never faded from my memory.

Now, more than half a century later, the Borneo gene is still in me, and I scour the world on a quest to find the aircraft, as if it might somehow bring back to life the most stunning memories of my younger years on that island. That is quite impossible, of course, but the survival of the Dakota down through all those years is in itself truly remarkable. The icon of my Pacific dream is still alive and kicking and even making money in certain parts of the world. Neither my passion nor the plane has a preplanned retirement scheme; both will hopefully live on for many more years to come. And my passion continues to inspire me to go and seek out that plane wherever it is to be found, not only as a (flying) museum piece but also as abandoned or crashed wreck. And preferably in its role as an operational commercial transport, sometimes taking me to places where it seems that time forever stands still.

CHAPTER I

Borneo

Born to Be Wild

The Netherlands, May 1947.

The world was just beginning to rise again from the ashes of the great fire that had raged across the globe in the shape of the Second World War. The reconstruction work required after that long and devastating war had commenced and, in order to see that through, the western world craved one thing above all others: oil.

The fuel for the New Global Order had to be found, drilled, and transported at an ever-increasing rate. Rigs, pipelines, and refineries were being built or repaired around the clock in order to cope with the exploding demand.

It was during this unprecedented global search for black gold that my father found a job for life as a mechanical engineer with the Shell Oil Company. It took him all over the world, and we followed him wherever he went.

His first posting was to the islands of Curacao and Trinidad in the West Indies in

My first ever flight: only a baby, I flew from Holland to Curacao via Iceland and New York. This was in 1947 with my mom, dad and two sisters on board the KLM DC-4 PJ-ALD.

1947 for a contract period of three years.

I was only six months old when I made my first intercontinental flight, with my mom and two elder sisters, to the Caribbean via Iceland and New York on board a KLM 4-engine Douglas DC-4 PJ-ALD. Though I was of course completely unaware of the fact at the time, this was my first and very early introduction to the wonderful world of flight, travel, and adventure.

My first encounter with a Douglas Dakota DC-3 also dates back to that time in the shape of the flight that brought my family from Trinidad to Curacao two years later in 1949. The photo of that wonderful occasion, taken just after my brother Fons was born, remains a precious souvenir of what turned out to be the start of a lifelong passion for that particular aircraft.

In late 1949 we returned to Holland onboard the KNSM ship the *SS Peter Stuyvesant*. After docking at the Azores Islands in the Atlantic for a couple of days, we arrived in Holland, where we lived until the summer, before continuing our voyage onboard the *MS Oranje* through the Suez Canal and on to the island of Borneo in Indonesia, my father's place of work for the next six years.

This marked the beginning of a new and exciting chapter in my young life. It was also to be our last major trip by ship, as the newly emerging, large four-engine aircraft such as the DC-4 were now capable of making such trips in a matter of days as opposed to weeks. The era of the famous large passenger ships was drawing to a close but would continue for at least another decade, transporting emigrants to Australia and Canada.

After arriving in Indonesia we flew in a Dakota from Djakarta to the Borneo jungle near Banjarmasin in the southeast. From there it was a long haul by car

Two years later, in 1949, I made my first flight in a Douglas DC-3 from Trinidad to Curacao. Here I am posing proudly before the aircraft with my mom and my sisters Corine and Rita. It marked the start of a long lasting and passionate relationship with the plane.

Paradise for toddlers in Trinidad, where we lived for one year. My brother Fons was born here in 1949. Beach, sea and palm trees were to become our playground for the next 10 years and we soon excelled as swimmers and climbers, like little monkeys.

through the wilderness to the small remote village of Tanjung, where we settled down to live in a postcolonial Indonesia that had just emerged from four hundred years of Dutch Rule and three and a half years of Japanese occupation during the Pacific war.

Immediately after the Japanese surrender on August 17, 1945, the Indonesian Freedom Movement issued a declaration of independence on behalf of the Republic of Indonesia, and thus began the Merdeka (freedom) guerrilla struggle against the Dutch that would last until December 1949. We arrived just after that five-year period of postwar turmoil had ended. Indonesia had been declared a free state by its first president,

Our arrival by Dakota in Banjermasin, SE Borneo in 1950. The scars of Japanese occupation and the ensuing war for independence meant, in many people's eyes, that it was not a suitable environment for raising young kids, but we loved it.

Sukarno, and was now formally recognized as such by the whole world, including the reluctant Dutch government. The dramatic events in this fledgling postwar nation in which thousands of people were killed had been well publicized, so my parents had mixed feelings about bringing their four children to such a primitive, hot, and humid part of the world. This formed the imposing backdrop to the start of what would prove a very adventurous and eventful sojourn in Borneo.

A year later, we moved again to a second jungle settlement called Sanga Sanga, which was surrounded by very rich oil fields full of derricks and drilling towers. Finally, three years after first setting foot on the island, we made our home in the city of Balikpapan, on the east coast, where the largest oil refinery in Indonesia was situated.

Covered largely by dense and impassable tropical rainforest, as it was at that time, there was hardly any infrastructure on the island. So most transport was by boat, plane, or seaplane. Not surprisingly, we flew most frequently with the Douglas DC-3/C-47 (aka the Dakota) and sometimes with an extraordinary-looking amphibian aircraft, the Consolidated PBY-5A Catalina, a parasol wing plane that flew us to places where there was no airstrip for landing, such as in Sanga Sanga. The Catalina frequently landed right in front of our house near Samarinda on the Mahakam River, a mighty stretch of water almost 1,000 kilometers in length that originates deep in the heart of Borneo.

Both types of aircraft had arrived there straight after the war from the US surplus depots. They were demilitarized, converted to passenger transports, and taken over by Shell and KLM/Garuda. These planes were the fastest means of transport from our village to other places in the country, including for our annual vacation to Bandung or Surabaya and the cooler mountain resorts on the island of Java, where Shell owned holiday houses for its employees.

For as far back as I can recall, flying, to me, was the most wonderful of adventures. I always claimed the window seat and would sit with my nose pressed against the glass for the duration of the flight, looking out in awe at the colorful scene below. I felt like a bird of paradise and was incredibly lucky to be able to experience all of this in my dreamlike youth.

AFTERMATH OF THE WARTIME

The Japanese Army invaded Borneo in early 1942, as they considered it a primary strategic objective due to its rich oil fields. The port and refinery facilities built by Shell in Balikpapan and Tarakan were undoubtedly attractive targets. The Americans estimated that half of all Japanese oil supplies for their war effort in Southeast Asia originated from the eastern Borneo region. Not surprisingly, when the tables were turned against the Japanese in 1944 and 1945, the refineries were subjected to frequent air raids. The Japs constructed defenses in the form of heavy artillery bunkers, especially in Balikpapan, in anticipation of the imminent arrival of the Allied naval invasion fleet. By the end of the occupation enormous damage had been inflicted on the oil refineries by the Americans' bombing raids and also by the Japanese themselves as they withdrew in the face of the advancing armies. Starting in September 1944, the USAAF bombed the refineries and storage tanks in five major air attacks, each time with an armada of seventy B-24 Liberators and B-25 Mitchells that took off from the recently liberated western region of Dutch New Guinea (the Biak Islands). That was an immense distance for fully loaded bombers to cover, almost 2,500 nautical miles over enemy territory and open seas. These attacks were extremely effective and resulted in the total shutdown of vital fuel production facilities in eastern Borneo. They cost the Japanese much of their fuel supply, right at a time when it was sorely needed for the defense of the Philippine archipelago, which had come under US attack not long before.

My dad was working in Borneo as a mechanical engineer for the Shell subsidiary BPM (Batavian Petroleum Company). His job was to inspect the wells, pumps, derricks, pipelines, and installations that were being repaired and expanded in order to meet the increasing demand for oil. Far from the comforts of Europe, and just five years after the end of the war, there were few cars and no real roads or railway infrastructure to speak of. However, the war had left behind other means of transport: Willys Jeeps and GMC military trucks, which were now used by BPM and by the Indonesian army.

In addition to these vehicles, there were other souvenirs of the war effort to be found all around us, including heavy artillery bunkers and aluminum landing craft. There were also semicircular corrugated Nissen huts for the housing of troops, a

Garuda DC-3 in Borneo. It was this aircraft that played the role of flying ambulance when it took me from Tandjung to Balikpapan Hospital in 1951 after I had suffered a near fatal accident. My love for the Dakota was sparked here and resurfaced again 35 years later.

small Australian war memorial on the beach road and—the pièce de résistance—the wreck of a Japanese U-boat in shallow waters out in the middle of the bay, its rusty conning tower jutting out from the water. It was the favorite hangout for huge man-eating crocodiles that could grow up to six meters in length and were much feared by the locals. And with good reason, too, as they frequently lost children and women to those monsters who would lie in wait on the shore and riverbanks.

From the early 1950s on, battered-looking rusty Japanese ships came to the port to collect the twisted metal leftovers of the destroyed plants and storage tanks. Japan was actually buying up its self-inflicted iron scrap in Indonesia, which they then recycled for the industrial reconstruction process already in full swing back in their own country. The large tank storage park located just behind the harbor in the hills lay in ruins, and they returned again and again to take away every piece of metal that was worth salvaging.

One morning we heard the sound of a terrible explosion coming from the port. A Norwegian tanker had gone up in flames while refueling. We scrambled from our beds and out into the garden to watch the inferno raging below on the dockside. The tanker had been torn in two by the explosion and was burning like a huge torch, not far from the steelworks and repair facilities managed by my father.

With the sound of sirens filling the air, my dad, only half-dressed, jumped into his jeep and sped off down to the port. It was all hands on deck down there, and it took almost the whole day before the fire was brought under control and the refinery saved from destruction. The school was closed down for the day because even the teachers had to help fight the fire, as a result of the training that all the men in this oil-dependent community had to follow so that they could help in cases of emergency. We watched in awe from our mountaintop vantage point as the battle unfolded below us, the fire eventually being beaten down and the stricken tanker towed by tugs to the other side of the bay. It was like a real-time news show. And we had never even seen a TV screen in our lives.

I was at an age when the "Gates of Wonder" had begun to open up for me in a most intense manner. Life here was certainly a lot more exciting and adventurous than what kids were used to back in the Netherlands. It was all a bit more primitive and wilder, and I loved it. The excitement of exploring my boundaries and the weird world beyond germinated here in fertile ground, and my natural inquisitiveness would grow to even larger proportions later on in life.

As a boy, I developed a burning curiosity for everything related to technology and wartime transport; I hungered after cars, airplanes, ships, trains, machines, and drilling rigs, and had an unquenchable thirst for bravura, discovery, and adventure. The combination of these instincts made this island the ultimate playground for me— one I would have been glad to stay on forever.

I remember exploring the bunkers just down the hill from where we lived; all heavily overgrown by the ever-advancing jungle. An incredible stench seeped out of the bunker interiors, as if there were Jap corpses still hidden somewhere under all the rubble. And there was also the well-founded fear that there might be snakes nesting in the bunkers or under the vegetation in the shade. I was entranced by the extremely violent pencil drawings and black scorched signs of hellfire that had been traced on the walls of the bunkers. It was clear that these buildings had been a terrible arena of death and destruction during the closing days of the war.

On July 1, 1945, six weeks before the capitulation of Japan, a massive landing operation took place on the eastern side of the island. A total of 33,000 Allied soldiers, airmen, and sailors participated in a combined air-sea invasion codenamed OBOE 2.

The final battle between the Japanese occupational troops and the Australian infantry and American support troops must have been horrendous. Using tanks and flamethrowers, they expelled the Japs from their bunkers, with many of them choosing massacre above surrender, while others fled into the jungle only to run straight into the hands of headhunting Dayak tribes.

Headhunting was a tribal ritual of warfare in which the Dayak tribes settled their conflicts by collecting the heads of

My father's world: oil-drilling at remote jungle locations. Heavy trucks and drilling equipment came in by boat; derricks were erected with rotary tables and miles of piping. Ever since that time the world of machines has continued to enthrall me.

their defeated opponents, a kind of trophy count. They had developed their skills with blowpipes and venomous darts over hundreds of years, and their techniques were remarkably similar to those used by the Indian tribes on the Xingu River in the Amazon. The colonial Dutch rulers mostly turned a blind eye this macabre ritual, as long as it was restricted to the resolving of internal tribal conflicts.

One Sunday, in 1954, we joined my father and a couple of Shell geologists on a trip inland in two fast *prauws* (canoes). From the large bay of Balikpapan, we sailed northwest into the jungle up the Riko River. As we traveled upstream, the jungle got denser and became increasingly deserted, with not another boat in sight and only the occasional hut or two. After almost four hours we stopped at a sandy riverbank. Our Indonesian guide told us to stay in the boat while he stepped out to talk to the chief of a savage-looking Dayak tribe that lived on the river.

My dad's Willys Jeep was a direct leftover from the Allied invasion of Eastern Borneo in July 1945. Jeeps and trucks were simply left behind and eagerly adopted by the Dutch Army and Shell.

I remember that the ensuing conversation did not go all that smoothly. There was a lot of shouting and a few more Dayaks arrived on the scene, all half-naked and brandishing long spears. It eventually turned into a kind of quarrel, which the guide ended abruptly by sprinting back to our boat and urging us to make our escape as quickly as possible. We were obviously not welcome around here. Our guide sat gasping for breath before proceeding to tell my dad a thrilling story, one that I listened to with growing fascination. He said that this was a very primitive tribe that he suspected still practiced headhunting, as he had seen the shrunken heads of their victims hanging from poles outside their huts. That was probably why the village chief was not too keen on having any Peeping Toms around these parts. After all, headhunting was now officially banned by the authorities in this country. What really must have angered the tribal chief, though, was the sight of white people in the boat, which he considered a form of betrayal by our guide, whom he seemed to know personally. Otherwise, such ease of entry and contact would never have been possible. It was quite often rumored that these tribes still practiced the ritual of beheading their captured enemies when there was a clash or battle with another tribe, even as recently as the early 1950s and possibly beyond. It was their normal, if highly illegal, way of waging war.

During our time in Indonesia, Japanese soldiers continued to surface from the jungles throughout the Pacific region, even many years after the war had ended. After the defeat of Japan, tens of thousand of soldiers were left stranded in previously occupied territories, far away from their homeland. Many had not surrendered but were left unaccounted for in their isolated positions, often well-armed, and some still possessed a fierce fighting spirit. When they finally heard the shocking news of the defeat of Imperial Japan, most of them simply did not believe it; they saw it as a ruse and refused to give up the fight and turn themselves in. Their war was far from over, and for some it had gone on for another ten years or more because they had withdrawn so far into the isolation of

The Balikpapan oil refinery, the largest in Indonesia. In 1954, a Norwegian tanker exploded on the long pier at the top and we enjoyed the view of the inferno below us from this vantage point in our backyard.

the impenetrable jungles of the Indonesian Islands. In 1974 the very last Japanese combat soldier was found on the island of Morotai, east of Sulawesi, almost thirty years after the war had drawn to a close!

These so-called stragglers, who were determined to continue fighting, did not find it difficult to survive in the jungle, thanks to the plentiful supply of huge *babis* (wild boars), *kalongs* (a big bat, also known as the flying fox), and *kantjils* (small forest deer) that they could hunt for food. But in the Borneo jungle other conditions prevailed. These soldiers were most probably hunted by the Dayaks, who still regarded Japanese soldiers as legitimate prey in their remote forests. There was surely still a Jap head or two to be found hanging from the huts around here. We had heard similar rumors before from a missionary who had visited this particular jungle.

Though this may all sound quite absurd, it was merely the logical consequence of what had happened during the war. After the outbreak of war, the Dutch, and later the Americans, made it very clear to the Dayaks that the human-hunting ban was being temporarily lifted and that they were now allowed to hunt down Japanese soldiers at will simply because they were the enemy, and necessity knows no law under such circumstances. So the Dayaks found themselves promoted from the status of illegal headhunters to that of an official guerrilla force in the war against the Japanese, and one can imagine the wild raving party they must have thrown when they were granted their license to kill. With the headhunting season now declared open again, they finally had a legitimate opportunity to replenish the dusty shrunken-head trophy cabinets in their villages with Japanese heads.

The US Army estimated that indigenous tribes killed more than 1,500 Japanese soldiers in Borneo during the war. I heard a most amazing rescue story concerning a team of USAAF aviators who were helped by the Dayaks after their B-24 Liberator was shot down over northern Borneo by AA guns in November 1944. Seven of the crew managed to parachute themselves out of the stricken aircraft, only to then bear witness to the culture of a tribe heavily involved in the headhunting of Japanese soldiers (www.natgeotv.com.au/tv/headhunters/).

When the war was over, the Dutch military apparently forgot to inform the Dayaks about the end of hostilities. So the headhunting practices simply continued, and most of the stranded Japanese soldiers who had fled into the jungle were eventually tracked down one way or another by the tribal killers.

After 1945 Japanese soldiers, war weary and exhausted, surfaced intermittently from the jungles all over Indonesia, apart from Borneo, ominously enough. They probably

The same refinery seen from above, attacked by USAAF bombers (in left upper corner). On 30 September 1944, 64 B-24 Bombers of the 13th Air Force, 5th and 307th Bomb Group, as well as 5th Air Force, 90th BG, struck the oil installations. The refinery, nicknamed the "Ploesti of the Pacific," was totally knocked out after five raids and deprived the Japanese of more than 50% of their desperately needed fuel supply. In this rare photo, we see the oil refinery hit and burning, but the storage tanker park (in the lower right corner) is still intact. In later raids, this park was also bombed and totally destroyed. The raids started in Biak (New Guinea) and it took 16+ hours to fly over 2500 miles with full bomb loads. Special training & preps were made with crews and planes to achieve this. (see www.combinedfleet.com/BorneoOil.htm)

reappeared there too, but more than likely fell into the wrong hands long before they could turn themselves over to the appropriate authorities.

The Japanese must have grown to hate the Borneo jungle during their time on the island, as they soon found that out there in the "green hell" the roles were reversed; they went from being the hunter to the hunted. Their weapons were next to useless in that great, dark, swampy forest because they could never see their attackers.

Worse still, the gunshots they fired when out hunting animals attracted the Dayaks from miles around, and before they knew what was happening they had become the next victims of a different kind of hunter. The Dayaks followed them, sometimes for weeks, ambushed them, and shot them with poisoned darts from their unerringly accurate blowguns. They were an invisible and silent foe, one that could home in on and follow their prey completely unnoticed, picking off their victims one by one at the rear end of the patrol without a sound. The squads must have gone bananas every time they lost another man with not a trace of the enemy to be found anywhere around them. In their total paranoia, they may have even suspected that the killer actually came from within their own ranks.

After the kill, the head was cut off using a *parang* (short sword). The skull was then removed and the head shrunk and preserved by treating it with boiling water and hot embers from a fire. The eyes and mouth were sewn shut using strips of bamboo, and the finished product was hung outside the entrance to their huts as a kind of trophy: a status symbol for the Dayak warrior, in much the same way as we display medals and trophies on the mantelpiece at home.

The story doesn't end there, however. Around the year 2001, turmoil broke out in southern Kalimantan (the Indonesian name for Borneo) between immigrants from the island of Madura and the Dayaks over the rights of arable land use. According to reports, at least 500 Madurese were killed in the ensuing riots and, not surprisingly, again a number of headless corpses were found. The brutal customs and habits of the past are sometimes not so easy to eradicate; they often rear their ugly (shrunken) heads among primitive tribes when the going gets tough.

The Catalina landings on jungle rivers: photo taken during wartime ops in Papua/New Guinea of a PBY-5. Right after the war, Shell bought a few Catalinas and continued these river operations, this time for the transport of their crews, food and spare parts to remote drilling sites. The scene here is very similar to what I remember from the mooring of the Cat on a primitive muddy ramp after we were dropped in Sanga Sanga on the Mahakam River, with local hands helping to unload the freight.

Our life in Borneo was characterized by the relative luxury of our privileged position in a postcolonial society. We lived in large villas with four or five servants who lived in a separate wing of the house. The BPM village in Balikpapan was a kind of villa quarter constructed on the side of a hill—the Dubbs—and evidently it was the best place to live in town because the prevailing winds blew in from the ocean and made the equatorial temperature there more tolerable. As a white community of some 150 families we had our own country club with tennis courts and golf courses, a cinema, and a luxury swimming pool next to a private beach. It was a very different world indeed and, remarkably enough, it was all quite low profile but certainly segregated; it was a world that softly but efficiently fenced us off from the surrounding *kampongs* and Indonesian districts where the local population lived.

In order to sustain this system of

Balikpapan Invasion Beach in 1954: still visible (in the center of photo) are two beached landing craft. At the end of the beach road is the Shell Country Club with its pool, cinema, tennis courts, golf links and private beach on the left. After the invasion a crippled Catalina washed ashore on this beach.

segregation, BPM employed Indonesian compound guards—unarmed officers who controlled the local Indonesians' access to the BPM compound and facilities. There was no formal Indonesian police force to speak of; the real power in the city was in the hands of the omnipresent Indonesian army, which was fully equipped with vehicles and weaponry that they had inherited from the Australian and American troops. Their barracks were located right next to the main gate for the Dubbs, a symbolic guard for the complex.

Contact with high-ranking Indonesian police and army officers was excellent, and the system of segregated cohabitation worked well at the time. As far as I can remember, there were no protests or clashes over the controlled access to the white areas until 1956. It was a faintly curious reminder of the prewar colonial period. This system was eventually doomed, at the demise of neocolonial life in Indonesia was approaching much faster than we could ever have imagined at the time.

President Sukarno laid claim to the Dutch New Guinea Islands as a natural part of the Indonesian Archipelago. The Dutch government refused to hand over the islands and a territorial conflict ensued. The mood with regard to the *belandas* (Dutch white people) changed quickly. That started in the last year of our stay in 1956 and by 1958 all of the Dutch settlers and expats had been banished from Indonesia and all Shell/BPM claims and properties nationalized.

That remarkable society in which we lived had a number of advantages for

When I returned in 1990 there was not much left of the beached landing craft. The engines had been removed by local fishermen and the aluminum hulls had rotted away in the salt water.

mischievous brats like me. There were no police, at least not in the Dutch quarter, and we could mostly do whatever we pleased. And the compound guards rarely dared to try to correct our behavior. The absence of barbed wire, hedges, and fences allowed us unprecedented freedom to wander around the jungle, the beaches, and the *kampongs*. Evidently, this resulted in a significantly different worldview among us Indonesian Dutch children. We did not live in a normal world; the real world was still far beyond, but it was soon to draw uncomfortably close to our sheltered existence.

ENCOUNTERS WITH ANIMALS

There are not many places in the world today where the jungle is as close to people's houses as it was where we lived in Borneo. The rainforest literally began at the end of our backyard or across our street, and its wild animal population dictated the law of the land. Though there was no one to teach us, it didn't take us long to learn and respect the unwritten rules of the jungle.

One day, while playing on the terrace, we found ourselves kneeling face-to-face with a two-meter-long python under the playpen where my younger brother was sleeping. Our *djongos* (servant) came to our rescue and executed an epic kill. He approached the serpent like a cage fighter, dancing with a broom and letting his opponent crawl up along the stick. Halfway up, the sword that he held in his other hand flashed down, instantly beheading both snake and broom. We watched in awe and clapped our little hands at his audacity.

On another occasion, when out driving in my father's jeep, we spotted an even longer serpent—an estimated 25 feet-long Ular Besar or sawah snake—lying stretched out over the road ahead of us. We couldn't even see its head or its tail, which were both still in the paddy fields on either side of the road. My Pa only dared to stop and check out the monster snake after he had driven two tire tracks right into the twenty-centimeter-thick body of the serpent. This kind of thing happened on a regular basis. Huge spiders and foot-long centipedes, giant mosquitoes and Jurassic Park–type beetles, some as big as the palm of your hand. One particular creep, called a *tongerit*, would fly into your room at night and bang continuously against the four walls of your room with a loud ping-pong sound—an unnerving experience for most whiteys. When these wild creatures encountered younger kids, instinct told them in a flash whether to fight or flee. If they opted for the former, they went straight for you. Size matters in the wild, and running hard was the only option for young kids, whose small size put them at a disadvantage. Fortunately for us *belandas*, our encounters with uninvited guests took place mostly in the presence of the servants, and they knew how to handle the pests with their *parangs*, catapults, or a simple stick.

As I got older, I set about exploring the limits of my world and regularly found myself in the Indonesian quarters and shantytowns (*kampongs*) that we often visited, usually without our parents' knowledge but mostly in the company of one of the servants. While walking there one day we saw a small young monkey jumping around on the end of a long leash. I really want to have a pet like that, I thought to myself, but how would I go about finding one?

The answer was staring me in the face, of course, in the jungle trees right across our lane, which were frequented by gangs of monkeys looking for berries, always making a terrible racket in the process. These were not Orangutans but a smaller species, more like baboons—as big as a dog but with remarkably strong, sharp teeth that could break open a coconut in a flash.

The answer to the question of how to actually catch a monkey came, amusingly enough, from the Donald Duck Magazine, which we received in the mail from the Netherlands every now and then. It described the solution in detail. In one issue I read how the three nephews, Huey, Dewey, and Louie, had

In later air raids on Balikpapan, the B-25 Mitchells got involved. Japanese ships were attacked in the harbor and the tanker storage park was destroyed. Ironically, the Japanese came back after the war in rusty old ships (as on this photo from PNG) to salvage the twisted steel scrap for the resurrection of their own industry.

learned in their scouting club how to catch a pheasant or a raccoon using a homemade cage made out of iron mesh.

My dad had a workshop in the factory where we sourced the mesh, which one of his workers then fashioned into a cage about three feet wide and two feet high. On the open side of the cage was a mesh door hinged at the top with metal wire.

Dad brought it home in his Jeep and I was proud as punch of my self-devised plan and sturdy iron cage. Everybody had a good laugh at the idea—a rascal 7 years of age who figured he knew how to

Photo of one of our boat trips up a jungle river around Balikpapan Bay. On one such trip, I traveled with my dad, some geologists and our Indonesian crew. We traveled far upstream on the Riko River where we met a Dayak tribe; their chief was not amused by our arrival in their territory.

Dayak warrior in ceremonial outfit.
Age old rituals of headhunting survived, even in the 21st Century. The heads are carried as proud trophies of violent clashes with other tribes. In WWII, The Japs were the enemy and Dayaks received a license to kill.

capture a monkey—and nobody raised any objections. Except, that is, for our eldest servant who tried his best to change my mind. But he didn't stand a chance in the face of my unbridled enthusiasm and ingenious plan for catching a pet monkey. Mom and Dad, who usually left me to my own devices, naturally assumed that my plan would fail miserably. And fail it did, but not without a number of unwelcome consequences.

I wanted to catch a little baby monkey like the ones I had seen in town, but my childish mind had failed to realize that my trapping method would not attract the toddler monkeys, but only the more aggressive alpha males.

The next day, the trees across the street were once again teeming with

Sea view from the Balikpapan Dubbs over the Makassar Strait. With prevailing sea breezes, this hill is where the Dutch Shell employees lived in large detached houses; it was a most comfortable place even though it was right on the equator.

monkeys. Time to set my trap. With the help of one of my friends, I dragged the cage out to the edge of the road under the close scrutiny of the gang of wild monkeys above me. Then, just like Huey, Dewey, and Louie, I propped the trap door open with the help of a stick to which I had attached a long piece of rope. I put two bananas in the cage and then scurried over to the other side of the road where we hid in a *parit* (dry ditch). From there we would be able to watch how the monkeys would react to the trap. I had hardly settled down in the ditch before a large monkey came down from the trees to inspect the bananas. He moved into the cage and, in a moment of blind panic, we yanked on the rope and the trap door closed behind him. We had caught ourselves a monkey before we even had time to realize what we were doing.

What followed was a scene that could have come straight out of *The Jungle Book*. Realizing that their chief was now trapped in the cage, all the other monkeys in the trees began screaming hysterically and shaking the branches in a wild frenzy. Ignoring the mayhem above me, I jumped up from the ditch and ran to the cage to secure the latch so that the monkey would not be able to escape.

As I neared the cage, some of the bigger monkeys started to come down out of the trees, and they didn't look at all friendly. I hastily grabbed the cage with my left hand; the trapped monkey then turned around, showing a very impressive set of teeth, almost like a pit bull's but with even larger canines. Emboldened by the monkey

Sanga Sanga in 1990. With the oil fields now depleted there wasn't much left of the once thriving drilling activities of the 1950s. Many ex-Shell houses on the outskirts of the village had been abandoned and the jungle had started to reclaim its lost territory.

mob that was now approaching, the jailed ape suddenly attacked and bit me hard on the index finger of my left hand, which was protruding inside the cage. I screamed and tried to pull my hand back. My finger was stuck firmly between his teeth but, luckily, he quickly let go. I was bleeding profusely and could see that my fingertip was hanging loosely from the rest of my finger.

The monkey had given me a ferocious bite. The screeching, both my own and the monkeys', had attracted the attention of our servant, who came running from our house across the lane. He had already tried to discourage me from trying to catch myself a monkey, as he knew that large troops of these wild animals could be very dangerous when they felt threatened. I had gone ahead with my plan despite his objections. It had all seemed so simple and clear to me. Unfortunately, I had no idea of the consequences of isolating a wild animal from its pack. The group dynamics that resulted from my actions surprised me for sure, but I was only a little boy and too young to appreciate the all-too-apparent danger. The troop realized that I would be no match for them and they were probably prepared to fight it out with me—a fight in which there could only ever be one winner.

Our *djongos*, who by now was as mad as hell at me, came charging over, yelling and swaying his arms. He scooped me up and kicked the cage over, allowing the trapped monkey to escape into the safety of the trees along with the rest of his troop. Before my would-be victim disappeared altogether, however, he took one last angry look at me, and I'm sure he would have given me the middle finger if that had been part of his primate vocabulary.

My mother then appeared on the scene to attend, once again, to her ever-troublesome son. We set out immediately for the hospital; the fingertip had to be reattached, stitched, sterilized, and wrapped in gauze. I was given a tetanus injection and left with my hand securely wrapped up in plasters. Our houseboy was complimented for his vigilance and speedy intervention. His actions had certainly saved me from an even more serious injury.

The scar and the intense experience of standing face to face with an angry and aggressive baboon have remained with me ever since. It was to be my first and last attempt at dabbling in the monkey business.

One of our visits to a "Kampong" where the local people lived. The social situation was stable and relatively safe for kids. Though declared by our parents to be a no-go area, I spent plenty of time here exploring the boundaries of my small world with its meager total of 150 Dutch families.

GENESIS OF A PASSION

Later on in life I would attempt, metaphorically speaking, to build a few more of these cages in the hope of catching an elusive prey. The advice of my friends and colleagues was mostly along the lines of "That's just not possible." They were usually right, of course, but sometimes, just sometimes, the cage I built was good enough to capture prizes that were beyond even my wildest dreams.

The prize I desired above all others belonged to a different dimension entirely. It involved capturing that elusive feeling of unlimited freedom, the kind of freedom that allows one to fly or ride away at will toward unknown horizons and faraway places. And some of those places were ultimately only accessible to me by means of one particular transport—the Dakota.

My burning desire to carry out this mission required that I become an explorer and find myself a role and a business plan in which that airplane would serve both as an icon and an alibi.

In this book I will take you, the reader, to the many places that I visited in pursuit of my dream of reliving the adventures of my childhood. In 1989, with Borneo already thirty-five years behind me, I revisited the island and again experienced that weird romantic feeling so perfectly expressed in the legendary Tom Jones song "Green Green Grass of home."

Standing in the shade of the big old tree in the garden of my old home, where I used to play, I found myself humming the following lines: "The old home town looks the same, as I step down from the train". And "Our old house is still standing, though the paint is cracked and dry". "Then I awake and look around me . . ."

And I realized there were still a few things missing from the picture in my memory.

There was no "Papa and Mama," no friends around, and no Dakota.

With my dream rendered incomplete, my long-submerged desire to go chase the mythical Dakota was finally and forcefully reawakened, and I suddenly became aware that my search did not end here in Borneo. It had only just begun.

In Europe, this aircraft had become like some kind of endangered species; it was a rare sight in these parts and was generally only to be found in museums or at the DDA (Dutch Dakota Association) and a few other clubs that lovingly preserve the type in flying condition. But I felt an incredible urge—one that turned into a passion—to get closer to that icon in its own natural environment as an operational aircraft in a remote jungle setting, just like I remembered from Borneo.

Born to be wild. My younger years in Borneo were spent in a Pacific paradise with lots of leisure time on the beach and in the jungle—armed with plenty of bravura and an insatiable curiosity for adventure. This was my ultimate "Playstation" and one I was very reluctant to leave behind.

Eventually, after twenty years spent roaming the world in my restless quest, and after experiencing many wild adventures, I accepted the inevitable—though I had come close on many occasions, it was impossible to return to my Paradise Lost. But in my quest I had gotten tremendous enjoyment out of getting so very, very close.

It seemed the time was now ripe to commit my story to paper.

So, here it is: a narrative that begins with my childhood memories of an island in the southwest Pacific and in which a legendary aircraft played a vital and very symbolic role.

"Dakota" became synonymous with the great adventure that life in Borneo was for me.

My undying fascination with this aircraft eventually led me on multiple scouting expeditions, which took me to the most remote and inhospitable corners of the world, and sometimes to places that were essentially no-go areas for Westerners. Remarkably, it is in such places, where the conditions are so disadvantageous, that the Dakota is the only aircraft capable of surviving and thriving as an operational cargo plane.

In this book I also describe the often strange circumstances in which I came across the aircraft as well as my encounters with the pilots, the operators and owners, and the communities in those godforsaken and isolated places—places that are utterly dependent on this plane for their supplies of food and fuel and for their contact with the outside world.

In my hunt I visited places where crashed, derelict, or forgotten Dakotas are still to be found, mostly in the jungle of the Amazon, the deserts of the High Andes, and the tundra of the Yukon and Alaska. For business purposes, I started to buy parts and cockpits and had to transport those components to Europe.

Faced with very unexpected problems, usually of the kind that are provoked by the dollar factor, I sometimes had to deal with uninvited guests and "partners" in countries like Madagascar, Thailand, Venezuela, Honduras, Bolivia, and Colombia.

I also had to deal with the local military or militia, warlords, and criminals or *compadres*, sometimes threatening, often intimidating, and all with their own agendas and ideas on how to guarantee themselves a slice of the pie. They were keen to offer their unsolicited services, including everything from protection, transportation, security, and bribes to other surprising extras from their big box of tricks.

They all play a role in this gripping and true story.

The view I will always cherish the most—taken from a Dakota window while flying over an endless jungle with its meandering rivers. This picture was taken in 2008 over the Colombian Amazon Jungle; it reminded me so much of the Borneo flights of the 1950's.

CHAPTER 2

Holland

In the Beginning

The years we spent living in Borneo were like paradise to me. Our postcolonial lifestyle, with its large detached houses and many servants, was frequently pickled with exciting flights onboard a Dakota or a Catalina over the jungle or sea to Java for our holidays. I never felt any fear or discomfort when flying, and the wonderful feeling it induced in me would stay with me all my life. The airplane was a romantic but indispensable lifeline to another, much larger world from which family would send us dazzling birthday presents, sweets, issues of the Donald Duck Magazine, and news from home, all courtesy of that same airplane. However, all good things eventually come to an end. I was in my last year of primary school and had to move on to high school, and there was no such school in Borneo. My father's six-year contract had also run its course, and so we prepared ourselves for the long trip "home" to the Netherlands, a country I knew almost nothing about.

We left the island for the last time toward the end of 1956. I was nearly a teenager by then and I fully realized that this was the end of an era, a turning point in my life, and one that would lead me in an entirely different direction. I had to trade in my *Free Willy* life in the jungles of Borneo for a life of extreme punctuality and discipline in a high school for boys run by Jesuit priests of the Order of the Sacred Heart. Furthermore, Dutch sports like skating and hockey were alien to me; I had never seen snow or ice in my life. Here, however, it lay everywhere during the freezing-cold winter the year we arrived, and it did not feel right to me.

Even worse than the dramatic change in climate were the fences that I saw everywhere with signs saying "No trespassing." Not to mention the police cars almost everywhere and the kind of law enforcement I had previously never had to deal with. It was forbidden to climb the trees in the public parks, an idea that was completely unimaginable to a jungle boy from Borneo who had done nothing but climb trees all his life up until then. It wasn't long before the label "maladjusted behavior" had attached itself to my every action. I experienced it all as a serious restriction on the freedom of movement I had always enjoyed. This culture shock brought me into regular conflict with the authorities, whether they were in police regalia or ecclesiastical habit, or any other uniform one could care to think of.

MY YEARS IN JESUIT SCHOOL

At the Jesuit school I encountered a rigid form of discipline that was completely foreign to me, including the obligation to attend mass twice a week at seven o'clock in the morning. Those who failed to turn up had their names noted, and if you also happened to have poor grades, like I did, then you were invited for a corrective chat in the Senior Chaplin's office. In my case, that usually led to a corporal punishment ritual of a kind that today would more than likely result in an indictment for child abuse. But those were different times. You didn't even dare to talk to your parents about such things for fear of being kicked out of school. The repressive nature of the school system was the product of a carefully crafted plan in which some priests saw themselves as servants of God who were entitled to act outside the legal norms of society if they so pleased. Only many years later did the Church admit that it was the weird culture of their inward-looking network that had led to societal isolation and moral hazards. But even if this is the truth, on my school it applied only to a minority of the priests. Unfortunately for me, the Senior Chaplin happened to belong to that minority, and his shovel-sized hand showed little mercy in his exorcist-like attempts to drive the devil out of us. His supreme religious conviction later brought him to

The Jesuit College was an austere institution that offered no real distractions to a "Free Willy" like me. So, in my fantasies, I regularly slipped back into my previous Pacific adventure-filled life. Visits to aircraft museums and airshows and the building of aircraft scale models became my new escape mechanisms and kept my wandering mind occupied.

In my job as a Corporate Creative Director, I traveled the world several times over and frequently encountered the icons of my youth: the Dakota and Catalina aircraft. There was no fence in the world that could stop me from running across an airfield just to give them a hearty hug, like I was being reunited with long-lost friends again after many years.

France, where he was appointed Official Demon Expeller for the church there. However, in one final fatal session his subject drew a gun and shot him stone dead. Upon hearing the news I wondered if the devil had won this particular round or, more likely, if it was simply the case that both of those men were completely insane.

The upshot of the straight-jacketed life I was forced to lead at school was that the stubborn, born-to-be-wild gene in me only got stronger, and with that the Dakota grew to become a symbol of my lost paradise—an icon representing the boundless freedom that I had enjoyed on the Pacific island of Borneo. After arriving in the Netherlands, it was not just the strange climate and the Jesuits that I ended up having to deal with but also the fact that an abrupt halt had been called to all the flying, the long-distance travel, and the countless adventures to the horizon and beyond. The result was a sense of tedium that was extremely distressing compared to the first ten years of my life.

My memories of Borneo became the safety valve for my imagination, which I drew on to escape the daily drill of complying with the bourgeois values of the late 1950s. My yearning for the pleasures of yesteryear led me to embark upon many imaginative initiatives that would eventually lead to my quest to find the Dakota again. The past was gone, sure enough, but that plane was and still is a tangible symbol of the glories of those times and, in many ways, my fascination with it was not unlike a surrogate love affair.

Herein lies the core of my story: my search for the Dakota. Long after I had left Indonesia, this quest stemmed from a passion that would only grow stronger over the span of fifty years. Looking back, I can trace a gradual development.

It all started in high school with the aviation books and magazines that I loved to read and that nourished my dream of encountering this legendary aircraft again. I also remember that my father managed to momentarily satisfy my insatiable appetite for plane-spotting by taking me to the air show at the Ypenburg Air Force Base, where

I saw several Dakotas lined up together alongside supersonic jets. It was the summer of 1959 and I was almost 13 years old; it must have been an emotional reunion.

In my second year at the Jesuit school, I joined a hobby club and built my first balsa wood scale models of warplanes. This interest progressively developed into visiting aviation museums, airports, and hangars wherever I could find them. Sharing a common interest with my friend Bally (who had also come from Indonesia), we often showed more bravado and daring than most other Dutch boys. We made increasingly adventurous trips to the many World War II "*Atlantik Wal*" bunkers in the nearby dunes, whose roughly bricked-up doors we would pry open, armed with no more than a chisel, a hammer, and a flashlight for peeking inside. We found ammo and many enigmatic paintings on the walls that enthralled us. We sneaked onto the Army's firing ranges in the dunes between The Hague and Wassenaar looking for adventure, which we then found in the form of rocket-like, non-charged canon shells neatly piled up and packed in cardboard boxes in a wagon on a narrow-gauge railway. We were gobsmacked by the fact that such a projectile could be found and had no hesitation in taking home a grenade or two for ourselves! We then hid these secret gems under the garage floor, as we were well aware of their flammable nature and did not want our parents to find them.

At the Reno Air Races, which I first attended in 1990, I felt a growing urge to somehow bring the planes of my youth back into my life. All I had to do was find a way of incorporating the aircraft into the sponsoring schemes and ad campaigns that I developed for my employer.

In November 1990, my company sponsored the Aloha Classic World Cup finals. Windsurfing in Maui, I produced a video clip featuring the last surviving Hawaiian DC-3, then being operated by Haveco. With the help of famous windsurfing stars (including on the left, Laird Hamilton), it was my first attempt at using the Dakota in a promotional campaign, though this one eventually came to naught.

One day we decided to go visit the Naval Air Station in Valkenburg, ten miles north of The Hague. We climbed the first low fence at the end of the runway and sneaked through the meadows where the cows were grazing to get closer to the runway. In awe, we waited to watch the submarine patrol planes and dive bombers taking off. We lay there stiff from the excitement and the thump of the Grumman Avengers' radial engines, which you could feel in every bone in your body. Those planes were later replaced by the Grumman Trackers and the legendary Lockheed Neptune, and also by a rare amphibian aircraft of the Martin Mariner type that looked to me like a cumbersome whale making a foolish attempt to fly.

The virus had infected me in Borneo, but it was in Holland that it really started to catch hold. Slowly but surely, Bally and I succumbed to an intoxicating mix of undying admiration for and fascination with the machinery of war, including transport vehicles in the form of aircraft, jeeps, and motorcycles. Apparently it was our way of providing our boring life in the Netherlands with some adventurous content on our free Wednesday afternoons and on weekends. Inevitably, our overenthusiasm when it came to climbing fences and scaling walls saw us being marched to the local police station after we had been caught trespassing—again—by a police officer or a guard, but through our adventures we were to become friends for life and still are to this very day. For many years now, we have been riding our Harleys and Jeeps on an annual pilgrimage to Normandy with the same group of sworn friends for the D-Day commemoration festivities and to see the museums, beaches, parades, air shows, and, of course, the Dakotas on display there every year.

My laborious, seven-year sojourn at the Jesuit school finally came to a happy end in June 1965. I passed my final exams—barely—and said goodbye to the slowly crumbling institute of the religious boys-only Jesuit school. I left it with conflicting feelings, thinking of the establishment both as a jail to be jeered at and also as the place where I wore my first pair of Wrangler jeans and played the first Rolling Stones music at school parties. Both these modernisms were much to the chagrin of the fathers, who must have regarded my friends and me as a pack of little devils that constantly pestered them for no good reason with all that noise and our worn and torn attire.

TRAVELS AND STUDY

It was the end of high school, and I could now look forward to dedicating my time to long-distance travel, something I had been dreaming about for years. In July of that year, I went to live with my parents in Yokohama, Japan. In 1967 they moved to Melbourne and I got used to frequently flying there, too, all flights onboard KLM's first intercontinental jetliner, the Douglas DC-8. Back in those days, intercontinental flights were punctuated by a number of stopovers, and everywhere I landed I would see Dakotas all around me. Whether it was the Middle East, Anchorage, Singapore, Manila, or Sydney, the good ol' Daks were there to be admired in large numbers. That always gave me a special feeling: the boundless curiosity of my childhood never ceased to rear its head, especially during the longer journeys.

Whenever we had a stopover and I spotted a Dakota parked somewhere in a remote corner, the naughty habit of climbing fences would simply take over again, urging me to risk all just to be able to touch the aircraft. I often gave in to this urge, too, much to the annoyance of airport security staff all over the world. I still feel that urge today and, to be honest, I am still a darned good fence climber.

After a year split between traveling and hanging around my parents' house in Japan, I enrolled at the Erasmus University in Rotterdam in September 1966 to study economics. It was the beginning of a fantastic ten-year period in my life; years that flew by far too quickly.

In between my studies and visiting my parents in Melbourne, I also found the time to set up a student club/bar/discotheque called The Westwood Club, in October 1967, together with a neighbor and friend of mine. From the outset it was a huge success; the money came in handy and we were quick to treat ourselves to cute-looking British MG-B sports cars and my own long-cherished WWII motorcycle, a Harley Davidson Liberator, upon which I spent my free time roaming all over Europe.

To be honest, my motivation to rush through my studies was low, to say the least. At the time I was more interested in devoting my time to expanding our club's business and bringing it to the next level by searching for a larger building. The joint we had was bursting at the seams as a result of its success. My parents lived in faraway Australia and they were not entirely up to speed on the situation regarding my efforts to combine the running of a student discotheque with the rigors of academic life.

In the end, it all worked out fine; nine years later I graduated from college and the club continued to flourish. It is still going strong today under the same name but with a new and younger management.

It is often said that your student years are the best years of your life. I loved every minute of that time but, in hindsight, the best was yet to come.

THE CORPORATE CAREER

After completing my studies at the Erasmus University, I was offered a position as a management trainee at the Turmac Tobacco Company (later Rothmans, and finally Batco) in Amsterdam. Thus began, in July 1976, an extremely interesting working relationship in a fascinating job, one that I would hold for the next twenty-four years.

The management and promotion experience that I had gained over the previous eight years with the Westwood Club also came in very handy.

I soon found that my abilities and interests lay primarily in the development of new and creative communication strategies for the multiple corporate brands aimed at the European markets, where the Turmac/Rothmans Company was very active. Given my background, it is probably stating the obvious to say that what I craved was a job that would afford me plenty of freedom, both in the creation of brand strategies and in terms of global traveling opportunities. I had knocked on exactly the right door; this multinational company had the perfect job for me.

I worked from the company's offices in Amsterdam and later on in Paris, and I spent six months of the year traveling around the world as sponsorship and promotion director. The job involved

As creative director for the PME clothing label, I shaped the "Cargo Pilot" theme for the brand, culminating in a photo shoot in Opa Locka, Florida in 1996. This iconic picture of the PME sheepskin pilot jacket was to become the most prominent image in the ad campaigns that would bring the label great success and continues to do so today.

organizing large sports-related events and parties that promoted the brand experience. In our role as sponsors, we were actively involved in tennis, golf, car rallying, motorcycle racing, the Paris-Dakar Rally, and windsurfing events, and later also in Formula 1 with the sponsorship of the British Williams team. In motorsports, we had a contract with the Honda team for the Motorcycle Racing World Championships, while in the Paris-Dakar Rally and in the Le Mans 24-hour race our company enjoyed great success with the Porsche team on behalf of the Rothmans brand name.

An important element of most of our promotion schemes was the setting up of a branded clothing line, which significantly increased brand and event awareness.

With races, rallies, tournaments, and world cups to be (co)organized and the design and sales of brand-linked clothing lines, I had a very busy agenda and, along with a fantastic group of colleagues, my travels saw me circumnavigate the globe ten times or more. My work brought me from Aruba to Athens and from Maui to Monte Carlo. It was precisely this aspect of the job that would eventually lure me to another, more distant world. One where I would finally go in search of the Dakota.

In 1989 I was asked to devise and submit a new sponsorship campaign for one of our main brands. In the course of studying a number of options, I visited the Reno Air races in Nevada in the summer of 1990. It was there that I first came across the fascinating world of vintage World War II aircraft participating in what is often dubbed "The World's Fastest Motorsport." But what really caught my eye were the operational piston prop aircraft still being flown on a commercial basis.

That same year, under the banner of Peter Stuyvesant Travel (PST), we again sponsored the World Cup Windsurfing Finals in Maui, better known as the legendary Aloha Classic. At the airport I encountered the last surviving DC-3 still flying freight in the Hawaiian Islands. This Haveco-owned Dakota inspired me to shoot an experimental promo video for the brand.

With the island teeming with professional windsurfers, I drew up a storyboard in which a group of windsurfers hired the local Dakota to take them and their boards to the hottest surf locations in Hawaii. The intention was to show this video at the Salon Nautique, a major water-sports related public fair in Paris two months later. Every year we had an impressive stand at that huge boat fair where we sold cartloads of event-related surf-style clothing under the PST label.

I probably could not have made the promo video any cheaper than I did, as even the film crew was on hand on Maui for filming the main event. Both the crew and the surfers loved the MTV-style film—which we managed to shoot in only three days—but, unfortunately, back home the film was less well-received.

In fact, the Ivory Tower (as the board was often dubbed)—the guardians of an advertising campaign that had been running successfully for over twenty years—was outraged. In their eyes, the existing brand theme with the Concorde Jet silhouette and the slick luxury style of traveling around the world was still a very valid one. A shift in image from the Concorde to an old vintage plane like the DC-3 was quite simply a bridge too far for them.

In hindsight, I had to admit that the video was poorly timed; it was too much of a change for most of the conservative board members. This video was primarily meant to be an out-of-the box tryout into new directions, as in the back of my mind I was convinced that the brand was rapidly losing its powers of attraction and relevance.

My first attempt at introducing the Dakota into the professional realm of a commercial promotional campaign had ended in scornful failure. But not long afterward a new opportunity presented itself, again involving a clothing line, but this time from a different perspective and for a different brand name.

In the mid-1980s, our company launched for the Dutch market a clothing label under the name Pall Mall Export Clothing Company (better known as PME). My colleague and friend Ron had come up with the idea of transforming the predominantly sports event–related apparel line into a more general men's casual brand. He was looking for a cool brand image that would suit their "vintage" collection's flagship: the leather aviator's jacket. Ron came to me looking for help with the creative pitch, one aimed at devising an advertising concept that would fit seamlessly with his newly designed leather and denim jackets and casual shirts and trousers.

The experience I had gained on my trips to the Caribbean and Hawaii proved very useful. I had come across vintage aircraft and their pilots, the rowdies of the tramp aviation world, who flew all kinds of cargo in their wrinkled planes to distant and remote locations, in particular Alaska, Northern Canada, the Caribbean, and Central and South America. I suggested that we should focus the repositioning of the PME clothing label around this little-known and unique phenomenon, a world characterized by the romance of unlimited freedom and one that could provide a fantastic image platform for a casual clothing label. For the sturdy leather aviator jackets and cargo-style trousers and shirts, the name Cargo Pilot seemed to be the perfect fit for the brand. In addition, as the brand's icon, I naturally proposed using the Dakota; what else?

This aircraft was, and still is, the predominant means of transport when it came to flying cargo to primitive and remote locations. I wrote a slogan for PME that incidentally also provided an apt explanation of how this veteran war plane had managed to survive in the modern world of aviation: "Dakotas fly in low and slow to places where no jet, truck, or boat can go."

That simple one-liner reflected precisely the image that PME wanted to communicate: we may be old, but we are still gold. The sentiment embodied in this phrase soon became a new and attractive value in the world of jeans and casual clothing. The concept of vintage and worn goods and attire was set to become more fashionable and, in that light, the Dakota turned out to be the prefect icon for the

PME became a favorite with retailers everywhere and the label went about extending its network through free "Shop Props." I contacted Basler in Oshkosh and bought two containers jam-packed with surplus DC-3 components. PME absorbed it all for use in retail window display in their appropriate "Old Hangar" style.

communication strategy around the PME brand.

The idea provided me with an alibi for introducing that aircraft once again into my world of advertising and promotion. It was enthusiastically received by Ron and his team, but the internal battle with the Ivory Tower was by no means won.

With the fiasco of the PST video film still fresh in my mind, I had to take a more intelligent approach this time. I needed the right visual imagery, and that meant carrying out a preliminary photo shoot. I flew to Arizona and Florida in the fall of 1990 in order to visit the Tucson aircraft graveyards and Opa-locka Airport just north of Miami, the home base of a fleet of operational Dakotas. Later on during that same trip I also visited the Caribbean islands of Puerto Rico and the Dominican Republic, where there were lots of Dakotas still operating as freight haulers.

Together with a photographer friend of mine, I went about the task of capturing on film the world of the workhorse Dakota. It was on this trip that we did the first test shooting for what would later turn out to be the genesis of the new Cargo Pilot advertising concept.

In the absence of any official budget, we followed the formula of the ultra-low-budget shoot. I looked around for suitable locations at the airports where the vintage planes were to be found, took on the role of photo model, subsequently dressed up as a cargo pilot, and did my best to look cool for the camera.

All things considered, the results weren't too bad, especially given the fact that everything was done without the use of any special effects or lighting whatsoever, never mind the help of a stylist. We got the photos blown up into large prints and I put the whole series of pictures under my arm and returned back home. This time, however, I did not go straight to the gallows of the entire board of directors with my idea. Instead I first went to see my CEO alone in order to discuss the concept with him upfront. Once I felt he was okay with it, I gave a presentation to the board at a meeting in Amsterdam. Different approach this time—the CEO was now an ally for my idea and that made a hell of a difference when it came to keeping the opposing forces at bay!

Almost two years later, in 1992, they finally gave their seal of approval to the new advertising campaign for PME. That may sound like sluggish decision making, but an important psychological hurdle had been taken. It opened new doors and, unsurprisingly in my eyes, it was a huge success from the outset and provided the label with an extremely relevant and original theme that is still very popular today. Their smart marketing mix of price and quality with relevant apparel design seemed a perfect match. Bolstered by the new campaign, the label grew to become one of the leading Dutch men's casual brands with a dealer network of over 500 outlets in the Benelux.

From the start of the PME Clothing Company, I was engaged as a creative director in charge of all photographic sessions on behalf of their campaigns and selecting the planes and remote locations for the shoots up until the year 2000, after which I worked on a freelance basis until 2004. I also began writing the scripts and text (in English) for their advertising, tags, badges & prints and brochures and gave support to a completely new phenomenon in the market: dressing up shop windows and corners with authentic brand-related shop props.

For the purpose of attracting and supporting potential outlets and PME dealers, we started to buy up cheap DC-3 surplus components in the United States from the aircraft junkyards that I had located on my earlier photographic trips. Using this scrap, Ron was able dress up shop windows in the unique "Old Hangar" style of the brand image, which included a special PME display corner decorated with a prop blade, cowling, or instrument panel, all in their original "as found" state so as to accentuate the vintage aspect of the clothing line.

Those shop props were low-cost but original eye-catching items supplied for free in order to lure new and reluctant outlets into the company's network, and it worked wonders. I flew many times to the United States, buying up one container load after another of scrap/surplus parts that I was able to find in the various traders and operators' corrosion corners.

In 1999, my employer Rothmans announced a merger with its major competitor, Batco, with the result that our entire board of directors, senior management, and staff were replaced in July 2000. The merger was partly due to the introduction of stricter

The photo shootings for the clothing brand were soon extended from Miami to Tucson and the Caribbean Islands, and later on to South American countries. In rare cases, I had to take on the role of photo model, like here in Tucson at the AMARC, the largest aircraft junkyard in the world. These yards were to become an important source of surplus parts for our free "shop prop" scheme.

European anti-tobacco legislation prohibiting all promotional and advertising exposure for tobacco brand names.

After twenty-four years, I left the company with mixed feelings. I had had a fantastic time and made many friends in my job as international promotions director and creative executive, but I felt it was time to move on to new pastures where I would be less exposed to the machinations of the corporate flow. Just as in my days at the Jesuit school, I knew that my skewed attitude toward the powers that be would always result in friction within any company culture. Where many people feel more comfortable treading the well-beaten, risk-free path, I usually wanted to check out the roads to my left and right to see if they might lead me to new horizons.

The Gates of Wonder through which I had first passed way back in Borneo seemed to be much more open to me than they were to many others, for whatever reason. Possibly, as a result of my extensive wanderings around the world up to that point, this lifestyle had provided me with a slightly different perspective than that of the average policymaker or board member of the decent "old boys network".

Many times I had to play the game in which certain members of the council of sages would agree with my ideas on the condition that I incorporated some reflection of their own ideas in the final result of a new concept. It was like trying to bake a new kind of pizza with six chefs standing around me, all of whom had to be in agreement on the recipe and also be allowed to add their own ingredients. The end result might look like a pizza, but we would never have a chance in hell of finding a customer who would want to eat it.

Creative processes are rarely enhanced by the democratic participation of an entire board of directors. Compromises were, of course, usually required, but in my view they did nothing but weaken the original concept, with the subsequent loss of impact, relevance, and soul.

But in hindsight, the results were not that bad at all. I was able to introduce the PME Cargo Pilot concept, which brought me close to the whereabouts of the Dakotas. Another major success followed on the tails of the PME story—they finally let me do the Catalina Odyssey TV series for our major brand Stuyvesant. The proposed vintage amphibian aircraft Catalina PBY-5A was finally accepted as the new image carrier for the brand in 1993 and 1994, replacing the previous Peter Stuyvesant icon, the Concorde, after more than twenty years. (For more details and photos, view also my friend Michael Prophet's website at www.michaelprophet.com/News_articles/News_articles2012/PSTravel.html).

In spite of all these successes, however, after more than two decades of boardroom cage-fighting—endless discussions with directors, councils, country managers, advertising agencies, bureaucrats, accountants, and many other prominent players—I decided it was time for me to leave.

I have often wondered why there was so much divergence in our respective views. Were they all too blind to see what I could see or had I maybe drifted too far

Dolph's purchase of the DC-3 wingtip at the Miami Art Fair marked the beginning of a whole new venture and the genesis of our company, Avionart. With four legs added underneath, the converted wingtip had the perfect shape for a luxury desk, one steeped in WWII aviation history: a unique combo of a wartime collector's item and a shiny polished desk.

away from the (sub) cultural feel for what really went on in our markets? As always, the truth lies somewhere in between. Sometimes I hit the bull's eye with my creative ideas and sometimes I was as mistaken as I had been with that monkey cage of mine in Balikpapan. I often figured I could snare dreams that, ultimately, were simply beyond my reach. And that misadventure with the ape wouldn't be the last time I got my fingers burnt either.

However, when it came to dreaming about searching for the legendary Dakota I had no doubts at all. The urge to go out, find that airplane, and retrieve it from the mists of legend was utterly irrepressible.

Ron and the people at PME stuck with me from the very start. They were a great source of support and confidence and I am still grateful for that. But eventually, in 1999, I found myself at the point of no return; I had to take on challenges in which I would not be able to rely on anyone for help. Americans have a neat way of putting it: "The eagle soars alone." When it comes to fulfilling your own dreams, you simply have to do the job yourself because no one else can ever feel as intensely as you do about those dreams.

THE ADVENT OF NEW OPPORTUNITIES

The announcement of the merger with Rothmans and Batco happened to coincide with an extraordinary telephone call I received from an old friend of mine, Dolph Bode. He had a curious tale to tell. Dolph had learned the ins and outs of the jewelry and art trade from his father, who had a reputable shop just behind the famous Hotel Des Indes in The Hague. Dolph was also an excellent salesman and did a lot of traveling through America and Europe, buying and selling high-end jewelry. I had known him since we were teenagers and had hung around with him a lot in the late

1960s and early 1970s. In 1975 he had married a girl named Susanne, who happened to be the granddaughter of the legendary Dr. Albert Plesman, the founder of KLM.

The Plesman family had amassed a fine collection of relics and unique pictures down through the years—all evidence of the rich aviation-related history of the family. Dolph had been collecting art and rare objects for quite a while, and with his background and that of his wife he soon developed a special interest in KLM- and Douglas-related artifacts from the past.

Dolph told me that he occasionally bought unique memorabilia that he came across during his business trips to America. These were usually posters or scale models, objects that were easy to transport. But one day, in 1999, he called me again with a somewhat confusing story. He was all excited about a very cumbersome aviation object he had bought at a fair in Miami on his last day in the United States, and he was very eager to show it to me.

It all sounded a bit mysterious, especially since he was not willing to go into any detail over the phone about this particular object. "Come over and see it for yourself," was all he would say.

I arrived at his house, just 100 meters down the lane from my own home, more than just a little bit curious to be honest. I went inside and saw that he had already unpacked this "big thing" on the floor. I immediately recognized what it was and said, "Wow, that's a Dakota wingtip! How did you get your hands on that?"

He was clearly surprised by my instant recognition of the object and so he came up with a counter question. "In Miami. I bought it at an antiques fair. But how the heck do you know it's a Dakota wingtip?"

"Well, the thing is, I've been flying around America for three years looking for Dakota stuff to supply the PME stores with shop props. So you don't need to tell me what DC-3 parts looks like. But why did you buy it?"

"Well, it was the last day of the fair, near to closing time, and I had been circling the thing for two days already. I knew the dude at the stand and he told me that this was the last remaining wingtip that was still for sale on the free market anywhere in the world. I just couldn't resist it. I had to have the damned thing. So we did a deal just before the fair shut down on the final day. It was only after I had bought it that I thought, "How the hell am I going to get this lump of a thing on board a KLM flight to Amsterdam?" One leaving that very same night too!

In a mix of undisguised boyish bravado and pride, he continued, "I told the staff at the KLM check-in counter that it was a gift for Prince Bernhard and that it absolutely had to come onboard, otherwise it wouldn't be there in time for his birthday."

Dolph was the kind of guy who could get away with a tall tale like this. He was an excellent salesman and a real charmer. To top it all off, at over six feet tall he made for a physically imposing sight and he had obvious connections with the founding family of KLM. His frequent flyer Gold Card also helped get the message across and,

We traveled to Coventry Airport, UK to visit the legendary Air Atlantique Company in our first search for surplus DC-3 wings. They operated a number of vintage Lockheed Electras and DC-3s for tackling coastal oil pollution using sprayer installations.

in the end, nobody felt compelled to investigate his story and refuse his request.

They swallowed the lot—hook, line, and sinker—and he managed to get this huge 2.30 meter by 1.75 meter (almost 8 by 6 feet) piece of "luggage" onboard as "odd size" without even paying a dime extra!

His Prince Bernhard story was clever to say the least. Almost everyone in the Dutch aviation world and beyond knew of the relationship that the Dutch royals had with that old airplane. It all went back to May 1945 when Queen Wilhelmina returned to the Netherlands after the German occupation onboard a Dakota. The picture of that landfall is printed in the collective war memory of the Dutch, and it was this connection that convinced the KLM staff to help him, because, if the story he was telling was true, then none of them would want to be responsible for failing to deliver a birthday present for the Prince on time! Dolph, of course, knew this.

But now that he had gotten it this far, what on earth was he going to do with it?

"Well, look closely at its mirror-polished surface. It would make a fabulous showpiece if I were to use it as a desk, here in my house as the pièce de résistance in my collection of historic aviation objects."

After the polishing job, the shiny protruding rivet heads reflected light like water droplets, making them look like a pearl necklace stretched out on a mirror.

It wasn't long before we had this incredibly beautiful wingtip standing on four legs in his living room, a pristine example of bygone aviation craftsmanship and a unique combination of a war relic and a designer desk with a fine elliptical shape at the wing's edges.

Moreover, it was an authentic piece of a Dakota, which just so happened to be *my* plane!

Familiar as I was with what could be bought at vintage aircraft scrap yards

We were taken to an old barn where we found our very first DC-3 wingtips and horizontal stabilizers for our new business. Without any expertise in paint stripping and polishing, we had a long way to go before we could sell our first shiny DC-3 Wing Desk.

around the world, I challenged him, half in jest.

"Well, I think the shark who sold you this took you for a ride by saying that this was the last wingtip in the world for sale. That, I know for sure, is certainly not true. I know where you can buy at least half a dozen of them."

A look of disbelief crossed his face, quickly followed by an attempt to cast doubt on my assertion. "Are you kidding me? Seriously? How do you know that?"

He was probably afraid that he had paid far too much for something that was not as scarce as the man at the fair had claimed. Nevertheless, in my opinion it was still a very special object and definitely worth a lot of money.

"I have been to places where the Dakota is still flying, and not as a kind of flying museum piece but as an operational aircraft. Places where they also have surplus parts—from wingtips to engines and everything in between," I replied.

Whereas I had always seen DC-3 parts merely as shop props in their original bare metal form, all dull, dimpled and wrinkled, Dolph had bought his object as a highly upgraded shiny version, an object fit for high-end interior decoration.

In any event, we were both greatly impressed by this stunning piece of work. A short while later, Dolph said, "Well, if it is true that wingtips like this one can still be bought, why don't you go and buy some? We can convert them together and I'll sell them."

That sounded like a very compact business proposal. We were quick to develop and expand upon our plan, no doubt driven by our mutual appreciation for this piece of furniture and our affection for the airplane that would provide us with the basic materials for such a wild plan.

We had both built up a wealth of expertise in our respective fields over the years and were ready to combine our talents to set up a business together. We reckoned that we would be able to source, design, produce, and sell an exquisite collection of vintage aircraft parts converted into high-end interior decoration objects and designer furniture.

We set up the company Avionart and decided, as a kind of trial, to travel to England in order to buy a small number of Dakota wingtips and then set to work on how to make them as shiny as the Miami wing panel. With that hurdle taken, we would then consider how we should go about selling them and for what price. We rented a van and took the ferry from Hook of Holland to Harwich. Our final destination was Coventry Airport in mid-west England, where we bought our first wingtips from the well-known aviation firm and Dakota operator Air Atlantique. This was the first Dakota-hunting mission undertaken in the guise of Avionart. It was the summer of 1999 and our business trip/holiday would turn out to have far-reaching consequences for the pair of us.

The trip to the hangars at Air Atlantique was a memorable one, even if only for the opportunity to admire their fleet of vintage aircraft, a fleet that existed nowhere else in Europe on such a large scale. To us, being back in England was like visiting the largest open-air museum in the world, with its rural villages where time seemed to stand still and factories and workshops that looked like they had been taken straight from the pages of an old picture book. We drove across the charming English countryside where the road system had an alarming lack of road signs and the coffee and beer we were served tasted like they had been brewed a few years before we ordered it.

The quaintness of it all was splendid, however, and the people most helpful in providing us with directions to our final destination, the door to Cargo Platform of Coventry Airport. At that time, Air Atlantique was often jokingly referred to as Air Antique. The company flew a breathtaking collection of vintage operational aircraft from the forties and fifties and also carried out maintenance work for museums, private collectors, and other aircraft owners.

Even this late in the twentieth century, we were able to witness the freight operations of 1950s-era Lockheed Electras there. In the large hangars we saw work being carried out on classic

For the promotion and advertising campaign of our new product line, we were allowed to use some stunning photos from the post-war Plesman Collection on our website. Here is a KLM DC-3 that had just landed at a Scandinavian airport, back when airport security was not yet a major concern. (Photograph: Plesman Collection)

airplanes like the De Havilland Dragon Rapide, the Avro Anson and, of course, a beautifully restored Dakota. There were also another four Dakotas parked outside, one or two of which were still operational, the others in greater or lesser states of dereliction and without engines.

This fleet stood on standby just in case an oil tanker ran aground on the English coast. In such a scenario these old aircraft, with their sprinkler systems mounted on the horizontal stabilizers, could operate as oil pollution control platforms. They were able to spray their chemicals over oil spills at sea. Later on these aircraft were used for charter and sightseeing flights for paying passengers who were flown to and from many major air shows in England and continental Europe.

However, what we had come for was not to be found in these large hangars but rather tucked away in an old farmhouse in the countryside, some ten miles from Coventry Airport. When we got there, we were taken to a big old wooden barn with huge doors that opened with a mighty creak and, after getting used to the darkness inside, we found ourselves standing in an enormous warehouse packed to the rafters with Dakota instruments, engine parts, panels, wings, wheels, flaps, cowlings, etc. You name it, they had it. It looked like the owner, in an inspired moment of historical awareness, or maybe temporary insanity, had gone to the considerable trouble of storing a complete arsenal of Dakota stuff. Most of it seemed to come from the many small Dakota operators that had existed in England in the 1960s. They, and others like them, including Freddy Laker and Danair, had gotten into the business of flying to the then newly emerging holiday flight destinations in Spain, the Canary Islands, and France. For the English, this was an attractively fast and inexpensive way of getting across the channel to the sun in the days before the Chunnel and major motorway networks.

After searching around in the gloom for a while, we suddenly found ourselves standing eye-to-eye with a row of dirty wingtips buried underneath many years of grime and dirt courtesy of the roof above them, which leaked like a sieve, and the multitude of pigeons' nests and cobwebs. The bird droppings were on every surface that we touched, but this did not suppress our great excitement. Here we were, staring at our first wingtip windfall. In their current state they looked no better than old demolition scrap, but we knew exactly what lay beneath the grimy surface thanks to the shiny wing adorning the living room back in Dolph's house.

Another photo from the Plesman Collection, with 3 different types: the tail of a Lockheed Constellation, a Douglas DC-4 in the background, and a DC-3 in between. (Photograph: Plesman Collection)

The Tragic Final Flight of the Dakota IBIS (BOAC flight 777A), 1 June 1943.
KLM was the first overseas airline company to operate the DC-3, with this first plane named IBIS, delivered in Sept.1936. The aircraft operated on the long flights from Amsterdam to Batavia (Jakarta). During the German Invasion of Holland in 1940, the aircraft happened to be in London, and it stayed there to be employed by BOAC with a Dutch crew for wartime flights from Bristol, UK, to Lisbon, Portugal. IBIS escaped 2 aerial attacks in '42/43, but the third time, while flying over the Gulf of Biscay, she encountered eight Luftwaffe Ju-88 fighters, who shot her down. The crippled aircraft was able to make a perfect landing on the sea. But while floating, the 4 crew & 13 passengers' ordeal was not over: in a series of appalling strafing runs, the German fighters came back again. No one survived the carnage, and as later developed, the camouflaged British/Dutch DC-3 had on board Leslie Howard--not only a famous actor from the legendary movie "Gone with the Wind," but also a talented British spy, who had just held a most secret meeting with Spanish leader Generalissimo Franco. Perhaps that this gave reason to German intelligence to employ a Luftwaffe squadron to shoot IBIS down and make sure of no survivors. In any case, this particular DC-3 stands as a fascinating tragedy with an even more intriguing background of spying and possible betrayal.

The man who was helping us told that four of the wingtips, which were slightly damaged, were for sale. The pigeon shit, which he threw in for free, turned out to have caused additional corrosion on the aluminum skin of the wingtips. Those birds shit a sort of acid that has a disastrous effect on aluminum when water is added to the equation. And there was water in plentiful supply thanks to the leaking roof. The corrosive effect on the skin where the birds had deposited their turds showed up as miniscule worm shaped wrinkles etched on the aluminum surface. Fortunately, the years of dust that had accumulated on the wingtips was like a layer of baked clay and it seemed to have absorbed most of the shit, thus neutralizing the worst effects of the droppings.

We loaded the four wingtips—our first ever trophies for the business—into the van and drove back to Holland. In our enthusiasm we were convinced that the production and delivery of our first wingtip desk was only a matter of a few weeks' work. We had no experience whatsoever when it came to the necessary production techniques, nor the slightest clue as to what lay in store for us.

This all soon became apparent when we started on phase one: removing the layers of paint from the wing panels.

The first three layers of conventional paint were stripped to reveal a layer of yellow-green anticorrosion paint that proved impossible to scrape off. We tried everything and asked everyone for advice. Many people offered solutions, but this paint was resistant to even the most aggressive paint stripper available. The only thing that seemed to have worked up to now was the pigeon shit in that barn in England, which, as it turned out, had actually worked too well.

Where the shit had landed, it had actually removed the greenish super-coat and also damaged the skin underneath, leaving zillions of tiny wrinkles. The offending paint turned out to be an electrolytically applied zinc chromate, which was fetched during the production of the wings in the war; an anticorrosive agent that works almost like liquid galvanized plating on the aluminum sheets.

We had to learn not only how paint stripping was done correctly but also how to polish the wing to give it a perfect mirror-like skin without grinding a hole in the weather-beaten and flimsy skin plating of only 0.70 mm of thickness.

A list of accessories and parts was required to convert the wing into a desk, including the aluminum legs, trimmings, and fittings. We needed certification plates stamped with identification numbers guaranteeing the authenticity of the wing as an original wartime Douglas/OEM product. And last but not least, we went out of our way to get our hands on the original Grimes navigation lights, which had to be sourced and then mounted on each desk before delivery to the client. It took a grand total of ten months from our first trip to Coventry to the delivery of our first table, complete with a high quality mirror-polished finish and all the extra trimmings.

We took our first wing desk to a photo studio, placed a Charles Eames office chair behind it, and let the studio photographer get to work with us looking over his shoulder in the role of critical art directors. The result was fantastic. The pearl-like longitudinal rivet lines on the top skin shone in all their glory after a day of experimenting with lighting and reflections on the shiny surface.

Satisfied with the results, we placed our first Avionart advertisement in a well-known international glossy publication published by Condenast, the famed magazine

The Dakota Wing Desk in all its glory. The mirror polishing of the desktop accentuates the lines of protruding rivet heads: they reflect ambient light like a string of pearls draped over a mirror. Minor dimples and spots on the surface are scars from the war and they underline the rich vintage texture of the skin and the heritage of this Dakota Wing panel.

called *World of Interiors*, and it wasn't long before we made our very first online sale. Moreover, an antique dealer from London, Bentleys of Walton Street, contacted us with a view to setting up a dealership. The owner, Tim Bent, has a unique Harry Potter–style shop that boasts a bewildering array of high-end interior objects and a matching collection of antique Louis Vuitton suitcases. He also sells old shotguns, ship models, binoculars, chairs, and other special objects in a shop that is more like a mini museum with all its quality memorabilia and collector's items. Our wing desk from the World War II era was the perfect addition to his shop window.

We made two more trips to Coventry to buy more wings. On one of those trips we also bought the horizontal stabilizers from a DC-3, which we then converted into an 8-meter long conference table that we sold to an aviation-related client in Toulouse! Not long afterward we even managed to find four forgotten wingtips in an old farmhouse in Northern Holland, also stored in a large barn out in the middle of nowhere. The owner was a collector and he wanted to trade his wingtips for the DC-3 propellers that we had acquired via a dealer in Arizona, still in their original crate and dating from the Korean conflict, November 1953!

Finds like these were exceptional, however, and could never form the basis of a viable business that required a steady supply of the main component of our trade—the DC-3 wingtip.

The production and sales of our wing desks started to pick up, and we were soon able to better estimate the product's sales potential; a product that would inevitably become scarcer with each passing year. All war production contracts with US manufacturers of military transport vehicles, including airplanes, trucks, tanks, and motorcycles, were cancelled overnight after the second atomic bomb was dropped on Nagasaki on August 9, 1945, forcing Japan to surrender only a few days later.

The production of Dakota/C-47 parts was also discontinued abruptly, although the DC-3 airplane continued to be assembled using existing stockpiles up until 1946.

This meant that we were basing our business model and all our investments in terms of time, money, and effort, on a component whose production had actually ceased in 1945.

Were we diving headlong into quicksand?

We had to consider very carefully exactly what we were getting ourselves into. Where in the world were we going to find sufficient supplies to keep our business going for several years? One thing was clear: Europe was an empty warehouse. We might be able to find the odd wingtip here and there that could be purchased or swapped for something else, but in order to be able to buy wings in any decent kind of volume we had to switch our attention to other potential surplus markets.

Thanks to the experience I had gained at my previous job with PME/Rothmans, I was able to call on a large network of contacts and locations on the other side of the Atlantic. This vintage aircraft was still to be found in respectable numbers in North and South America; it was there that the Dakota continued to fly as a commercial airplane. I knew where we needed to go and where we could start our quest. The best part of the story was about to begin.

The DC-3 Horizontal Stabilizer was also mirror polished and converted into a boardroom conference table. Boasting a staggering 8m wingspan, one of these tables was delivered to the Dutch Institute of Technology in Delft (TU) as a symbol of the groundbreaking aircraft design and manufacturing techniques that changed the world of aviation forever in the late 1930's.

CHAPTER 3

The US Gulf States

Jackpot and Quicksand

In 2000 we sold the seven wingtips we had bought in Coventry and were faced with a growing demand for our product. The supply line from England had quickly dried up, however. There was no stock left; we had bought (and sold) everything we could get our hands on across the Channel. I decided to get in touch with my friends from Florida Air Cargo (FAC) at Opa-locka Airport near Miami, the air cargo company I had come across a few years earlier when looking for good photo shoot locations in America for the PME label.

After leaving my job at Rothmans in July 2000 I continued to work on a freelance basis for the PME clothing company as a creative consultant, enabling me to capitalize fully on the combination of this job and my new role as Dakota Hunter. Though it was still the same game, it was now serving a dual purpose.

Opa-locka Airport, an old military training airfield dating back to World War II, is located north of Miami not far from Fort Lauderdale. These days it functions as an airport for smaller-sized air cargo carriers and the US Coast Guard. It also houses a number of demolition companies that scrap old aircraft, mainly outdated jetliners, including Jumbos, and recycle the aluminum.

It had always been a very informal airport where you could simply walk in through the front gate without too much trouble, but all that changed after 9/11 when security became much tighter. I re-visited the place in 1996 to do a major PME photo shoot after having done some preliminary test shooting at locations in Holland and the United Kingdom. It was a fantastic spot. The place was a hive of industry, with cargo aircraft being loaded nonstop, and it boasted an impressive collection of operational vintage propeller aircraft.

In addition to a C-45 Twin Beech or Expeditor, Florida Air Cargo also had two operational Dakotas parked there plus a third redundant one that served as a source for parts for the other two, whose fuselage was always full to bursting with all kinds of wing and body parts. Anything that didn't fit inside was left lying on the ground around the old airplane. In the good old days, when training aircraft were relatively small, there was little need for parking space or paved runways, so tall trees and grassy areas still formed the backdrop to this scene. This particular corner of the field was filled with old-style hangars that had huge sliding doors. The whole picture made this part of Opa-locka the ideal location for our photo sessions thanks to the vintage feel of the place, the sunny weather, the beautiful, lazy Florida light, and the backdrop of aircraft from bygone days all still working and flying as if time had somehow stood still there.

The founder and owner of FAC was Paul Kupcke, an extremely amiable and big, chubby man. He was quick to appreciate my admiration for his vintage aircraft. Most modern-day pilots looked down on the kind of junk and flying scrap metal that stood in his yard. But luckily, every once in a while, "Hans from Holland" came along and paid good money for a photo shoot or a flight to the island of Bimini, that little gem just offshore from Miami.

Paul flew us himself on our first trip over Miami in one of his Dakotas with a smaller aircraft, a Cessna 172, flying next to us filming everything. He sat there with that great big body of his squashed into the tiny pilot seat in the cramped cockpit. He could barely get the belt across his belly, and any movement other than handling the steering column was almost impossible. The DC-3 cockpit had obviously been designed at a time when Americans were smaller in general and, in any case, certainly less voluminous.

Despite this handicap he was very attached to this oldie, which he had been flying all his life. His younger operational managers, on the other hand, were much less forgiving when it came to the whims of this flying barrel. They hated having to dole out the attention and daily cuddles a Dakota requires in order to keep it going.

When I returned in 2003 and 2004 I found exactly the same friendly atmosphere and the same complaints among the ever-changing team of cargo masters and

Opa Locka airport, located north of Miami, is the Gulf States and Caribbean hub for vintage prop liners. Pictured here is a Twin Beech (aka C-45 Expeditor), an operational DC-3 on the left, and on the right, a couple of DC-6/7s.

The DC-3 N-15MA on the right with PME nose art, was the mainstay of Florida Air Cargo's operations from Opa Locka. It was the first Dakota we flew in to Bimini, and our photogenic star featured in many of the ads for the brand. The aircraft has since returned to its original nest.

managers. They all thought it was a time-consuming and costly affair to keep the plane in the air, and it was especially difficult to find certified mechanics who could work on the demanding piston engines. Many of those wrench jocks moved to Alaska, where it was easier to earn good money. A lot of the managers I spoke to told me that the Dakota was now really in its last days and would soon be replaced by a more modern airplane with more speed, more payload, and more profit. Such a plane would have to be propelled by turboprops, for only then could you get all these benefits along with a higher degree of dependability and less time spent on maintenance.

Those young dudes could dream all they liked. A medium-sized turboprop aircraft capable of transporting twenty-eight passengers or three tons of payload costs up to eight times more than a DC-3. Moreover, a turboprop engine requires a much higher level of maintenance and the total investment has a higher rate of depreciation. Whereas you can tinker with a radial piston prop engine out in the open air, the work on a turboprop requires a hangar, and if you don't have your own hangar then you have to make use of an expensive FAA-certified maintenance facility. That means you can't carry out the maintenance work yourself, which makes the price tag of a turboprop aircraft far too high for nonscheduled flights or tramp aircraft operators whose main business is flying to the small islands of the Caribbean.

So the load managers' fortune-telling abilities let them down in this case. The DC-3 remained in service in their fleet, even long after Paul had sold the business. The cargo depot was eventually moved to a more central location in the airport complex. I always dropped by to visit them at this cozy little airport whenever I was in Miami. The place simply oozed the spirit of the fifties, and one day, in 2006, I

Opa Locka was the ideal airfield for our photo shoots. A laid-back atmosphere with hardly any security checks, it was also a demolition station for phased-out jets. With vintage hangars and aircraft all around, this ex-military pilot training center even had trees and lawns, a rare sight these days at any airport.

found myself there again, this time face to face with five Dakotas standing on the cargo platform. Oddly enough, I had been able to walk straight onto the airfield without being stopped by any security guards, and I made a direct beeline for the Dakotas, camera in hand. The cool shade of the trees had been replaced by the shadow of a huge new control tower—a rather disturbing feature in this near perfect picture of yesteryear. It was not as informal a place now as it once had been. Furthermore, the all-American image was distorted somewhat by the presence of a pair of old Antonov AN-26s at the rear of the airfield, both with their turboprop engines removed. These Russian aircraft had obviously been standing idle for quite a long time, a sight I had previously seen in many other places around the world. These cheap import aircraft from Eastern Europe had once seemed to be the ideal successor to the seriously aging Dakota. The AN-26 is fitted with turboprop engines, which makes it much faster. And its cargo was not loaded via two impractical doors in the side of the aircraft but via a wide rear tailgate ramp, just like on a truck; much more convenient and capable of handling larger payloads than the Dakota.

However, no one had accounted for the possible onset of Soviet Sickness—an ailment that within no time immobilized much of the Antonov fleet. This ailment was brought on by the lack or poor supply of engine parts and the high level of maintenance that the aircraft required due to the poor quality of its parts. Not unlike the Trabant syndrome of old communist industrial rubbish that never worked when you needed it and for which no spare parts were ever available in any serious quantity or quality. Though Florida Air Cargo and other operators tried to keep them flying, they usually had to fall back on the services of their good old Dakotas just to keep business going.

Florida Air Cargo only stopped using the DC-3 in 2008 or 2009 and then relocated to Fort Lauderdale where they flew exclusively with the Cessna Grand Caravan, a single-engine turboprop aircraft that, even secondhand, can cost up to one million dollars. That plane can handle only one and a half tons of payload, while the Dakota does double that number at a price that is less than 20% of the purchase price for a Cessna.

It seemed to me that the end was now definitely nigh for the DC-3 on the US mainland. The most famous transport aircraft of the twentieth century continued to fly into the current century, but the signs for its future were not good. However, while writing these very words, I got a call from my good friend Michael Prophet informing me that there was still no stopping the Dakota at Opa-locka Airport and that as of October 2012 there were three operators still flying regular operations with the DC-3 and its successor, the C-117 Super DC-3.

Even the name Florida Air Cargo popped up again on one of the planes in 2014, albeit very small and under the tail, and the company is now flying cargo from Opa-locka with a DC-3!

Amazingly, this aircraft is the legendary C-47 N 15 MA, the first plane that we ever chartered at Opa-locka for the PME shoot, with Paul Kupcke as our pilot. For that epic shoot we fitted out the aircraft with PME nose art decals on both sides of the cockpit. This logo had been the PME trademark for years and is the one used in PME's iconic advertisement with the model posing in front of the airplane clad in a sheepskin flight jacket.

In my never-ending search for wingtips I went back to Florida Air Cargo at the end of 2000 and told Paul Kupcke about my new business: looking for airplane parts. In their scrap yard under the tree and in the derelict plane we found four slightly damaged wingtips, which I purchased straight away. Paul explained to me that the tankers and trucks, which had to back up close to the doors of the Dakota for loading, often bumped against the wingtips, as they were two meters above the ground and thus out of sight of the drivers. The result was usually a little light damage and a lot of cursing and swearing,

Florida Air Cargo used a derelict C-47 airframe as a depot for their surplus parts. Inside, we found the wing tips that we were looking for. Our first US deals were made right here with the owner, Paul Kupcke.

On our first trip, we came across the legendary Tradewinds scrap yard in San Antonio, TX. There were DC-3 components piled up everywhere by the ton. And the prices were sky high, too!

because even the slightest dent in the wingtip meant that the airplane could not fly, which called a halt to all operations until the wingtip had been replaced.

That costs time, money, and customers, but the clever design team at Donald Douglas had anticipated such mishaps and designed an easily detachable wingtip when the plane was still at the drawing-board stage, a feature similar to the rear fender on a truck. This outer wing panel is not riveted to the main wing but attached using 120 screws. In cases of damage, these can be unscrewed and, after disconnecting the electrical wiring to the navigation light, the wingtip can be removed and exchanged for a fresh one. On the condition, of course, that there are both left- and right-hand versions of that wingtip on stand-by.

Changing the wingtips took about an hour for experienced mechanics. The plane could thus be restored to operational status reasonably quickly, the repair work on the skin of the damaged tip being a concern for later. In reality, these slightly damaged wing panels often ended up on the surplus heap or in the junkyard. Spare wingtips were more easily acquired from old airplanes and were less expensive than repairing the damaged tips. This practice of "swap and store" opened up a substantial supply channel to us of redundant, slightly damaged wing parts. We would now be able to track down surplus wingtips in the corrosion corners of Dakota operators all over America.

One day Paul introduced me to a business colleague of his, a man who worked for him as a trader and parts locator. His name was Andy Downs, from Nashville, Tennessee, and he had a vast network of customers and parts suppliers in the American Midwest. He soon became our agent, helping us in our search for wingtips and propellers in North America and Canada. We rented a depot at Opa-locka where we stored all the stuff that we found in that first year. Andy took the Midwest Trail while Dolph and I went searching in the Southern states—Florida, Texas, and Arizona. We flew to many locations in those states looking for traders, bone yards, dumps, and demolition sites that might deal in old aircraft.

Andy set to work as a kind of bounty hunter for us, as he had the expertise and the connections required. However, one day he had a terrible accident with a Dakota that was being started up. He was turning the propeller by hand—the normal procedure when starting cold—but through a lack of concentration and communication the pilot in the cockpit had already set the ignition switch to "on." The engine started up when he was turning the blade, the propeller burst into life, and Andy suffered a terrible blow to his shoulder and neck that seriously crippled him. It was years before he had made any kind of recovery from the physical, psychological, and financial damage inflicted.

A few years back he contacted me again to tell me that he was getting married and was working hard at getting his life back on track. We may be able to do some business together again in the future, but the US market has been grazed bare over the past ten years, and we contributed to that depletion ourselves. At the locations that we have already scavenged there is virtually no new supply of surplus wingtips, simply because the number of operations with these aircraft has dwindled rapidly in the United States.

Then, unexpectedly, we stumbled across a rare source of parts at the reputable Odom's Aircraft Parts located in the southwest of Miami. There was no sign of an airport for miles around but that did not stop the owner, Glenn Odom, from establishing a maintenance workshop for aircraft starter motors and generators in an old railway station and building up a huge stock of Douglas parts and components for the DC-3, DC-4, DC-6, and some Convair types, all of which had flown in the Caribbean until well into the 1990s, Miami being the hub of their operations.

The presence of a huge number of relatively small island communities in the vast ocean to the south and east of Miami ensured that flying vintage piston propeller airliners remained a viable business. Speed, time, and payload were not as decisive factors here as they were on scheduled intercontinental flights. In places where small scale and short distances are the norm, a Dakota, despite its limited load capacity and

Our final stopover was in Tucson, AZ, where we found 5,000 redundant airframes in the AMARC desert storage facility, but not one single surplus C-47.

speed, will get the job done. You do not need a lightning-fast turboprop for a flight to a small ring of islands.

In that atmosphere of low speed, low investment, and snail-like depreciation a man like Glenn Odom with his parts and repair shop was still able to survive up until the beginning of the new century. Though the services that he offered vintage aircraft operators were still viable, it was clear that those planes were now performing their swan song after more than half a century of reliable operations.

SAN ANTONIO, TEXAS

After this visit we flew further west. San Antonio, Texas, was our next port of call, as that was where we knew we would find another well-known Dakota Trader: Tradewinds Aircraft Supply. Driving up from the airport over the North Loop out on the city limits, we spotted the familiar sight of C-47 airframes off in the distance, their noses stuck high in the air like they were begging for one more opportunity to fly. When we entered the premises we saw a huge collection of parts scattered all over the place, almost as if a couple of Dakotas had just fallen out of the sky.

What looked like a disordered heap of scrap was in reality a well-sorted array of parts: cowlings, propellers, wheels, and flaps by the dozens, bits and pieces of DC-3s everywhere. We walked around, stunned by the quantity, and suddenly I found myself standing face-to-face with a whole row of wingtips all neatly stacked upright next to each other.

"Holy smoke, get a load of this!" I whispered to Dolph while trying my best to suppress my enthusiasm. I had never seen so many wingtips together in one place before. We had hit the jackpot.

The boss was very friendly, and after giving us tour of the place and serving coffee he said, "Before we get down to business, I want to introduce you to the taste of a real burger. Not that tasteless rubbish at the Big M, but the original burger with pure Texas Beef."

We were hungry and he was right; we had never eaten such a tasty burger before. That helped us through the day, and we needed every ounce of energy it provided, as it turned into a long day during which he gave us an unsolicited and lengthy rundown of how they do business in Texas.

After lunch he drove us around the area of San Antonio, where he had a number of old barns and farmhouses that he wanted to show us. The sun was shining brightly in a clear blue sky but it was freezing cold out in the open country. The barns were filled with parts of old aircraft, mostly DC-3 stuff that he had acquired thirty years previously from Delta. When the airline stopped all operations with this particular aircraft he took over the entire stock from them. We stared at it all in gobsmacked awe. This looked like what we had seen before in Coventry, but here in Texas, where everything comes bigger and better, there were at least five barns fully packed with parts, compared to only one or two in England. We were bewildered by the scale of it all and tried to silently calculate how many wingtips we might be able to take from this treasure trove.

But the truth can be deceptive at times; what you see is not always what you get. It quickly became apparent that most of his stock was operational stuff, complete with yellow labels. FAA certified solid wingtips, ready for use, but not our use. The price he quoted was stiff, very stiff.

I tried a different tack: "You wouldn't happen to have a few surplus wingtips for us with a little corrosion or slightly damaged skin, non-operational, for a nicer price than this, would you?"

The man had gotten a whiff of our appetite for wingtips during our long lunch. He was a shrewd trader, first filling us up with alcohol under the guise of "Try this meat. Nice, hey?" and, as we nodded in agreement, ordering three more beers with a big smile. That went on for a while until he figured we were ready to see his Aladdin's cave. In the meantime, he phished us slyly about our budget so that by the end of the "magical mystery tour" we were simply gasping to buy from him and he was able to hit us hard in the nuts with his exaggerated prices. Back in his office we had sobered up a bit and tried to negotiate, but we were in no position to reject or even haggle over his prices.

It was a lesson in humility for two smart asses from the Netherlands who had waltzed in displaying a little too much interest. With our combined years of experience in negotiating and haggling we thought we would have no problem bargaining with him for the lowest price possible. But the situation here was different. We found ourselves trying to do business in an unfamiliar setting, and the simple fact that we had come all the way from Holland just to buy some wingtips surely weakened our negotiating position. Before we knew what was going on we had shown all our cards, even before the bidding had begun. Not a good idea when you find yourself sitting at the table with an experienced Texas Hold'em poker player.

Our stock at home was completely sold out and acquiring more wingtips was clearly going to be more difficult than we had anticipated. That made us more desperate in our search and too eager in our approach; and this businessman had certainly seen us coming. However, if you make mistakes like this only once and learn from them, then everything is easier the next time around. And the good news, in any case, was that we had found what we had come looking for—wingtips—and despite the exorbitant price it felt good to be back in business again with new stock.

TUCSON, ARIZONA

The next day we flew to Tucson, Arizona, leaving the cold Texas plains and traveling to the milder temperatures of the Coronado desert near the Mexican border. Tucson is home to the largest airplane graveyard in the world: the AMARC (Aerospace Maintenance and Regeneration Center), which fans out over an infinitely flat sandy field. There are over 4,000 old military aircraft lying around in the desert here and it takes a bus tour lasting many hours to see everything. But it is definitely worth the effort, if only to take in the mind-boggling vista of thousands of old airplanes stretching off to the distant horizon.

Contrary to what many people think, you cannot buy anything here as a private individual. The US government uses this facility to park all of its redundant aircraft (from the air force, army, marines, navy, and coast guard), and upon arrival the planes are sealed against corrosion and insect and bird nests (they know all about bird shit and its devastating effects here). In addition, each aircraft is drained of all liquids, such as oil and fuel, and stripped of any weapons and hi-tech avionics before being put into outdoor storage for an indefinite period of time. The idea behind it all is to park these aircraft so that they can be restored to operational status in case of a national emergency. But any aircraft that remain there for more than ten to twenty years are declared surplus and demilitarized. These written-off aircraft are then sold in special auctions, at which only screened and certified traders or friendly foreign air forces are allowed to buy them (Iran and North Korea are definitely not on

The wreck yards around the storage facility are worth a visit: this is a paradise for vintage airplane and car lovers, in a desert with the lowest rainfall of all North America.

The dreaded smokestack—signifying the conversion of most of the aircraft parked out here into aluminum ingots. The 2 Super DC-3s (C-117 D or R4D-8) in the foreground were reserved for clients, a lucky escape from the perpetual aluminum recycling process.

that list). Upon purchase, the aircraft are towed to the site owned by the trader, which usually happens to be right next to the AMARC. A handy setup, because how otherwise could you be expected to transfer a non flying B-52 bomber to your yard? Scrapping on the AMARC premises is not permitted, but transport on a deep loader can be arranged and some aircraft can also be flown out.

Most of the planes that are sold go to the adjacent private demolition firms where they are then stripped of usable parts. The rest of the airframe is shredded to scrap metal and transported to the ovens at the nearby recycling facilities, who then sell it on in the shape of aluminum ingots to the heavy industry sector.

Despite the largest stock of flight equipment ever beheld by us, it was a huge disappointment that there were no C-47 airframes at the site ready and waiting to be dismantled. We did manage to find four Super DC-3 frames at the site of one of the traders. This particular aircraft is an upgraded and stretched C-47 built immediately after the war as a C-117, but that plane's wingtips have a totally different shape and were not suited to our purposes of conversion into a magnificent personal desk.

It was shocking to discover that there wasn't one single C-47 to be found anywhere at this sacred place; a place where all the historical icons of aviation come together one last time for a kind of grand finale, albeit a finale holding no promise other than eventual cremation into blocks of aluminum that end up as soda cans.

The setting winter Arizona sun, at least, with its streaks of "mellow yellow," helped soften the blow somewhat. As did our realization that the absence of the Dakota from this scene indicated that there was still sufficient demand for the aircraft, as it was obvious that it still belongs to the very select club of vintage propeller aircraft flying commercial operations to this very day in far-flung corners of the world.

Regardless of our disappointment, the visit had certainly been worth our while, if only to see the huge array of planes standing there waiting for the cutting torch of the executioner to put a definite end to their existence. That process can take years and years, but a macabre end is guaranteed for all of these flying machines unless, as happens once in a blue moon, someone comes along looking for a suitable museum piece or a relic to put on display at an air force base or in a public park.

A visit to the nearby Pima Air Museum and the demolition sites for civil jet aircraft in Avra Valley, Marana, are also well worth your time and a veritable Walhalla for any true aviation enthusiast.

The presence of such large numbers of aircraft (and also huge numbers of old cars) has everything to do with the fact that the Catalina Mountains have the lowest rainfall in all of North America. With only about six days of rain per annum this is the best and driest outdoor storage location that you could hope to find anywhere north of the Rio Grande or the Sonora Desert.

We arrived back in Miami with the batch of wing tips that we had scored at Odom's and Tradewinds. Andy had not been idle either and soon afterward we were able to take stock of the fruits of our joint quest. The counter stopped at a very satisfying final score of fifty-three wingtips, which we stored in our warehouse in Opa-locka, Miami.

Avra valley, where hundreds of commercial jets and a few prop liners await the fate of the cutting torch and the smelting oven. Even as a derelict, this Super Constellation still displays its majestic beauty under a thundercloud sky. The sheer elegance of this aircraft never failed to impress me.

Eventually, nearly six months later, a container arrived in Rotterdam carrying the stock. One single trip by three men around the United States had produced a result far beyond our initial expectations.

We were finally in a position to start advertising and selling our precious metal, but this was to be the first and last time we would ever hit the jackpot in such a spectacular manner. We all realized this immediately, of course, based simply on the stories that we heard from the many dealers we had met. The stock we had purchased and taken away with us would never be replenished.

ISLANDS IN THE SUN

One day when I was back visiting Opa-locka Airport, I finally found the owner of a very beautiful and unique four-engine DC-7C that was parked in front of the Florida Air Cargo facilities. This DC-7C was flanked by two DC-7 Bs—a special fleet of large "prop liners" in the possession of one man: Carlos Gomez, a native of South America. I had been eyeing this elegant collection for quite a few years already. These aircraft belonged to the greatest of the intercontinental propeller planes, famous in an era before the Jet Age started, with the arrival of the DC-8 and Boeing 707 in the late 1950s. The DC-7C was the final version of the legendary Douglas DC-propeller aircraft, a production line that started with the DC-2 in 1933, followed by the DC-3 at the end of 1935. The up-scaling or "stretching" continued: in 1942, the four-engine models were introduced with the DC-4 and DC-6, and finally the DC-7 and DC-7C in 1956. The latter plane marked the end of the era for large piston prop airliners.

Now, forty years later, here they stood looking like museum pieces but all still operational and, most amazingly, flying for a commercial company and making money for their boss.

I expressed my admiration to Carlos for his fine collection and told him that I had flown in these planes as a boy. When he asked me why I was here at Florida Air Cargo, I told him about my frequent trips in search of Dakota wingtips. In the ensuing conversation he informed us that his aircraft flew three times a week to the small Turks and Caicos Islands, north of Haiti, supplying fresh food to the shops and luxury hotel resorts on the islands. Of particular interest to me was his story about the devastating effects of the many tornados that frequently raged across the islands and that had wrecked many an aircraft over the years. He couldn't be sure, he said, but he thought there were two battered Dakotas still lying abandoned on the island of Providenciales, a small pearl of an island straight out of the movie *The Blue Lagoon*.

My undisguised admiration for his flying monuments quickly forged a strong bond between us. Where someone has put his heart and soul into such preservation activity, that effort prompts strong admiration, and the appreciation expressed can sometimes produce surprising spin-offs, as I had experienced previously with Paul Kupcke and many others. Similarly here, Carlos and I shared a passion for these

The US Navy R7V-1 MATS Super Constellation in all its glory. This aircraft was hired for a PME photo shoot and I enjoyed a short flight on board for the photography. It reminded me of my perilous flight in 1956 in a similar aircraft (a KLM L-1049) that almost ended in disaster after an oversea engine explosion.

aircraft. That was probably what prompted him to invite me on a flight the next day to the island where he had to deliver his cargo and where we could look for those lost Dakotas. That was a real bonus and one that I had not even been fishing for: a flight I had only ever made in my dreams. Now Dolph and I had been invited to take a trip in this rare and beautiful Seven Seas, as the DC-7C was often dubbed.

We were up before dawn the next morning—not my favorite pastime—but with such a unique flight before us we were naturally eager to go. At the airport, with the morning still dark, the cargo of fresh fruit, eggs, and meat was being loaded using a large forklift. The DC-7C has a nose wheel and huge propellers, and is so big that the aircraft stands high on its legs in order to keep the prop tips clear of the ground. As a result, the load floor is much higher than on the DC-3. In terms of dimensions this is a totally different kind of aircraft, even though the age difference between the DC-3 and DC-7C is only twenty years—a sign of how fast aviation technology had developed since the early 1930s.

To step on board you need a long ladder, somewhat different from what we were

used to with our cuddly DC-3, the primal father of this mastodon.

Once on board—with a little extra help from the forklift—we were assigned seats right behind the cockpit, the only ones available in what was essentially a long tube stuffed to bursting with pallet upon pallet of cargo. The sun was just creeping over the horizon in the east when we climbed into the deep black sky with its magnificent aurora of orange light, our ears filled with the typical heavy droning sound of the plane's four giant radial engines, each delivering 3,400 horsepower at full speed. The equivalent of 14,000 galloping horses pulling you off the runway is quick to knock any lingering sleepiness out of your system, and I felt the hairs on the back of my neck standing promptly to attention.

We flew over a still drowsy Miami and headed out toward one of the small islands of the Bahamas for a stopover with a landing on a half-paved stretch of beach. The hotels were just a few miles from the beach, waiting patiently to serve their guests the breakfast we were flying in: milk, bacon, eggs, tomatoes, and bananas. Fresher than this early morning delivery you simply couldn't get.

After this brief stopover, where the pilots did all the unloading themselves, we climbed into the sky again on our way to our final destination, the island of Providenciales. The scene below you on the way to the southern Caribbean Sea truly defies description. Turquoise colors that constantly change in tone and accent, interspersed with the bright white of the beaches and the almost arctic blue of the

The awesome flight that we made with the Gomez brothers from Opa Locka to the Turks and Caicos Islands was on board this rare DC-7C. Like most vintage prop liners here, it was used for supplying fresh food to the many luxury hotels and resorts on the small holiday islands of the Caribbean.

deep ocean, and every shade and hue you can imagine in between. Surveying this palette of colors from above, you cannot help but think that the Great Painter was well into his stride when he was working on this bit: a surrealistic artwork of unprecedented beauty with a mystique and romance that calls to mind the Harry Belafonte song:

Oh, island in the sun, willed to me by my father's hand,

All my days I will sing in praise of your forest, waters, your shining sand.

The small islands beneath us all had their own wreath of white sand, like some kind of ring they wore signifying eternal union with their Creator. It reminded me of my fabulous flights over the Indonesian Archipelago fifty years earlier. We enjoyed the panorama in blissful silence, broken only by the monotonous drone of a plane that flies slower and lower than a jet. This made the experience even more dramatic, as if we were flying in our own private plane over small pearls with exotic names like Ragged Island and Crooked Island.

When we landed a few hours later on Providenciales and went looking for the wrecks of the Dakotas, we soon discovered that we were too late. The remains that Carlos had seen years ago at the end of the runway had been shoveled unceremoniously by a bulldozer into the sea at the end of the beach road that runs around the island perimeter. I had seen exactly the same scene years earlier in Tortola on the British Virgin Islands, where many aircraft had fallen victim to hurricanes that were detected too late before they made landfall. Aircraft on local airstrips, even ones the size of a Dakota, that were often parked unprotected and unanchored were sometimes simply blown over during these storms or severely damaged by flying debris, including corrugated iron roof plating and smaller aircraft that had come flying in, often minus their pilots, only to be smacked against other planes.

Something similar must have been the case here too. Damaged aircraft were written off, stripped of their instruments and engine parts, and then dragged to the beach. Sadly, we had arrived too late. Everything was now sitting at the bottom of the sea—a fatal situation for the planes' aluminum skin due of the swift corrosion caused by the warm, salty waters.

Back in Opa-locka after this magnificent flying experience, we expressed our genuine gratitude and said goodbye to the Gomez brothers, who had taken us on a truly memorable flight.

San Juan, Puerto Rico

Having been put on the right track by Carlos Gomez, we soon became aware of the existence of another dump location in the Caribbean, in Puerto Rico. We flew to the capital, San Juan, and met representatives from Four Star Air Cargo and TolAir at the island's international airport.

Both of these companies flew with a fleet of five Dakotas throughout the southern region of the Caribbean, including to Aruba, Curacao, and the British and US Virgin Islands. Their business model was identical: cargo flights to the smaller islands with luxury hotel resorts that needed fresh fruit, meat, eggs, milk, etc. every day, supplied by aircraft that could land on very short airstrips.

Oh Island in the Sun. On our flight south, we took in the view of the Paradise Islands at a speed and altitude half that of modern jet airliners. This enriched the fabulous sight tenfold!

In Caicos, we arrived too late to be able to retrieve any components from a tornado-damaged DC-3. The derelict airframe had simply been shoved into the sea at the end of the runway. (Photographs: Rico Besserdich)

We started at the TolAir premises, where we were introduced to the boss. I asked him casually whether he might have any surplus DC-3 parts. As we had already learned in San Antonio, all talk of wingtips was best kept until the very last moment. Displaying any more evidence of our eagerness would only end up costing us dearly, as we had already learned the hard way.

The next stop was at Four Star, where they had quite a stock of wingtips but none for sale, unfortunately, as they felt they needed to keep them as backup for their own operations. They also had to deal with a relatively high incidence of "touch and crush" accidents during cargo deliveries by trucks and vans to the aircraft on the island's smaller airstrips.

Unfortunately, both of these C-47 operators are now defunct, though many of the airframes are apparently still standing at the Luis Munos Marin International Airport of San Juan, Puerto Rico.

OPERATION PINK DAKOTA

Though we didn't find any wingtips, we did get an excellent lead from a TolAir manager who showed us a picture in an aviation magazine of a number of pink or purple painted Dakotas that had become damaged beyond repair during a tornado that had raged across the island. For whatever reason, the hulls of the Dakotas had been transferred to a nearby swamp just behind the beach and dumped. Next to a weird photo in the magazine, we saw a vague description of the spot where they could be found. We decided to drive down to the east coast of the island the following morning in the direction of the city of Ceiba. The Jose Aponte Airport is close to the city, and the manager figured that the dumped Dakotas had been stationed there as operational aircraft.

Operation Pink Dakota was launched, and after a journey of more than one hundred kilometers across the tropical island we were quick to notice that even dream islands sometimes have blind spots. It was a phenomenon that I had seen in many other places: the total ignorance of the locals when it came to environmental issues. They tend to litter their own backyard indiscriminately with all sorts of rubbish, like old refrigerators, cars, bottles, furniture, and mattresses.

We saw it everywhere along the way, in ditches and in the woods, and soon we were going to experience this pollution in its most extreme form: the frames of abandoned aircraft.

We came down a hill and drove along a forest road that led to the beach that we saw looming in the distance. We knew we were close to what we were looking for because of the swamp on our left-hand side. Yet we were unable to see anything that looked even remotely like a bunch of purple Dakotas, despite driving up and down the road a few times. Suddenly, however, I spotted what looked like large bubbles rising from a field in the swamp about fifty meters off the road, completely overgrown with a kind of swamp ivy. I yelled out, "Bingo, I think I see them! Look, over there, those four big humps covered in vegetation."

Beside ourselves with excitement, we jumped out of the car, and after an hour of

For many years, the airport of San Juan, Puerto Rico had been a beehive of DC-3 flights operated by Tolair, Four Star and others who flew cargo to and from Miami, the Dominican Republic, BVI, USVI and many other smaller Caribbean islands. By 2010, most such operations had ceased.

searching we finally found them. We stood on the edge of the road; between us and the aircraft there lay a submerged field of tall grass. There was no trace of pink or purple paint to be seen anymore; the metal was completely covered in weeds that obviously thrived in this wet ground. I knew from my Borneo years how to walk across boggy fields like this and told Dolph, "Just walk behind me. Push the tall grass flat with your feet and your stick, then you can use that as a kind of carpet to walk on." We slowly waggled out over the water without getting our feet wet. My plan worked perfectly; step by careful step we got closer to the spot where the Dakotas were dumped. We saw that the wings had been removed and that the two hulls were lying right next to each other with two more hulls behind these, slightly further away from the road. One airframe was still standing on its wheels with its central wing section between the engine nacelles, which were still in place.

In Puerto Rico, we found 5 airframes dumped in a swamp. Dolph felt confident that he could walk through the dense vegetation to reach the overgrown Dakota hulk in the background. The smile on his face had vanished not long after this photo was taken.

We had to be very careful. You couldn't really stop walking, because if you did you would instantly sink into the mud. Maneuvering slowly but surely, we tried to find out what had happened to the wings; were they still lying somewhere nearby maybe?

When I arrived at the first hull I went to inspect the interior of the cockpit to see if any of the instruments were still intact.

The cockpit windows of the partially sunken front section were at chest height, so I bent over and stuck my head inside, twisting my way through the open window frame.

That way I could take a closer look inside, but my pleasure at what I saw was of very short duration. I suddenly heard a hissing whoosh coming toward me. Definitely bad news, and I quickly pulled my head out and yelled, "Snake! Get out of here."

When I had extracted myself from the small window frame, I was instantly faced with another surprise: Dolph was busy doing something that looked like an Indian tribal dance. Between all the jumping and swaying of arms I noticed something I had never seen before in my relatively action-packed life. I knew exactly what it was

The airframes in the marshland were completely covered in ivy and inside lived a security force that stopped us dead in our tracks. Happy hour was over and we had to switch very quickly to survival mode.

though, thanks to the weekly Donald Duck Magazine I had read in my younger years.

A swarm of wasps was busy attacking Dolph and, although the insects were small, their sheer number and fierceness made them a real danger. I saw the little beasts spin around his head and attack him. They produced a scary hissing sound and had Dolph hopping around in a frantic attempt to keep them from stinging him.

Barely recovered from the surprise of what I was witnessing, I was then suddenly attacked as well by a new swarm that emerged from the plane. Fortunately, I had a cap on my head and so managed to keep the creeps at bay by swiping wildly at them. But it was clear that we were fighting a losing battle. Tactical retreat was the only option, but there was no route that could be taken in a prompt and orderly fashion, just those wetlands with tall grass where you had to watch every step you took.

However, we didn't have time for any kind of pussyfooting around and so we ran in blind panic trying to escape from this prickly situation. With splashing steps, we galloped as quickly as we could back to the spot where our car was parked, our shoes soaked through and dripping with mud. We were still under attack, so jumping in the car was not an option. Remembering the Donald Duck stories, I yelled at Dolph, "Run to the beach and dive into the water!"

It must have been a hilarious sight, and while we were waving our arms about furiously trying to keep the wasps at bay, a bus carrying a load of Japanese tourists

came driving up the road. We saw them waving back at us in amused excitement. Nice people, these, with their nodding heads and oriental smiles. We had other worries, however, and we ran off down the road in the direction of the beach. We had just set foot on the sand when we noticed that the pesky buggers were suddenly nowhere to be seen. They had vanished as quickly as they had appeared, into thin air.

Exhausted and dazed, we sat on a bridge next to the beach with sore arms and necks. Dolph had suffered most from the attack, with at least twenty stings to his face, neck, and arms. Further down the beach road there was a small bar with a veranda where we took refuge and tried to recover from the shock. We had never imagined that Dakota hunting could be this scary.

It was a bizarre experience, and while we licked our wounds the bartender came over to us. Intrigued by the marks of the stings he asked us what kind of jellyfish had stung us.

"Jellyfish? What are you talking about? We were attacked by a swarm of wasps," we replied.

"A swarm of wasps? Are you kidding me? I've lived here for years and I've never heard of people being attacked by wasps around here, so what are you guys talking about?"

I told him what had happened and that the red swell of the stings was proof that we had been attacked. He told us that he had once taken a look at those airframes but that he had used a different route along the beach to get there and had never seen any wasps.

The Bimini Islands, 50 miles East of Miami: an illicit US-Colombian trading station.

Some time in the early 1980's, Colombian drug runners identified the tiny Bimini Islands as an ideal station for smuggling cocaine and marijuana into Florida. With no law enforcement or border control in effect, the smugglers flew Dakota's/C-47's and Commandos C-46's in at night, coming in low over the sea from Northern Colombia via Cuba. Flying under the radar, they landed on the South Bimini airstrip right next to the beach. From there, the precious cargo was reloaded onto the waiting Go-Fast Powerboats, which headed straight to the Florida coast to deliver their goods to lorries waiting on riverbanks and remote beaches.

Half the population of the island must have made a living from this trade: the local marina was stuffed with extremely expensive and fast powerboats with fitting names like "Midnight Express" and "Blockbuster." However, one day the US Coastguard and DEA picked up the scent of the Colombian's smuggling route via Bimini and set up a trap to crush this illegal trade. Awacs systems were used for early detection of low flying intruders and those planes were then pursued by American Coast Guard patrol aircraft. Many a pilot opted in panic to land their cocaine-packed planes before daylight, and soon the beaches and lagoons of the Bahamas were "littered" with crashed wrecks and abandoned airplanes from Colombia.

We had approached via the inland road; he had come in from the beach—could that make a difference? An hour later, with all the stingers removed and the pain now thankfully less agonizing, we decided to go back again, this time with the bartender as our guide along the beach path. We returned to the scene via the "backdoor" and came upon the second row of aircraft, where we also found the planes' wings lying around.

This was exactly what we had come for, so we did not have to search and inspect any further than here. Unfortunately, however, Mr. Bartender was quick to throw caution to the wind as the macho man in him suddenly surfaced. After looking around the place and not spotting even a single wasp, he became overconfident and joked, "So, where are all those honeybees, guys, the ones that attacked you so badly?"

The word "honeybees" came out of his mouth as if he were addressing a bunch of whining wimps who had been stung by nothing more harmful than a couple of mosquitoes. He obviously didn't take our story very seriously—an underestimation that he would soon pay for, and painfully. I gave him more details about the scene of the crime: "We were attacked more to the front; over there near the first row of DC-3s. But be careful for God's sake." He didn't listen, however, and just ploughed on ahead.

Somewhere deep inside me I'm sure I must have entertained the evil thought, "Go ahead you braggart; you don't know what you've got coming to you."

Swaggering like a genuine terminator, he pushed on through the sludgy grass over to the half-sunken airplane fuselages just to show us how tough and daring he was. Suddenly, he came under attack and a swarm of wasps started streaming toward him as if out of nowhere. I had a front-row seat and saw the swarm appear like a mini tornado right out of the derelict fuselage, accompanied again by that ominous hissing sound.

Crashed Curtiss Commando C-46 in Bimini Bay.
According to a tale recounted by the local bartender at the "End-of-the-World" Bar in Alice Town, this
C-46 came in at night to land on the Bimini airstrip, which locals had lit up using torches. As the heavy
aircraft approached over sea, suddenly, out of the dark, a US Coast Guard patrol boat appeared on the
scene like an uninvited party pooper. In the full glare of a searchlight, the pilots realized the imminent
threat and opened the throttle in an attempt to escape the trap, but the aircraft was too heavily loaded
and was flying too slow for this kind of panic maneuver. The result was devastating—the plane stalled,
rolled over its port wing and crashed upside down in the shallow waters just south of the airstrip. The
crew were all killed, and the Americans salvaged the valuable cargo and left behind only what you can
see in this picture as a warning to others. It marked the end of this illegal trade station, one that
ironically had had a similar history in the early 1930's with the smuggling of alcohol into Florida.

They fell full upon him from all angles; these little monsters know exactly where they can hurt you. They do not even try to pierce your clothes or your jeans. Instead, they go straight for your head, arms, mouth, and eyes. Curiously, they only attacked him, he being the intruder this time on their territory. They didn't come near us as we were standing further away from their nest. However, that did not stop us from running away just as fast as the barman did. We felt a little bit sorry for him, watching that deadly flying squad buzzing around his head as he ran back to the beach in panic, just like we had told him to do in case of an attack. The assault was now well and truly

A majestic water landing on the Bimini Lagoon. During our 1994 Catalina Odyssey with a British Catalina flown by Capt. Paul Warren Wilson, we landed here at the spot where Chalks Ocean Airways moored its Grumman Turbine Mallards.

in full swing with the wasps attacking him like kamikaze pilots: strafing from above and behind, trying to stab him, and being very successful in their mission, too.

Once he reached the beach, the little critters suddenly disappeared. Our daredevil bartender was in shock, like he had looked death straight in the eye. There wasn't a trace left of the swagger and bravura he had exhibited ten minutes earlier. Though we were sorely tempted, we refrained from asking him what he thought of the "honeybees" now. He had been stung all over, including on his face, even around his eyes, and on his lips and neck. His face was all swollen and we really did feel sorry for him then, because it was our story that had lured him into this trap.

We shared a drink with him at the bar and discussed our chances of getting the wings out of the swamp. During our second visit I had been able to get a brief but good look at the wings. They were lying next to the hulls but, unfortunately, some of them were partially sunken under water and that is not a good sign in a warm climate. The corrosion had probably eaten into the aluminum already and almost certainly to such an extent that a costly salvage operation would not be justified. It was obvious that this was the end of the line with regard to these wings. Operation Pink Dakota was cancelled; the airframes would remain forever in the realm of the wasps and would eventually rot away in the warm and salty swamp waters of eastern Puerto Rico.

I frequently flew with this Grumman Turbine Mallard from Miami Cruise Boat Port to Bimini. After the landing in the turquoise lagoon, the wheels were lowered in the water, the aircraft drove up to the ramp and parked in Main street of Alicetown. Such idyllic scene only existed here, but in Dec. 2005, it all came to an abrupt end. The Mallard crashed just off Miami South Beach after a wing collapse, killing all 20 people on board. It was the fatal blow to the oldest existing air carrier in USA, Chalks, since 1919.

We had made the find of the century in the United States, but here in the Caribbean the results fell bitterly short. No shortage of adventure and stunning experiences, but zero return in terms of what we were actually looking for.

I had to readjust my focus back onto new horizons because we realized that with the purchase of the wingtips in the United States we had more or less exhausted the supply available from the dealers, operators, dumps, and graveyards there that we knew of. A new supply of wingtips from these sources was unlikely and certainly not in the numbers that we had found this time around.

Nevertheless, thanks to my previous experiences with the PME photo sessions, I knew where I had to go next: Central and South America.

During those trips to that part of the world I had come across many weird characters, but I rarely saw a Westerner in the more remote areas of that great Latin continent. Not surprising, of course, as there is often something quite shady about the place, and conditions there can be very primitive, intimidating, and sometimes even downright dangerous.

Many of the countries in Latin America have a dodgy reputation—outside the controlled tourist attractions and fenced-off resorts the safety situation can be awkward, to say the least, and often just a step too far for the average traveler from Europe or North America.

I didn't have much choice in the matter, however. The rapid drain of DC-3 parts from the US market initially appeared to be a major setback, but it ultimately proved to be a blessing in disguise. The Dakota Hunter could now literally spread his wings and head for new territories in South America. That was where the real challenges and adventures were awaiting me.

CHAPTER 4

Venezuela and Honduras

Angel Falling from the Sky

In April 2000, I traveled with a team to Venezuela to do a photo shoot for a new advertising campaign for the PME clothing label. We had chosen Venezuela as our location because of the country's exotic and scenic landscape and the large number of Dakotas still flying there. I didn't have to think twice about returning, though this time not for the scenery but primarily to hunt down wingtips.

In the autumn of the same year, with our own company, Avionart, now in full swing, Dolph and I planned a search and salvage trip to Venezuela, followed by a flight to Honduras.

We kept our options open regarding our flight schedule and started our tour in Caracas, the capital of Venezuela. From there we planned to fly east to the cities of Puerto Ordaz and Ciudad Bolivar. Both towns had active Dakota operators at the local airports, and we were keen to find out what surplus parts they might have in their depots and corrosion corners.

There was a network of tourist shuttle flights between the popular Caribbean

We flew in the oldest flying DC-3 (with right hand side entry door) from Caracas to Los Roques, a tourist island close to the Dutch Islands of Aruba, Curacao and Bonaire. The company Aero Executivos has since ceased operations.

holiday destination of Margarita Island off the northeast coast and the jungle location Canaima in the southern region, between the Amazon and Orinoco rivers. That spot is a truly perfect sightseeing location for tourists, as they can admire the natural wonder of the place in a real *Jungle Book*–like adventure from the comfort of their seats in a Dakota circling low and slow around the mountains.

The fabulous scenery here is of an unprecedented grace because of the mix of tropical rainforest and savannah, meandering rivers, lakes, and rapids, and the very impressive vertical cliffs from where the highest waterfall in the world plummets to the foot of Table Mountain.

JIMMIE ANGEL

That impressive 1,000-meter-high waterfall is called Angel Falls. The name suggests a connection with winged heavenly creatures, but the cascade is actually named after an American adventurer, Jimmie Angel. Angel, who was a friend of Charles Lindberg and almost certainly a role model for the later Hollywood hero Indiana Jones, came here in 1937 looking for gold and gems in his brand new five-seater Flamenco aircraft, accompanied by his wife and two fellow adventurers. Weighing his options on how to get to the summit of the almost inaccessible Table Mountain, he bluntly decided one day to land his aircraft on top of it, on the Auyan-Tepui crest, as if they were flying in with a glider, provided with a sled rail.

The mountain's Indian name means "house of the devil," and it wasn't long before Jimmie discovered why; he should have known better with such a macabre name.

In his attempt to land on the very swampy terrain on what from a distance looked like a flat top, he damaged the landing gear and propeller when the aircraft nosedived into the soft ground, with the result that he would never be able to take off from that godforsaken place.

He and his passengers were literally trapped in a Lost World, a sort of Jurassic Park where man had rarely, if ever, been before. They had to deal with rare species of jaguars, snakes, frogs, and insects that had evolved in splendid isolation from the rest of the world. The summit was almost always shrouded in clouds and incessant rainfall fed the dozens of cascades that rushed over the rim of the huge tabletop. More depressingly, there was no sign of the gold or precious stones that Jimmie had imagined would be lying around waiting for him to simply scoop up—a fairytale that existed only in ancient Indian legends. He knew this area from previous expeditions and had

Jimmie Angel "discovered" the highest falls in the world while searching for gold on a table top mountain. The daredevil landed his light aircraft right on top but nosedived it into the boggy ground. He found himself trapped in a "Lost World" and it took him 11 days to find an exit from this Jungle Alcatraz.

already looked for gold there, and he claimed to have found it. During that first trip in 1933 he had "discovered" the waterfalls, though they had long been known to the local Indian tribes, of course.

It must have been a crushing disappointment for him not to find the promised El Dorado. After spending a few days searching for the elusive gold, he and his group decided to quit and descend the mountain, but it was not easy to find a path down; the walls of this mountain are almost perpendicular and completely bare of all vegetation for the first few hundred meters below the top plateau. After a long search they finally found a way down the mountain and they eventually arrived, completely exhausted, in the Indian village of Kamarata below. It had taken them eleven days to escape from their jungle Alcatraz.

THE LOCAL DC-3 OPERATORS

Immediately after the war, the world had an insatiable appetite for iron and steel, in order to meet the demands of large-scale reconstruction work. Huge deposits of iron ore were found in a vast mountain range along the eastern Orinoco River. In collaboration with the major US steel giants, who at that time were still very welcome, a massive reclamation plan was drawn up. The iron ore (and later on also bauxite) was taken by train to the Orinoco River, where it was loaded onto ships destined for Baltimore. This required the dredging of the river so that large seagoing vessels could penetrate deep inland. As a result of all the mining and the construction of new ports, the cities on the river expanded rapidly, as did employment levels in the eastern Orinoco basin.

Servivensa and Rutaca were the two main regional airline operators that

The magnificent Angel Falls. The highest water falls in the world with a free drop of almost 1000 m. from the Table top mountain Auyan Tepui, translated as "House of the Devil". Jimmie should have known better with such name.

flourished alongside the industrial development of the Orinoco iron region. For many years they flew with a fleet of Dakotas—an airplane that was relatively cheap to acquire and also perfect for use in the primitive conditions of the remote settlements, with their short, unpaved landing strips.

But the need for the Dakota gradually dwindled. By the end of the 1970s the airports had been improved all around the country—a development that resulted in longer, paved runways and better maintenance facilities. This opened the door to the turboprop and jet aircraft, and they rapidly replaced the Dakota because of their higher speed, greater range, and greater payload capacity. It was the same story all over the world at that time, but here and there one could still find notable exceptions to the downgrading of the DC-3, some of which still operate to this very day.

Just as the Dakota was coming to the end of its operational career in the Orinoco region, the new phenomenon of mass tourism was exploding on Isla Margarita, a development that would significantly extend the life span of this vintage airplane.

In the early 1980s, the Venezuelan government decided to create a major tourist resort on the island of Isla Margarita, and the "Costa del Caraibe" was thus born off the northeastern coast of Venezuela. Every week, jumbo jets from Europe, America, and Canada delivered thousands of tourists to the international airport of Porlamar on the island, which was only a three-hour flight from the magical jungle spot in Canaima.

Local operators spotted a golden opportunity for their still-operational but otherwise redundant Dakota fleets, as the faster jets could not land on Canaima's tiny gravel airstrip.

The DC-3 could bridge the distance in a one-day round trip, carrying 24 passengers. In a country where fuel is almost cheaper than bottled water and labor costs are low, tickets could be offered at very competitive prices and a new daytrip/sightseeing market opened up.

Canaima airstrip, with Auyan Tepui and cascades in the background. The DC-3 YV-224C was our transport and motor home for the photo shoot out here, just months before she suffered a fatal crash.

The route was a huge success. Every day, six to twelve aircraft operated by the Rutaca and Servivensa firms flew planeloads of tourists from Porlamar to Canaima. When Dolph and I went there in 2000, we were just in time to experience the heyday of a business that single-handedly extended the lifespan of the Dakota in this region by at least ten to fifteen years. Until suddenly, in January 2001, that dream came to a dramatic end.

Just a few months prior to that fateful date, we had booked our flight from Caracas to Puerto Ordaz, the home base of Servivensa. On the morning we arrived, the first thing we saw was the fleet of Dakotas with their distinctive black and white striped noses.

It was here that our trip began in earnest. Gauging from the number of aircraft we could see before us, we figured that there had to be a pile of damaged wingtips lying around in a warehouse somewhere. This was a realistic expectation, based on our experiences in the United States, but we were in a different country now, on a different continent, dealing with different laws. It soon became obvious that nothing here was ever declared surplus, so there was virtually nothing for us to buy.

So what made this place so different? In contrast to North America, Venezuela is not a land of abundance—in oil and iron ore maybe, but definitely not in goods. Everything they have and use here will continue to stay operational until the end of time; in Venezuela nobody throws stuff away. Old smelly Jeep Wagoneers from the

1960s and 1970s are still driven around in the thousands, similar to what one sees in Cuba with old 1950s sedans. Buying a new car in this country is simply not an option.

And it was the same with wingtips—they had them in heaps, but they kept every last one for possible future use. The fact that wing parts needed no recertification for repair or reuse was the main reason they never dumped them or declared them surplus to requirements. In America, each and every repaired aviation component must be certified by the FAA (Federal Aviation Administration) and can only be overhauled by a certified repair station or mechanic. That obligation does not exist here and this encourages the operators to carry out repairs themselves, which of course is a lot cheaper.

So, were the Dutch dudes disappointed? You bet. But not defeated. We decided to travel along the Orinoco to the west, to Ciudad Bolivar, where we were soon knocking on the door of the other operator, Rutaca. For more than twenty years they had been operating a fleet of five Dakotas, and they were very proud of their superb safety record. The owners insisted on showing us the workshop, the hangar, the depot, and their airplanes, which were parked on the north side of the airport. Bolivar City was their HQ, from where they flew both to the coast and inland. It quickly

For many years Rutaca and Servivensa had operated the profitable tourist line from Isla Margarita to Canaima, with its impressive table top mountains and waterfalls. The attraction of the Angel Falls to tourists extended the commercial life of the DC-3 right up until 2001.

became clear to us that the tourist flights from Isla Margarita were the mainstay of their business, their real source of profit.

The place was a hive of activity. In addition to the Dakotas, which always needed lots of tinkering, they also had an old Antonov AN-2 biplane that could carry twelve passengers. Propelled by a large Russian radial engine with a four-blade prop, it is an archaic-looking beast of a plane and not very attractive or inviting to western tourists. If its single engine quits while flying over the jungle (and former Soviet stuff does have a reputation for suddenly doing just that) then you have little chance of survival. With this in mind, the aircraft was relegated to flying shorter cargo runs only. The ungainly biplane was not a commercial success here, but I did come across it quite often in Peru, Colombia, and especially in Cuba, where I flew in one several times from Havana to Santiago.

It was the Dakota that made Rutaca a commercially viable business. They had been using the plane since 1974 for scheduled flights, but also for "tramp freight" and nonscheduled sightseeing flights. The Rutaca premises were all very neat and tidy, with four DC-3s currently operational and two undergoing overhauls. They kept a heap of damaged and worn parts in the back of their yard. Unfortunately, everything here was also predestined for reuse. "*Disculpa signores, niente para comprar,*" or "Sorry boys, nothing for sale here."

To alleviate our disappointment we decided to spend the weekend in the legendary jungle camp at Canaima, chilling out near the waterfalls and the lake. After booking a flight for the next day, we had the afternoon free to take a tour of Bolivar's

The gravel airport platform of Canaima, with 10 to 12 Dakota flights per day. The airport was the exclusive domain of the DC-3, as it was the only aircraft that was able to handle the primitive conditions and short landing strip. The low speed and maneuverability of the aircraft added much to the spectacle when it flew close to the table top mountains.

Jimmie Angel's Flamenco Aircraft was salvaged in 1974 by helicopter from the table top mountain and erected as a monument in front of Ciudad Bolivar airport. The plane was in a remarkably good condition despite its grand old age of 80.

old city center. The old town up the hill has been preserved as an old Spanish town, complete with cobbled streets and a beautiful old cathedral, and next to that a small colonial-style fortress. From here we had a splendid view of the mighty, muddy Orinoco River, which flows all the way from Colombia right across Venezuela, more than 2,000 kilometers, before spilling into the Atlantic Ocean.

With a width of up to 15 kilometers in the rainy season, the river in some places looks just like the Amazon. The city's small airport is not far from the city center, and on the way there we saw a small park in front of the terminal building with a vintage sports aircraft mounted on concrete blocks as a monument or gate guard.

Once again, my curiosity got the better of me. I ran across, climbed over the low fence without a second thought, and scrambled up onto the concrete blocks looking for any titbits of information I could find. I saw the name "El Rio Caroni" painted on the bodywork. I tried the door, which opened easily, and inside I saw a wonderfully well-kept, if somewhat dated, interior, complete with leather upholstery: a roomy five-seater cabin and cockpit, still in good condition and with all the instruments in place and a storage compartment in the door marked "Maps"; clearly of prewar signature but with a single aluminum high wing. My curiosity grew immediately because the name seemed quite familiar.

Suddenly it dawned on me: this was Jimmie Angel's plane, the one he had landed on top of Table Mountain in Canaima in 1937!

According to the text on the pedestal, the aircraft had been salvaged in 1970 and airlifted by an Air Force helicopter from the top of the mountain. They had repaired the damage to the landing gear and then put it on display here as a tribute to the man who had given his name to the highest waterfall in the world. The twist in the story is that the company flying the Dakotas here at this small airport owed its survival in part to the adventures of Jimmie Angel, the man who had contributed so much to the fame of the place, including his name, of course. I suddenly felt an urge to find out for myself the kind of circumstances he had had to face on his adventure.

Sad ending for a Servivensa DC-3 that was forced to make an emergency landing in the river. All 24 passengers emerged unharmed, but the co-pilot was decapitated by this propeller that entered the cockpit after the aircraft's starboard wing hit the riverbank.

ANGEL FALLS, CANAIMA

The next day we had an early flight to Canaima on board a Douglas C-47 YV-224C, coincidentally the same aircraft and crew that I had hired for a PME photo session earlier that year, in April. After a scenic 300-kilometer flight over the vast Embalse de Guri reservoir lying below us in the endless savannah country, we landed on the gravel strip of Canaima. While we were taxiing to the small wooden terminal building, I spotted the wreck of a Dakota on the opposite side of the parking platform. It had gone down in a controlled crash landing on the river near Canaima in 1998.

Immensely fascinated, as I always was by crash sites, we decided to go and take a look at the site. We found a guide who could take us there in a *curiara* (a long slender canoe). This canoe was not the smaller type usually paddled by Indians but a faster and longer model with an outboard engine, one designed with lazy and impatient tourists in mind.

Our guide told us that the unfortunate Servivensa Dakota had just completed a flight around the Tabletop Mountain and was on its way back to land on the strip. With twenty-five guests for a private party on board, the aircraft was heavy but not unduly overloaded. In the last few minutes of its approach to the runway the plane suddenly lost altitude, possibly due to engine failure. The captain decided to abort the approach immediately and to make a controlled crash landing on the river below him. With the wheels retracted again he managed to put the plane down on that fairly broad river, wide enough certainly to land a plane with a thirty-meter wingspan. However, at the very last moment the plane's starboard wing hit the side of the elevated riverbank. The aircraft listed sharply to the right, whereby the wing and engine nacelle broke off and the rotating propeller penetrated the cockpit, beheading the copilot in the process. Three other crew members were injured in the crash, but all of the guests on board survived. It must have been a terrible shock for these passengers to witness this happening while so close to landing at the airport.

After the accident the wreck was dismantled using cutting torches, and a helicopter airlifted the larger chunks to the Canaima airstrip, where they were dumped for the final salvaging of useful parts and scrapping of the aluminum skin and frame. As is usual around these parts, nothing was thrown away; anything that could be repaired was repaired and used again as an operational part in another flying barrel. The FAA abhorred this situation, of course, but it was the law of scarcity that applied here, making the Yankee rules a distant and uninteresting formality.

The wingtips were nowhere to be found in the pile of twisted aluminum that was dumped at the airport. They had more than likely been taken to Servivensa's home base in Puerto Ordaz.

The sun was burning on our necks and we had no real business left here, so we decided to take a boat trip to the place where the towering Angel Falls plunge into the river. I was keen to see what the place looked like and I knew this would be my only chance to capture a sense of the adventures Jimmie had been through.

Unfortunately for Jimmie, he didn't have a canoe with an outboard motor like the ones we have today, so the only way he could get upstream was by paddling or

The top of the table top mountain Auyan Tepui. Usually covered by clouds, the semi-permanent precipitation escapes down the mountain via dozens of waterfalls. Can you imagine trying to land an airplane here?

walking along the river bank, which made for a long and arduous journey. Our adventurer was not known for his patience, however, and maybe that is why he made the fateful decision to make the trip by plane. At least that was better than having to walk and climb in the kind of stifling heat and humidity that makes you feel like you are dragging a boat up a river on a rope around your neck.

We had come in the dry season, and the local boatman wondered whether we would be able to make the trip successfully in the long canoes over the Rio Caroni, as the level of water in the river was alarmingly low.

Dry season or not, we decided to set out on what would turn out to be a unique canoe ride up a hot jungle river.

Everything seemed fine when we left Canaima, with the open savannah still everywhere around us. After an hour or so we made a short stop and disembarked so that we could hike up to another Dakota wreck, one that had also made an emergency landing here years ago. This one had been luckier than the C-47 that had crashed into the river and it was almost completely intact. The aircraft had been carrying a mining team and heavy drilling equipment when one of its engines failed. This is normally not an immediately threatening problem but they were unable to maintain their height, probably due to the heavy load on board, and the captain decided to land here in the savannah. In this infinitely flat prairie, you can land a Dakota almost anywhere. The plane landed on terra firma without further incident and another aircraft arrived to pick the men up and take them on to their destination. For whatever reason, it was decided not to repair the engine. Instead, they removed all of the plane's useful parts and instruments, including the other engine, and left the stripped airframe behind to stand there forever all alone and forlorn in the Gran Sabana.

We noticed that the wingtips were still attached. But we could not do anything out here in the jungle without tools or transport and, most importantly, without prior permission from the military, the omnipresent force that you are required to consult before you even consider undertaking such a salvage mission. Hopefully one day I will get the chance to return to this intriguing location.

Back in our boat and off up the river again, the relative comfort of the savannah was soon replaced by the tumult of the rain forest with more insects, monkeys, and birds, and an increasingly treacherous river that soon threw up its first serious rapids and small waterfalls. We suddenly found ourselves wondering just how on earth the helmsman and his helper sitting on the bow of the canoe were going to take us safely over the wall of water rising right in front of us on a river that was getting narrower by the minute and filling up with large boulders and fallen logs.

The long *curiara* headed straight for the four feet high rapids at full speed, and the minute the nose of the canoe hit the waterfall the boat pitched sharply upward at an angle of about twenty to twenty-five degrees. With its stern still in the water behind us, the propeller dug itself deep into the water, thrusting the canoe forward.

The bow of the boat continued to rise and, as it reached its tipping point, the

Another derelict Dakota in the Savanna. This one made a perfect emergency landing on one engine carrying a full crew and a cargo of drilling equipment. All survived, but the plane was abandoned after they salvaged the good engine and all instruments.

longer front dropped down with a smack onto the upper level of the waterfall. The propeller was now suddenly clear of the water, but then came the tricky bit. We would be fine as long as the boat had enough forward speed to plough on slowly against the current for a second or two, sufficient time for the propeller to be able to grab the higher level of water again and provide us with the forward thrust we needed to carry on across the waterfall.

But this only works under specific conditions; a high water level produces currents that are too strong for this kind of maneuver, while a low level of water will not give the canoe the crucial "screw bite" needed for maximum forward propulsion.

It is quite an experience, especially the bit where the boat slows down and you can feel it struggling against the current while the screw spins freely in the air. Several times, the nine-meter-long canoe only barely managed to sputter forward again at the last moment. We carried on like this through various obstacles for an hour or so, until suddenly our luck ran out. At one particular point on the river, the boat was not able to accumulate enough forward thrust to allow the screw to catch up with the higher level of the rapids. We started to go backward, pushed back by the current, and the boat was about as manageable as a piece of driftwood. The canoe turned sharply to one side and rolled over on its longitudinal axis, allowing water to rush into the boat over the lower sidewall. My first reaction was "Oops, now we're done for." But apart

Fast long canoes with outboard engines make river transport easier here; they can handle cascades of 3–4 feet without difficulty. However, on our trip upriver to the falls we had to give up after only one day due to the low water level on the Caroni River.

from a wet ass and soaked luggage we were all right; the canoe somehow stayed afloat and eventually ran aground on the river bank, from where we could drain the penetrated water with plastic buckets. Fortunately, we didn't flip over. That would not necessarily have been life-threatening, but you do need to be a good swimmer in such a situation, given the strong currents, if you want to bring both yourself and your luggage safely back to shore. And you also need to remember to check your legs for leeches when you reach the safety of the riverbank. You will be truly sorry if you forget this minor lesson—one I had previously learned previously the hard way in Indonesia!

Eventually we had to disembark, luggage and all, in order to make the boat lighter. The boatman and his mate then attempted to negotiate the next set of rapids, while Dolph and I waded on up through the river until we got to a higher level. It was very impressive watching them struggle to get their hollowed-out tree trunk up over the waterfalls, but eventually not even their best tricks would work for them. We had been stopped in our tracks. We were soaked to the skin and utterly exhausted, and we had not even covered a third of the distance we needed to travel.

We could have continued our journey on foot but that would have taken a whole day, or even longer, so we didn't have time for that option. We were on a business trip, hunting for wingtips, and not off on some wild treasure hunt following in Jimmie's footsteps. We had only three more days before our flight back to Holland, and our wingtip score thus far was zero. So we had no choice but to turn back, however disappointing that was to me.

After this memorable weekend, we flew back to Ciudad Bolivar and then continued our journey via Caracas with a flight to Tegucigalpa, the capital of Honduras, for our last Dakota hunting trip of the voyage.

HONDURAS

My Dutch friend Michael had tipped us off about a large number of C-47s still flying in Honduras for the Honduran Air Force. He had heard that the Hondurans wanted to build a giant roof for their air force museum and they were looking for sponsorship for the project. It seemed like a good opportunity to see whether we could possibly swap some surplus wingtips in exchange for a cash donation to the museum.

Normally you have to be very careful in these countries with cash payments, as they are often considered a direct form of bribery, especially when it comes to the purchase of military or government property. For our overseas transport we always have to have an export document, and that requires an official invoice with a payment procedure that can be traced. With this in mind, we were looking for an acceptable way of transferring funds and officially sponsoring the foundation that was financing the air force museum seemed like a safe bet. We decided to go there and meet the man that Michael had said could bring us into contact with the military.

Via Panama City, we first flew to the small country of El Salvador and from there continued our long overnight flight to Tegucigalpa, a typical Central American boomtown in the middle of the steaming jungle. It is a modern city, with shopping malls next to huge concrete office complexes, surrounded on the outskirts by the

Honduras, Toncontin Airport in Tegucigalpa.
One of the most dangerous international airports in the world, with a guaranteed "white knuckles" approach during which passengers pray loudly for the blessing of the Lord. That didn't help this big TACA jet, however, which somehow managed to miss the stop sign at the end of the runway.

favelas or slums that, though not as large as those in Rio or São Paulo, are expanding rapidly.

The city is located on a fertile hill, parts of which, where the slums have not yet taken over, are still completely overgrown. Treacherous hilltops surround the airport, and the final approach seems very dicey when you fly in for the first time.

As we came in, we could see the mountaintops flashing by very close to the plane. To make things worse, the pilots added to the tension by pulling the engine throttles back and forth. The sudden howling of the engines provoked quite an unnerving feeling among us and, before we knew it, it seemed like we were caught up in the middle of an airborne church service. All the other passengers were praying loudly and repeatedly making the sign of the cross as we came in to land, and they carried on doing so until we came to a stop at the airport ramp. We had arrived in a very religious country; that much was obvious. But that would be of no help to the victims of a big jetliner crash here later in 2008.

Upon our arrival at the airport we noticed another interesting feature: the air force was very visibly present on the other side of the terminal building where we collected our luggage. Our contact man picked us up and we drove in his car to the heavily guarded air force base, named Toncontin, and then went straight to the site of the museum. There we saw a huge collection of vintage fighters and training and cargo aircraft, all parked out in the open air.

A roof over this collection would clearly be no luxury in this tropical country, given the heavy annual rainfall and scorching sun. The lack of protection from the extreme tropical elements had already had a visibly devastating effect on these aircraft. The absolute star of the exhibition was a fabulous dark-blue single-seat fighter from the final years of World War II—a Vought F-4U Corsair. The career of this robust aircraft spanned the time from the war in the Pacific against the Japanese to the Korean Conflict (1950–1953). It was a very reliable and strong propeller-driven (and often carrier-based) fighter that was sold overseas to many air forces, including the French Aeronavale.

But by the mid-1950s her time on the front line was up, due to the arrival of much faster jet fighters. A small number of the type ended up in museums and with private collectors in America, but there was also another market for the plane: the countries of Central America, for whom the modern jet fighter was simply too expensive. Many discarded Corsairs quickly found their way to the second-tier air forces of third world countries with the aim of satisfying the needs of their military forces with written-off combat planes that relied on vintage technology.

What no one had anticipated might happen did happen here, against all the odds. A number of these phased-out pursuit planes would come to star in a role for which they had been built twenty-five years earlier: winning dogfights by shooting other planes out of the sky.

In July 1969, a war broke out between the neighboring countries of El Salvador

The Salvadorian C-47 that opened the four-day war with Honduras by flying a tricky solo bomb run over Toncontin airport in an attempt to destroy the enemy's pursuit planes parked out in the open. This plane was never designed as a bomber and it was no wonder that their mission failed, considering that they had to roll the bombs out by hand through a cargo door!

and Honduras in which aerial dogfights were fought with these WWII Corsairs and other vintage fighters. This minor but deadly conflict started after Honduras lost a football match against the national team of El Salvador in a qualifying match for the World Cup. In the ensuing frustration and with the national pride of the dominant Hondurans seriously dented, El Salvador's generals felt threatened and, against all the odds, initiated the conflict with a surprise air attack on the enemy air force base at Toncontin, where we had just landed.

In the buildup to this idiocy, both countries had secretly amassed a fleet of about twenty extremely fast and agile North American P-51D Mustang propeller fighters, which they had purchased from private American collectors in order to circumvent the US ban on the export of arms. These former parade planes of the North American air shows were quickly reconverted to a military configuration, with machine guns, targeting equipment, and jettisonable fuel tanks under the wings. They went from "toys for boys" back to "killers for colonels" in a matter of days.

Neither country had any bomber planes, but there was a handy solution to that problem. The Salvadorians converted a Dakota into a makeshift bomber that they sent on July 14, 1969, to knock out half of the Honduran Air Force in their first Mickey Mouse–like air strike. The Mustang P-51D fighters that had been sent along to escort this bomber/C-47 during the opening raid of the conflict missed the rendezvous in the initial chaos and the Dakota soldiered on alone into hostile airspace.

Once over their target, the Salvadorian pilots made a low pass over the undefended air base, saw all of the enemy's fighters parked out in the open on the platform, and must have concluded that this was a once-in-a-lifetime chance to carry

The F-4 U Corsair piston prop fighters were at the heart of the action in the ensuing dogfights against an enemy with similar aircraft. While in the rest of the world, supersonic Starfighters and Migs ruled the skies, here in Central America an insignificant mini-war brought back memories of WWII-style combat 25 years after that war had ended!

out an annihilating hit-and-run. It seemed almost too good to be true, and they probably found themselves dreaming of their arrival back in El Salvador to a thunderous ticker-tape reception as national heroes.

However, although Dakotas are versatile and rugged planes, they were never designed for the role of bomber. On the second low pass, two crew members rolled a few bombs out by hand, over the threshold of the open gate-cargo doors that had already been removed. While the bombs flashed down under their enthusiastic shouts of "Geronimo," they quickly found out that this was not the most accurate way of hitting a target.

After two more passes and with all of their bombs gone, they had merely hit the runway in spots here and there but had missed every fighter plane below. Those fighters were now being prepared for a counterattack, and as soon as the Salvadorians saw the pilots scrambling to their aircraft they decided it was about time to hightail it back home.

The Honduran Corsair fighters were quickly airborne and set off in hot pursuit of their attackers. But, thanks to the fading daylight, the Dakota made it back home unscathed. The ensuing euphoria was short-lived, however, as it would not be long before things would take a turn for the worse in the conflict for the impoverished country of El Salvador.

In what was later dubbed "La Guerra Futbolistica" or the "Football War," this beautiful blue Corsair standing right in front of us had knocked two Mustangs out of

Cavalier Mustang P-51 D's, purchased from US civilian war bird, circles in order to circumvent the US weapons embargo. With wingtip tanks, weapons and gun sights, the Mustangs were reconverted from Airshow stars into deadly fighters of bygone days.

the air in just four days and was the highest scoring "ace" of that particular aerial combat theater. She is now part of the national heritage of Honduras and the pride and joy of the air force museum.

Bizarre detail: in the retaliation raids that followed, the Honduran Air Force also flew bombing missions with Dakotas against El Salvador, escorted by these now long-retired fighters. And those makeshift bombers from bygone days were now standing right here before our very eyes at this air force base, still operational as military transport planes! It is a testimony to the ongoing value of the C-47 in the air transport business today, whether for military or for civilian use, on a continent where primitive conditions still prevail and where the versatility of this aircraft was and is sometimes stretched to the limits of the (near) impossible.

In that short war, the much larger Honduran Air Force was quicker to get its military machine going and was soon shooting enemy fighters out of the sky like clay pigeons. But the watchful referee from the North, who had once delivered all those fighters under the illusion that they could do no more harm, brought the game prematurely to an end, and with that the last serious aerial dogfights between WWII propeller-driven fighters were consigned to the history books.

At the military air force base we kept gazing at the impressive row of military Dakotas painted in camouflage colors and in white. Most of them seemed to be operational, with a few in various states of disrepair or undergoing overhauls, though it was difficult to say for sure given the distance from which we had to view those C-47s. We desperately wanted to see them up close but our every attempt at doing so was thwarted. Eventually, I could no longer hold my tongue and asked the question that was burning inside me: "How many wingtips might you have for us to buy or swap?"

The colonel who was showing us around threw me a look of disdain but failed to provide me with an answer. What had we done wrong? Everything seemed so close to a perfect deal as we stared in awe at the row of beautiful Dakotas. We had come all this way just to see them in the distance, and they no doubt had a large stock of parts lying around somewhere, but it all just seemed to go up in smoke before our eyes.

The colonel wasn't very communicative or cooperative when it came to our sponsorship plan, which we and our middleman had thought would be very attractive. They kept us as far away from the hub of their air force base as they could, confining us to the museum, and for whatever reason they abandoned their original idea to do business with us. It is possible that the story of the scarcity of parts had reached the military here in advance, making them reluctant to sell, or that the plan was simply rejected by the generals upstairs.

This brought an end to our trip to Venezuela and Honduras. We had seen many Dakotas, both in civilian and military roles, and we had traveled to incredibly scenic places with unspoiled nature, but in the end we returned home empty-handed. We had not been able to buy one single wingtip nor had we picked up any clues as to other possible sources.

However, we had encountered one phenomenon that was hitherto unknown to us: surplus does not exist here; every single wingtip here is predestined for reuse one day. As long as it still looks a bit like a wing, it will fly again as a wing.

And as for the Air Force of Honduras, we never heard from them again despite our many letters and e-mails to them and the efforts of our local contact.

I learned a valuable lesson: The military and business don't mix all that well together here, and that would prove to be true of many of the other places I would visit in the future, places where the military played a dominant role.

But no complaints; it's all part of the job of the Dakota Hunter.

THE FATAL ACCIDENT

Just a few months after our visit to Venezuela, I was watching the news at home in the Netherlands when the newscaster said something about a plane crash in Venezuela in which some twenty American, Dutch, and Italian tourists had been killed. The plane had been flying back from Canaima to Isla Maragarita after a sightseeing daytrip.

I saw the dramatic footage of a smoldering Dakota lying between some sheds and immediately recognized the registration number 224 on the tail. My worst suspicions were soon confirmed. It was our beloved Dakota YV-224C that was lying there, having crashed on January 25, 2001, after a refueling stopover in Ciudad Bolivar. It appeared that eighteen minutes after takeoff the plane had fallen out of the sky due to an engine fire or malfunction in the right-hand engine. According to witnesses, a fire had broken out soon after takeoff and the fire extinguishers had either not been employed or had malfunctioned. In any case, Captain Lopez had tried to return to the airport for an emergency landing. While making a right-hand turn the aircraft lost too much speed, stalled, and crashed upside down on a slum and burst into flames only three kilometers from the airport.

With the tanks full of high-octane fuel, an unnerving conflagration resulted in which all twenty-four passengers and crew perished, including our friend Captain Lopez.

The angel had fallen from the sky, and that single incident turned out to be a fatal blow that would eventually put an end to all Dakota passenger-flight operations in Venezuela.

The Safety Council of the Ministry of Aviation ordered an inspection of the twenty Dakotas still flying in the country. In spite of its high safety record with the type, Rutaca was instructed to ground all its aircraft until further notice. This accident almost finished the company. However, they were able to switch over to using older Boeing 737-200s, which could still be bought on the cheap in America.

We landed in our hired aircraft on the open savanna field here for a photo shoot next to an Indian village. The co-pilot almost spoiled the fun while trying to start the starboard engine again during our lunch break. The captain saved the day with his swift reaction to the impending disaster.

They kept the company going by focusing more on cargo and passenger flights between the big cities of eastern Venezuela. Their Dakotas were left to stand idle for good in Ciudad Bolivar.

The year before the accident, I had hired the same Dakota YV-224C for a photo shoot for the PME brand. With our photo team of seven on board, we flew the plane with Captain Lopez to Canaima. The Dakota was our motor home, lunchroom, dressing room, and makeup studio, but also our brand icon and thus the prop and backdrop that we used in almost all the pictures taken there. It was a memorable trip with many eventful moments. Upon hearing the news of the fatal accident, I was reminded of a minor incident that we had experienced with this same airplane.

For five days the DC-3 had flown us around the big tabletop mountains near Canaima that loomed majestically above the jungle in the background of our shoots. On one of those days I was surveying the endless savannah below me, completely flat and overgrown with tall grass, and I asked the captain to make a landing on the plain. We spotted a sort of cart track leading to an Indian village situated near a river. It was a very idyllic location and only minutes later the captain executed a perfect landing on the hard *sabana* soil next to the track. We stepped out and looked around in awe, impressed by the unspoilt nature, and got our photo work done early in the morning when the light was at its best and the temperature still pleasant. After a few hours we took a break and sat in front of the Dakota for lunch. Then, for no apparent reason, the inexperienced copilot walked to the airplane, crawled inside, and settled himself into the captain's seat in the cockpit. He had decided, after consultation with the captain I assumed, to begin the full engine start-up procedure in the belief that it was time for us to go.

Suddenly, the right-hand propeller started to tick around. The copilot then switched on the ignition in order to start the engine. After a lot of clatter he eventually succeeded, but the exhaust barrel began spitting out white smoke, and when a flame appeared the engine stopped again. What the copilot could not see from his seat on the left-hand side, however, was that a puddle of gasoline had formed and, possibly due to over-priming, the exhaust flame had ignited this highly flammable fuel under the engine cowling. The fire grew quickly and soon there was a bulging black cloud of smoke, indicating that the flames were burning rubber or the wiring harness. That was not a good sign and, in a flash, everyone jumped to their feet and shouted to the copilot that there was a fire developing under the engine. The copilot did not understand what was going on and, worse still, there wasn't a fire extinguisher to be found anywhere.

The stupidity of the copilot's actions suddenly became clear to the captain. The old man jumped up and ran to the cargo door screaming, "*Incidencio, incidencio.*" He climbed aboard and scrambled through the cabin over the unpacked trunks to the cockpit. The copilot was still sheepishly wondering what had unnerved everyone so much. The fire was beginning to rage out of control and there was smoke everywhere around the engine.

In January 2001, DC-3 YV-224C crashed just after take-off from Ciudad Bolívar. Attempting to return to the airport on one engine, the crew could not keep her in the air. The plane stalled and fell out of the sky over one wing and onto a shantytown where it burst into flames, just 3 miles from the airport.

When Captain Lopez reached the cockpit, he dragged the foolish copilot out of his seat, took over, and made the correct decision by trying to start the burning engine again. After six turns of the prop, the ignition kicked in and, with a loud bang, thankfully started producing its familiar rattling sound—*po-ta-to, po-ta-to, po-ta-to*—at first quite sluggishly but getting faster with every second, until we heard the comforting drone. With the airscrew up to speed, the prop blast extinguished the fire in a matter of seconds and a huge plume of black smoke billowed out from the rear.

The rest of us had stood there paralyzed, watching the imminent burn-up develop, powerless to do anything; we couldn't even get our hands on a simple bucket of water.

With the fire now starved of fuel, the captain switched off the engine. But then all hell broke loose in the cockpit as he started mercilessly whacking the copilot about. Meanwhile the mechanic, who had climbed on board, quickly jumped back out with his toolbox and a ladder to remove the engine cowlings. Obviously, a thorough inspection of the engine, the electrical wiring, and rubber hoses for motor oil, hydraulics, and fuel supply was now crucial if we ever wanted to get airborne again in this nearly stricken aircraft.

I had become more than a little bit curious and went to have a look under the hood (as if my presence could be of any help). The fight in the cockpit had subsided; the copilot sat in the cockpit like a beaten dog and did not dare come out to face us again. The captain emerged and with the mechanic made an assessment of the damage that the fire might have caused, especially to the engine's electrical wiring and the onboard fire extinguisher.

It took more than two hours to change a few clamps, hoses, and cables and to do an extensive test run with the engine. Eventually, it all seemed to be okay and we were ready to return to Canaima, a flight of only ten minutes. Everyone climbed back on board, not without some anxious feelings, the engines were started, and we rolled across the field, gaining speed before we became airborne. I'm pretty sure that everyone onboard had one eye on the starboard engine hoping that it would hold up during the full throttle takeoff run. Without any further incident we arrived in Canaima and, two days later, flew back to Ciudad Bolivar in the same Dakota YV-224C.

The accident in January 2001 with that aircraft also centered around the starboard engine, and I was immediately reminded of the engine fire that we had experienced nine months earlier in May 2000. However, the probability that the two incidents were in any way related was extremely remote, as the engine that had suffered the first fire had more than likely been replaced in the meantime.

The days of the Dakota in Venezuela are now over for good. Servivensa went bankrupt and Air Executivo, which operated Dakota tourist flights from Caracas to Las Roques Island, is also defunct. It doesn't seem that long since our trip to Canaima, during which we spotted no less than seven tourist-carrying Dakotas and an AN-2 biplane in one single day, but in hindsight that was the heyday of these sightseeing flights and the fleet of over a dozen DC-3s in Venezuela.

The Rutaca aircraft were considered to be very reliable and meticulously maintained. The company had a solid reputation in relation to flight safety and the airworthiness of their vintage aircraft. Their vintage airplanes operated in a booming market of tourist flights, one that demanded more frequent use with more landings and takeoffs and the flying of more payload. Over the years, the planes had nudged their payloads closer and closer to the official maximum payload weight, a limit that was established for the military C-47s before and during the World War II. This begs the question as to whether it was wise to allow these planes to transport their maximum payload given their advanced age. Some suggest that it would have been more realistic to gradually reduce the maximum load as the aircraft got older.

Flying a Dakota on a single engine leaves very little room for error, particularly if that plane is loaded with the maximum weight of three tons of cargo or passengers and full tanks. Depending on external factors, such as wind speed and direction, altitude, outside temperature, engine condition and power output, and pilot experience, the Dakota is capable of flying for some (even extended) time on a single

Angel fallen from the sky. While some reported that they saw the YV-224C's starboard engine on fire, others later denied that. Whatever the cause, the fatal accident cost all 24 souls on board their lives and grounded all Dakota operations in Venezuela for good (photo is of an unidentified DC-3).

engine, but only when conditions are ideal. But if an engine quits immediately during or after takeoff with the maximum permissible payload onboard, the required rate of climb becomes problematic and the risk of a crash increases greatly if a safe altitude has not yet been reached.

Based on the many reports and articles on crashes that I found on the Internet, the conclusion seems justified that if one of the engines quits, in many cases the Dakota will slowly sink and, depending on the altitude and other factors, a rapid decision must be made whether to perform a controlled crash landing. When faced with this problem in the past, many pilots grossly overestimated their chances and ended up with a lot less flight range than they had bargained for, while other pilots immediately sought a landing zone straight ahead and made an emergency landing, mostly successfully, on land or on water.

The Rutaca pilots were faced with this nightmare scenario when one of their engines quit shortly after takeoff at barely 600 feet above the ground. Evidently, they tried to return to the airport, but even that turned out to be a very critical decision, as this involved making two 180-degree turns. The plane most likely stalled during the second turn, which was needed in order to line up with the landing strip ahead. At the very moment when the starboard wing was banked downward for the turn, their already marginal airspeed slowed even more and caused this right-hand wing to stall. It thus lost its lift and simply slipped further down and out of control.

The aircraft ended up in a spin, resulting in a terrible crash upside-down on top of a shantytown. However, it may also have been the case that the engine fire, which for whatever reason could not be put out, eventually weakened the starboard wing so much that it simply folded, thus resulting in the spin that took the stricken aircraft down.

Whatever happened, it was clear that engine failure immediately after takeoff was the primary cause of the accident.

Critical to flying the Dakotas with their Pratt & Whitney 14-cylinder R-1830 aero engines is a full throttle period of fifty to sixty seconds. In that first minute, the aircraft has to get airborne, climb out, and reach a minimum airspeed of 120 miles per hour, after which the first step in throttling back can be taken. It seems clear that overloading the airplane can lead to a longer full throttle run, in much the same way as a heavily loaded car takes longer to reach a speed of 75 miles per hour.

According to most experts, it is this factor of overloading that can result in a dramatic increase in the risk of engine failure and, if such problems occur, a very heavy aircraft has fewer options to choose from when it comes to an (emergency) landing due to its more limited flight range.

Some even go so far as to say that, given the age of the engines, you actually double the risk of engine failure with every ten seconds spent above the sixty-second limit at full throttle. True or not, it seems sensible not to tempt fate: flying a maximum payload of three tons of cargo or passengers on a frequent basis is, in many experts' eyes, a somewhat risky business for a vintage WWII Dakota. Whereas in the United Kingdom the Air Atlantique Dakotas are allowed to fly with twenty-five passengers, the air safety authorities in Holland recently limited the number of passengers to a maximum of twelve for the DDA Dakota PH-PBA, and in France the Dakota was permitted to fly with only nineteen passengers. The Swiss Breitling DC-3 is certified for twenty passengers.

All payload specifications as originally certified for the DC-3 before and during World War II are now under pressure from the authorities and insurance companies. The MTOW (Max Take Off Weight) of the aircraft was set at nearly thirteen tons. With full tanks at near sea level and normal temperatures this allowed for a payload of twenty-five to thirty passengers and their luggage.

For commercial operations with the Dakota, any substantial limitation of their maximum payload would be a major blow to the profit-making capacity of the plane. I don't see any restrictions happening any time soon in South America, as the plane's operations are not a luxury or nostalgic leisure activity, as they are in Europe, but a serious method of air transport to isolated locations, places that cannot be reached by any other form of transport, such as trucks, trains, or boats. The lack of any real alternative, even other types of aircraft, makes the Dakota a lifeline for many, and any changes to the present situation or regulations would only result in more expensive ticket prices.

The burning question is how long can such a complex engine, with its prewar design, built in the 1940s, keep going when operated several times a day at full throttle?

You would not subject your classic Harley Davidson 1944 WL 750 cc flathead motorcycle or your Jaguar XK 120 1948 sports car to that kind of (mis)treatment. In the case of those vehicles, we can start them gently and gain speed at low revs without causing too much stress to the mechanical parts. An airplane engine, however, does not have that option; the aircraft can only get airborne with the engines at full throttle. So there is no way to spare the engine by running at half throttle or less during takeoff.

The mechanical and thermal stress exerted on these aero engines by the peak load in the mandatory full throttle slot of 60 seconds needed for takeoff is so intense that the engines have to be completely overhauled every 1,000 to 1,400 running hours. This is the equivalent of putting an overhauled engine in your car every 70,000 to 90,000 kilometers. That is rather extreme for modern automotive engines but, as stipulated, a vintage aero engine should be seen more as a high performance racing motor, one with a much higher stress factor.

But even with that level of maintenance there is no getting away from the fact that (many of) the plane's components are now over fifty or sixty years old and so will not always adhere to the laws of wear and tear of the early 1940s. In addition, the engine design is outdated, the alloy of the materials used in the gears, pistons, and crankshaft cases is obsolete, and the engines run a lot hotter than modern engines do. Today's piston engine designs have efficient fuel injection systems and advanced electronic motor management that yield a leaner and cooler burn of gas, and they use very advanced synthetic oils that greatly reduce internal wear and tear.

Nevertheless, some operators are able to achieve extremely good safety records with these aircraft, and the performance scores for their vintage engines are barely inferior to those of their modern brethren. I have seen excellent scores in plenty of places, especially in Colombia (not the most obvious country you would think of when it comes to the priority of safety) where I met the best-trained and most disciplined of pilots and mechanics and found the best-maintained operational Dakotas.

FINALLY

It was time for us to make new plans. We needed to explore new markets, and my thoughts soon turned to another South American country, one I had already visited in 1994: Bolivia, the country I had been to as part of one of my first TV documentary trips with the PBY-5A Catalina. The vintage aircraft I had seen at La Paz International Airport still made my mouth water. It was time to renew my acquaintance with the land of the Incas.

CHAPTER 5

Bolivia

El Condor Pasa ...

After the trips to England, North America, and Central America, which I undertook over a period of one year, it became almost impossible to find any more derelict Dakotas or surplus wingtips in those regions. We had come across lots of other types of vintage aircraft, both operational and scrapped, such as the Douglas DC-4, DC-6, and DC-7, the Beechcraft B-18 (Twin Beech or C-45), the Convair 240, and the Curtiss Commando C-46, and we had considered the option of adding wing panels from other aircraft types to our collection. But there was simply no other wingtip on the market that came even close to the beauty of the Dakota wingtip. With its curved lines and fabulous skin texture, it was the perfect match and size for conversion to a desk. Therefore, we had to press on with our search. I turned my attention to a relatively unknown and insular country—Bolivia, in the heart of that great continent of South America, half Andes Mountains and half jungle, a mysterious land with a double identity.

It was not my first trip to this particular country and its omnipresent Inca culture, as I had already been there in 1994 during the Catalina Odyssey when we tried to film a water landing on the highest navigable lake in the world, Lake Titicaca. That adventure would have a very bizarre, almost fatal end for our PBY-5A Catalina amphibian aircraft.

Bolivia is in all respects a very strange yet enchantingly beautiful country. First, there is the extreme altitude, which grabs you by the throat upon landing at the airport of La Paz, El Alto Airport, at almost 4,200 meters above sea level. The name El Alto (The Heights) is more than appropriate for this airport, as it is the highest international commercial airport in the world.

After landing, you quickly suffer the very unpleasant effects of acute oxygen deprivation, especially if you are a Westerner who is not used to this kind of altitude. I had previously climbed Mont Blanc and had experienced great difficulty climbing the last 18 steps up to the mountain's half-way-up weather station at 3,400 meters. Both the view and the climb were literally breathtaking. But here in Bolivia you are 800 meters higher and stepping out of a plane with jet lag. So how does that feel? Not great, I can tell you. Altitude sickness hits you really hard when you have just flown in from the "lowlands" of Europe.

Once you have arrived at your hotel in La Paz, it is usually a little easier thanks

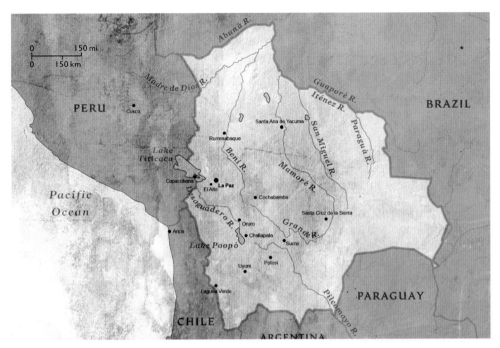

to the descent to 3,600 meters in the middle of the city. But be warned—do not try to climb the stairs. Take the elevator, and take it easy when it comes to alcohol and tobacco.

Freshly arrived from abroad, people often suffer terrible headaches, dry throats, dizziness, and a general uncomfortable feeling of "Get me outta here!"

There is a good local remedy called Mathé, a tea drink made from coca leaves; highly illegal stuff in Europe and North America, but here it is available in all the hotels and restaurants. It is the cheap substitute for aspirin and helps combat almost everything, especially altitude sickness. It tastes like green tea and it really does relieve the headaches and the pop-out pressure on your eyeballs.

Seven years after my first visit in the Catalina, I was back again in this alien country. I stayed in the same hotel in La Paz, a typical old Spanish city built in a mountain bowl and with the colonial architecture of the nineteenth century. The old city is surrounded by suburbs of sprawling favelas—the kind of slums characteristic of most developing countries. More than one million people live in this gigantic crater in a climate that can bring you four seasons in a single day. During the day the temperature can rise to 28 or 30 degrees Celsius (82 to 86 degrees Fahrenheit). At night it can freeze to 6 degrees below zero (21 degrees Fahrenheit). Rather extreme, to say the least, just like everything else here.

In El Alto, the temperature fluctuations are even worse, but for a serious aviation aficionado like me all that discomfort and climatic turmoil is compensated for by an unparalleled array of vintage aircraft. Next to the modern international airport lies a kind of clandestine airfield brimming with exiled and derelict aircraft from bygone

El Alto airport, at the High Andes of Bolivia.
The Jurassic Park of the aviation world: the show is over, but these relics of a glorious past are still
standing out here. The DC-3 played an important role in this region, but at this high altitude airport it
was the Curtiss C-46 Commando that dominated the scene due to its stronger piston engines with turbo
blowers, enabling it to transport larger cargo loads over the capricious mountains.

days. As you get closer it is like crossing the mythological River Styx, a gateway to the
Underworld. An unreal image unfolds before your eyes of an airplane graveyard filled
with zombie planes, including a number of completely dilapidated DC-6s.

A bit further down the road I came across a collection of derelict Curtiss
Commando C-46s and more Dakotas in various stages of decomposition. And, in the
middle of all that decay, a few still-operational C-46s and a twin engine Convair 240.
All of the aircraft were scattered across an oil-soaked sandy surface that only added
to the picture of total desolation. The surrounding buildings were reminiscent of a

The world's last Boeing B-17E Flying Fortress cargo transport was stationed at El Alto.
B-17E reg. nr CP-753 (2682) El Tigre was brought to Bolivia in July 1964 by Compania
Boliviana de Aviacion. Previous operators had included Lysdale Flying Service and Canadian Kenting
Aviation. She was involved in several mishaps, including a port undercarriage collapse while taxiing at
La Paz (1974) and a crash landing at San Borja (1976). She was rebuilt and sold to new owners in the
USA and ferried to Florida in March 1990. Her sister ship, B-17G reg. nr. CP-891 (22616) ex-CP-
627, also operated in Bolivia. This aircraft was saved from the scrapheap and brought back to the US in
1981 and is now on display at March AFB museum, CA (photo Ron Mak, text Michael Prophet).

scene from *Mad Max*, a disorderly mess of corrugated roofing sheets and brick walls
where Bolivian women in traditional dress with their peculiar crinoline skirts and
bowler hats shuffled around like trolls. Stray dogs slunk around in the high grass like
hyenas, keeping a respectful distance from the blonde stranger.

Rambling around in total bewilderment, I bumped into an old Bolivian man
wearing a beautiful vintage leather aviation jacket. He turned out to be a captain and
owner of two derelict Dakotas parked up among the moribund carcasses of airplanes.
He told me that the aircraft were for sale and that their parts could also be bought

separately. That was exactly what I wanted to hear, so together we walked over to his planes, through a time warp, into this unreal open-air museum. Out of the corner of my eye I spotted the ruins of the old terminal building still standing among all these flying relics, the perfect backdrop to this surreal scene.

I immediately noticed the difference from when I had been here in 1994 with the Catalina. Now, seven years later, there was much less activity. There were still plenty of old prop liners standing around, but there was no evidence of any cargo flights, no trucks, and hardly any people to be seen. In particular, the daily *carne* (meat) flights to the jungle provinces were obviously not operating any more. The old airplanes—dubbed the *carniceros*—had served as the capital city's main source for its meat supply until only a few years earlier.

For a long time Bolivia had managed to get by without any proper road infrastructure. The country had a reasonably good railway network in the west and south, but there was no reliable train or road network going to the north from the higher-lying Altiplano, the vast Andean Highlands upon which La Paz is perched.

Cattle cannot survive on the high plains here, but they do thrive in the pastures along the rivers in the lower-lying regions, especially in the Beni province in the northeast of the country. In order to cater to the needs of the more than one million inhabitants in La Paz, an aerial transportation system was invented—one that could bring in meat and other foodstuffs on a daily basis, thereby circumventing the shortcomings of the all but nonexistent road system. The unpaved roads to the capital were frequently plagued by heavy rainfall and mudslides, which inevitably led to transport delays due to blocked roads and impassable bridges. Perishables, including meat, could not be transported in such difficult conditions, and refrigerated trucks were a rarity in the country.

The flying "meat wagons" first appeared on the scene in the early 1950s. Old military cargo planes that had been used in World War II were bought in the United States and set to work as sky trucks flying between the ranches of the Beni and La Paz. The flight back and forth could be done in one day, so there was no need for expensive refrigeration equipment.

Later on, other foods, such as fruits and vegetables, were flown in using the same transport system courtesy of the large "aluminum condors" of the Andes: a fleet of Curtiss Commandos and Dakotas and even one converted Boeing B-17 Flying Fortress. For half a century they played a crucial role in supplying fresh food to the capital.

It became an industry in itself and I presumed that the amount of traffic over the years would have left an inevitable trail of wrecks, either crashed or abandoned, given the extreme weather conditions and the high mountains of the region that probably caused many accidents. I frequently enquired among the pilots I encountered whether they might know of any Dakota wrecks along their regular flight routes.

DC-6 (43035/61) CP-1654 (ex-American Airlines) rolling from the meat haulers' gravel ramp to El Alto main runway. This DC-6 had the pink panther on its tail. The old AA cheat line is still visible. The DC-6 met its end at Santa Rosa Airport (Bolivia) in March 1993 when its no. 2 engine backfired just after V1 on takeoff. The pilot aborted the takeoff but the DC-6 overran the 1,500m grass runway. The engine caught fire and destroyed the aircraft (photo Chris Mak).

THE MEAT HAULING FLIGHT

One day, when I was in La Paz on another search expedition, I got a phone call from the old captain saying that there would be a meat flight the following day from El Alto to the Beni region. He asked me if I would like to come along. Apparently, there were one or two wrecks that had been abandoned there years ago at the end of the jungle airstrip in Santa Ana. Dizzy with delight, I couldn't believe my luck and jumped at the offer.

The next morning, at the crack of dawn, I climbed on board a Curtiss Commando C-46 with a charming man, Captain Antonio, at the controls. Everyone called him Antonio because he bore a striking resemblance to the actor Antonio Banderas—slightly older but with the same charm and shapely Latino face. He was also very well dressed in a sheepskin pilot jacket and cowboy boots with high heels. The archetypical Latino Lover and undoubtedly very popular with the local beauties. He arrived at the airport in a vintage 1960s light yellow Mercedes 220S, the car's color faded by the sun but immensely suited to this scene with its old planes, hangars, and buildings.

I had flown with him many times before, back when I had come here for the first PME photo shoots in 1998. He recognized me instantly, as together we had twice experienced fairly crazy incidents in a C-46 Commando that were still imprinted on both our minds. And here we were flying together once more, this time on the *carne* tour on a flight that would turn out to be one of the last meat flights that this big Curtiss would ever make. These flights had almost come to a standstill due to the construction of proper mountain roads at the end of the 1990s and the arrival of modern refrigerated trucks that made it possible to transport perishable cargo by road, the death knell for the faithful meat wagons of El Alto.

I was very excited about taking this flight, as I knew that this would be my one and only opportunity to experience an authentic slice of Bolivian prop liner aviation history.

We left El Alto airport with two pilots, two mechanics, myself, and an otherwise empty C-46 rolling down the endlessly long runway. This 5-plus kilometer stretch of tarmac is one of the longest runways in the world. Due to the high altitude, standard piston engines have to deal with an acute shortage of oxygen and thus lack a lot of the normal horsepower and thrust even at full throttle. The long runway gives them the time they need to gain the required airspeed to take off and climb out safely over the nearby Cordillera mountain ridge.

The Curtiss Commando C-46 that we flew in had much stronger piston engines than its smaller cousin, the Dakota C-47. It was equipped with big turbo blowers to give it better lift in the thin air at this high altitude. Soon, the bulky beast was airborne and we flew off in a northeasterly direction. I sat on a jump seat between the pilots against the cockpit aft bulkhead; there was markedly more space than in a Dakota.

With a fantastic view through the large, glass, bullet-shaped nose, I watched the pilots as they resolutely worked the sluggish aircraft from one valley to the next. Perilously close to rock formations, cliffs, and canyons, they climbed slowly to the 6,000 meter altitude required to escape the clutches of the high Andes Mountains. To my surprise, we often flew no more than fifty meters above the barren landscape and sometimes even lower, with the extremely hostile-looking mountains, snow-covered plateaus, and glaciers directly beneath us.

It was a breathtaking flight—literally. I hadn't figured that the flight over the Andes could be so marginally tight for this airplane. However, it is also possible that the infamously macho Captain Antonio was actually flying the plane so low in an attempt to scare the wits out of me. I knew from my earlier flights with him that he had a reputation for showing off, but I didn't afford him the pleasure of seeing me throw up or turn green, although I have to admit it was a close call on a number of occasions.

Without the luxury of a pressurized cabin and with no insulation or heating in this old flying barrel, it was bitterly cold in the cockpit at this altitude, and at a certain moment I fell victim to the shortage of oxygen while we flew over what looked to me like a powder-white moon landscape at 5,500 meters. When we reached the mountain ridges, the big aircraft was rattled by the strong turbulence and rolled over by the downdraft winds that tested the structural strength of this old aircraft to its limits. In my twisted mood swings it all felt really scary. But the pilots, both dressed in vintage

The meat flights were an air bridge that flew 4 tons of beef each day in a C-46 back to La Paz, without any interference from meat packers, fridge installations or sanitary regulations. It all worked fine as long as the blood-red beef was picked up immediately after the butcher had finished his job. The beef was simply dumped inside the aircraft where an internal gutter system collected any spilled blood and drained it out over the tail wheel. (Photograph Christian Volpati)

sheepskin jackets, remained very calm under the difficult conditions while all hell broke loose around them. The deafening noise of the engines, combined with the howling wind that seeped in through every crack and joint in the airplane, felt almost apocalyptic.

Occasionally, the pilots took a puff of oxygen out of a plastic tube connected to an old rusty gas bottle that was strapped next to me against the bulkhead. They looked to all intents and purposes as if they were sitting back leisurely enjoying a hookah in a Marrakesh tea room. Antonio offered me the tube and I took a grateful and healthy swig from the bottle.

I instantly felt better and became less worried about the rigors of the biting cold and the fuzzy feeling of not fully realizing where I was. I had begun to experience hallucinations and strange fears that were completely alien to me. The lack of oxygen had been working like a dangerous drug and a paranoid feeling slowly seeped into my mind that we could at any moment slam up against the mountain ridges in our heavily buffeting airplane as it skimmed precariously over the glaciers.

Then Captain Antonio suddenly pointed forward: right in front of us there was a huge mountain range, with a notch between two summits on the right-hand side. After a slight roll the Curtiss headed straight for the pass. I took a closer look and found myself wondering if we had enough height to slip through the narrow gap. The pilots sniggered; they could smell my fear. We flew through the pass with the ground less than 100 meters below us.

Once safely through, the airplane was hit by one last blast of turbulence before we suddenly found ourselves flying into a scene straight out of a Walt Disney movie. Instead of a wall of snow-capped mountains, our view was now one of a large green carpet that stretched far beyond the horizon. It was bathed in glorious sunlight that shone in my face in a thermonuclear explosion of light, warmth, and colors. Wow! My paranoia quickly subsided and my body and mind shifted back to normal.

This was the other face of Bolivia: the gloriously green one, where the jungle prevails and where livestock graze on huge ranches that cover thousands of acres of lush pastures.

We immediately started a sharp descent in order to make life more comfortable in the cockpit, and both the temperature and the supply of oxygen rose dramatically. We headed for the village of Santa Ana in the province of Beni, named after the meandering river below us. We saw more pastures, here and there a ranch, and roads winding their way alongside rivers to small settlements.

After a further descent to 500 feet, we made a sudden sharp turn over the village. The plan was to land here for a short stopover to pick up some passengers, which would give me a little time to go and see a crashed Dakota that had tried to make an emergency landing nearby. We stepped out into a wall of heat—a more extreme opposite to La Paz was hardly conceivable, and that was only a two-hour flight from here. I went in search of the wreck, which couldn't be all that far away.

We found her quickly, but unfortunately the C-47 airframe had already been stripped to the bone. The wings were separated from the hull, which had been dragged to the end of the runway by a tractor. Everything had been plundered and the wingtips were gone, too. All that was left was an empty aluminum shell partially overgrown with vegetation.

Antonio made some enquiries and learned that another plane had landed with a wrecking crew on board. After two days spent shredding the plane they had eventually left, taking with them everything that was of any value. They were the plane's rightful owners, so there was no point in me crying over a missed opportunity.

We got back onboard and continued our flight to a nearby hacienda, over which we first made a low pass during which I spotted a corral teeming with cattle. There was no real runway, only something that looked like a cart track, and we prepared to make a landing similar to the one I had previously experienced on the Gran Sabana in Venezuela. Captain Antonio dropped the wheels and the flaps, gently landed the plane in the high grass, and parked her right next to the corral. It was hot, hot, hot, and the air was swarming with vicious horseflies. And the smell! Where on earth had we landed?

It turned out to be one of the many open-air slaughterhouses in the Beni region. Earlier that morning, the preselected cattle had been rounded up and shunted into the corral to await their bloody fate. The local cowboys and butchers worked quickly

El Alto Airport (4,100m) is the highest-lying international airport in the world. Right next to the slick jet scene is a vast corrosion corner from where cargo and meat flights operated to feed the capital. Derelict prop liners from bygone days are still scattered all over the field, like some kind of weird open-air museum. Here I found many spare parts for my business: wing panels, instruments, cockpits, etc. all abundantly available, as most of the DC-3 s had long since ceased flying.

and efficiently with their terrifying array of tools. When the Curtiss had crossed the Andes, the captain had sent a radio message saying that they were on their way and that signaled the end for the beasts.

By the time our aircraft had landed they had already butchered and axed five tons of beef into large bloody pieces of 60 to 80 pounds each. That was the maximum weight that one man could carry over his shoulder.

I had no idea how many cattle had been slaughtered, but there was an incredible mountain of waste consisting of innards and cows' heads. It was a bloody mess all around us. The animals' skins were piled high, destined for the tannery further down the road, a smoking shed that smelled even worse than this spot.

A narrow timber ramp was attached to the cargo door of the Curtiss Commando, up which the meat carriers then ran carrying their loads of beef. They dumped the chunks in the fuselage of the plane from their blood-soaked shoulders. The meat was still dripping with blood that ran off into a central gutter in the floor and down to the rear of the plane, where it was discharged via an opening in the tail. A deep, dark-red pool was beginning to form on the ground around the tail wheel. Everything smelled of blood, which explained the millions of horseflies buzzing around in a wild frenzy.

When all the meat had been piled up in the hold, the men threw in a severed bull's head to top it all off. I wondered if this was some kind of ritual. Inca superstition perhaps?

The four emergency exit hatches in the cabin were removed to provide better aeration for our cow cargo. I had never before seen nor smelled meat as fresh as this, nor in such quantities. The cabin was full to the brim, and after a stop of more than two hours it was time for the return flight to La Paz, back to where the customers would be waiting for this load of meat.

In order to get back into the cockpit we had to clamber over the sticky and smelly meat mass, now completely covered in black flies. The captain didn't want to soil his expensive snakeskin cowboy boots in this fleshy swamp so he had the cowboys make a kind of path using old burlap bags draped over the meat mountain, across which he then scrambled with surprising agility.

Within fifteen minutes we were back in the air after a long roll down the grass runway with our five tons of freakish freight. Soon, the sweet smell of blood and most of the flies had disappeared from our flying hearse thanks to the draft blasting through the cabin courtesy of the open hatches.

Now came the effort required to gain enough height with a full load onboard so that we could cross over the massive Andes mountain range again. It took quite a while before we reached our flight altitude of 6,000 meters with the heavy aircraft. The engines struggled at first in the scorching midday temperature but it became easier as we got higher and the air got colder.

In contrast to the outbound flight, we now had enough airspace and freedom of movement to climb to a higher altitude and we crossed easily over the same pass we

Once back in El Alto, the vans and trucks waited to take the beef straight to the shops in La Paz. From live bull to the shop in only 5 hours—fast food Bolivian style—it was a system that worked well until about 10 years ago when the roads were improved and refrigerated trucks arrived on the scene and took over the trade of the carniceros.

had flown through so precariously earlier that morning. That was the highlight of the flight, and from there we glided our way smoothly back to El Alto, now with sufficient altitude to stay away from the ridges and the turbulence.

Less than an hour later, we landed gently on the endlessly long runway and taxied for almost ten minutes before reaching the eerie parking field full of doomed aircraft at the very end of the runway, out of sight of the visitors at the international airport.

There were a few old Chevrolet pickup trucks waiting for us, obviously the clientele who had ordered the meat. The cargo doors opened and the first thing the mechanics did was to throw the bull's head as far out into the open field as they could. The hundreds of flies that had survived the cold of the flight were still clinging to the bull's head. They filled its nose, mouth and eyes—the warmest spots. Dumping the huge head with its massive horns got rid of the flies and so the unloading could commence, insect-free. Food hygiene Bolivian style.

This ritual of throwing out the bull's head also attracted stray dogs. To them the sound of the engines was a sign that food was coming. The dogs fought ferociously over the head—no doubt a delicious treat for them, especially with all the flies thrown in for free, like French fries.

In the meantime, the Curtiss cargo was distributed over four trucks parked right next to the plane. Only one hour after landing, the meat load was already in the shops in La Paz and ready for sale; the same beef that only a few hours earlier had been a living, walking bull. The steak on display at the butchers in La Paz had been transformed from live bull into a juicy dinner in less than a single day, without any need for a freezer or meatpacker. All thanks to the flying meat wagons of El Alto. The concept of Fast Food might actually have been invented here.

COCHABAMBA

On a later trip to Bolivia with Dolph, we were tempted to set out on further quests for the Dakota because we were sure that we simply had to stumble across a treasure trove of parts somewhere one day, given all the crashed and discarded wrecks we had heard about. It was a random search in a strange land, and we were not unlike the Spanish conquistadores who had come here 400 years earlier looking for gold and glory.

We flew from El Alto to Cochabamba, a city situated in the warmer green plains in the center of Bolivia. Upon arrival at the city's modern airport we grabbed a taxi to the other side of the complex and were confronted with a totally different scene: a faded old terminal building with rusty hangars, cobbled streets, partially collapsed walls, and a large wrought-iron entrance gate that was hanging half open.

A fabulous scene straight out of the history books; South America has a patent on such surprises. We walked onto an Indiana Jones film set complete with all the dazzling grace of an authentic vintage airport and the sinister, silent feel of total abandonment, as if the place was contaminated, like an exile colony.

We went through the gate and immediately spotted two Dakotas standing next to a hangar bearing the name of a long-defunct local aviation company. An old green Dodge sedan was parked in front of the hangar. There was no one around; the place looked like it had been abandoned a few years back, what with all the high grass and rust everywhere. The Dakota on the left was in a derelict state, with its engines and wingtips missing, probably cannibalized for parts to keep the other DC-3 flying. That one still looked reasonably complete. The scaffolding next to the engine nacelles was still there and there were even toolboxes and oilcans still lying around on the ground, as if the joint had been open up until yesterday. We could almost get the smell of wingtips inside the hangar but, unfortunately, it was locked.

Where was everyone? It all felt rather spooky, as if the owner had simply decided one day to pack up, lock the door, walk out the gate, and not come back to tidy up the place or even pick up his car.

Bankrupt, repossessed, impounded? We couldn't tell, but it all looked very forlorn indeed. A few more Dakotas were parked further down the field, also totally abandoned. It seemed that the glory days were long gone here, too, just like in Venezuela, with the expansion of the airports and their longer, paved runways meaning that larger aircraft could now fly in everywhere. The results of that change could be seen on the other side of the airfield where modern jet airliners now held sway.

Cochabamba, a city at a more moderate altitude in the center of Bolivia, had long been a hub for piston prop liners flying to every corner of this vast country. Again we found a ghost airfield from bygone days right next to the modern airport. This company had gone broke and had left everything lying around behind them, as can be seen here in this photo of two Dakotas, eerily surrounded by scaffolds and toolboxes. We could almost smell the presence of spare parts, but where had everybody disappeared to?

Curiously enough, there was one small airline company still operating in Cochabamba, owned by the Canedo family, and we decided to pay them a visit. When we arrived, they were working on the complete overhaul of a truly stunning Curtiss Commando C-46 and a Super DC-3. Both aircraft were more than likely destined to be used to fly international tourists in nostalgic style to the major sightseeing attractions of the country, such as Lake Titicaca, Sucre, Potosi, the Rurrenabaque jungle post, and the Uyuni Salt Flats. Painted in their fabulous livery with the eagle's head logo of Canedo on the nose, the aircraft looked brand new, but in commercial terms it all seemed a little too ambitious in a country where international tourism would not really start to develop for another ten years or so.

Apparently, their fleet is now up for sale but I couldn't ascertain whether that also meant that they have stopped their charter flights altogether. It would be sad if that were the case, as the Canedo family has poured years of love and dedication into keeping these museum pieces in the air.

Cochabamba did not provide us with what we had hoped for. It was impossible to track down any of the Dakota owners in the short time we had, and any deeds of ownership would probably turn out to be dubious at best.

COCKPIT AND INSTRUMENTS SCORED!

We returned to El Alto, where we met up with the captain and owner of two Dakotas. He was planning to overhaul one of them using parts from the other. Anything that remained after the job was done would be scrapped, and we had arrived just in time to experience firsthand the work of the cutting torch as it went about slicing up the airframe.

The C-47 that was being dismantled was an ex-TAM (Transportes Aero Militar) plane that had operated in the years after the war flying both military and civilian passengers, a common phenomenon in these vast countries. With hardly any road infrastructure, local passenger air traffic was often left in the hands of the military, a lucrative industry that continued right up until the late 1990s.

The TAM Dakota was being slaughtered. The wings, tail section, and cockpit had already been separated from the hull. It was like a crash site, with severed parts strewn all over the place. The captain offered to sell us the wingtips from this heap and suggested that he might be able to find more for us in Bolivia but that he would need more time to search for and collect them.

We had not had much luck so far ourselves so it seemed like a good idea to contract him as a parts locator, given his expertise and connections in the country. In much the same setup as we had employed with Andy in Florida some years earlier, the depot of the captain at El Alto was to be used for storing any wingtips he might eventually gather. When he had collected enough stock to fill a container, I would then come back to organize transport to the Netherlands.

During my earlier trips to Bolivia with the PME team, and before that with the Catalina Odyssey Tour, I had gotten to know an Englishman who would become my agent and outfitter in Bolivia for my photo sessions. His name was Martin Proctor, and he was a skilled and creative travel and film agent who had been living in La Paz for many years. He was married to a Bolivian woman and had plenty of connections. Prior to each trip, I contacted him to make appointments and arrange the aircraft needed for the photo shoots.

Our new parts locator, the Bolivian captain, spoke only Spanish and was very difficult to contact from abroad. Martin would play an extremely important role as an intermediary in our negotiations for the acquisition of wingtips and in setting up a shipping plan.

South America operates at its own pace and, according to Martin, this is especially true of Bolivia, where everything works slower in the human body and brains primarily because of the lack of oxygen. We eventually had to wait two years and I had to make three more trips to that country before we could finally transport our harvest.

Just around the corner we found the Canedo family. Their company is the operator of an immaculate Curtiss C-46 and this Super DC-3 (C-117 or R4D). Previously used for tourist flights to Bolivia's scenic spots, both of these planes are now up for sale and the future of their operation seems uncertain. Note the difference between this plane and the normal DC-3: higher tail design, stretched fuselage and wheel well covers.

For the last delivery we had enough components to fill a twenty-foot container, but our score of wingtips remained modest at only eight pieces, a rather miserable result given the effort and number of trips I had made. I planned to go back just in time to seal the deal, while Martin would take on the task of arranging a container in El Alto for our trophies. The empty container was scheduled to arrive at our El Alto depot on a Thursday but, once again, things did not work out as planned. Nothing would materialize until the following Monday. Delays are one of those things that you just have to accept as part of the culture and the *manana* mentality was very well cultivated here.

I had the nagging feeling that this would probably be my last trip to Bolivia, as there were no more Dakota parts to be found in anything like numbers sufficient to justify a new mission.

It was not all doom and gloom, however. Thanks to our growing network of contacts in Europe we had tapped a new source that might help improve our score of wingtips: war and airplane museums. Most of these museums have one or more Dakotas on display and they often have surplus wingtips that come with the aircraft. That is stuff they usually do not want to sell, but they might be prepared to swap with you if you could offer them something very special, something really scarce that they would love to get their hands on.

We discovered that these museums are always on the lookout for authentic military WWII cockpit material like dashboards, old radios, direction finders, and other instruments from that era. Most of these vintage instruments and radios are almost impossible to find nowadays. Except for, that is, in Bolivia, where they had

Thanks to 50 years of thriving prop liner operations in El Alto, there was no lack of scrap and Dakota parts here. This ex-TAM DC-3 was just about to be shredded for its aluminum. The makeshift smelting ovens were ready to consume it for the manufacture of household utensils like pots, pans and spoons. We arrived just in time to save the cockpit and took it to Holland for delivery to a museum, along with the wings and instruments.

kept all this stuff stored since the war.

In this country that time forgot, they had used these archaic massive lamp radios and phosphorous light-emitting instruments for many years after the war and then removed them all from the planes and stored everything in a chilly warehouse in El Alto, a shed called the Big Fridge. When Dolph and I walked into that shed one lucky day we saw a surplus dump jam-packed with old meters, radios, artificial horizons, compasses, and everything else we could ever hope to find in a WWII C-47 cockpit interior.

We had been put on the right track by the Wings of Liberation Museum in the town of Best in the Netherlands. They had expressed a willingness to trade (not sell!) their surplus wingtips for WWII gauges, panels, and radios. We hadn't forgotten their offer and now here we were, standing face-to-face with probably the world's largest and last inventory of precious wartime instruments. Jesus, it was like finding an old Jaguar XK-120 sports car in a broken-down hayshed, its aging owner prepared to offload it for 500 quid in cash. The owner was sitting in a chair inside his little house when we knocked on the door, apparently waking him up in the process. He took us to the adjacent barn and showed us around.

I stood there, nailed to the floor, asked him to quote us a few prices, and left him to mumble some figures to himself while we looked around. Within ten minutes we had bought the entire contents of the shop without even blinking. The owner continued mumbling away to himself but now with a big smile across his face. He closed down the joint for good, all of its stock sold in one fell swoop, and we left him there counting his fistful of dollars in total disbelief. He had done the deal of his life and decided to retire on the spot, while we saw our number of wingtips shoot up by 50% after swapping the instruments to the museum in Holland for four wingtips.

THE SALT LAKE OF UYUNI

Now back to the delay of the delivery of the container to our depot in El Alto. Faced with the prospect of a long and boring weekend with nothing to do other than sit around and wait in La Paz, I decided to take a trip to the southern part of the country, a region I had not visited before. I drew up a plan to check out the airstrips at Potosi, Uyuni, and Sucre in a three-day weekend round trip. I called the hotel's front desk to ask them to book me a seat on the train, but it turned out to be fully booked for the weekend. A flight then, maybe? Non signor. A bus? Ditto, all full, too late signor Wiesman, disculpa.

There was only one other option: a rental car. With the help of the hotel manager, I rented a Suzuki Vitara 4x4 for the trip without having even the slightest idea of what might be in store for me on the 500 kilometer stretch of road between here and the

The capital of Bolivia, La Paz, is situated in a huge mountain bowl at 3,500m above sea level. Despite the marked lack of oxygen at this altitude, there is no shortage of residents, with over one million souls living here in a climate that can bring 4 seasons in one day: the temperature variations are extreme and no cattle can survive on the Altiplano of the High Andes.

southern desert plains of the Altiplano. On Friday morning I went to the car rental garage and checked the car carefully, especially the spare tire and the jack, as this country with its primitive roads has a reputation for wreaking havoc on tires.

By noon, everything was ready for the long trip, and my first task was to fight my way through the hectic traffic of the city and then on to El Alto. From there, I planned to take the Ruta Nacional across the plateau to the city of Oruro (at 3700 meters) and then continue via a relatively good road along the enormous Poopo Lake, with another 100 kilometers to go to the last city, Challapata, before I hit desert country.

I had barely driven out of Challapata when civilization seemed to stop abruptly. Jeez, I still had some 200 kilometers to go on this road of hard sand and gravel (if I was lucky). Of course, no one had told me how bad it really was, but it quickly dawned on me that my planned arrival time of 7:00 p.m. in Uyuni was optimistic to say the least.

It was now 5 o'clock in the afternoon and the only other traffic left on the road consisted of big trucks driving in the opposite direction. Suddenly, the gravel road that I had been following along the railroad since leaving town ran out at a riverbank. What the hell was this? All I could see in front of me was a shallow but fast-flowing river. No road, only a long pillar bridge for the railway but no crossing for cars.

As I was trying to figure out how on earth I could get to the other side, two girls came walking over the railway bridge. I asked them where I could cross the river in my car. After overcoming their initial shyness, one of the girls pointed straight down into the water and said, "*Aqui*, keep driving along the railway bridge."

"*Donde*, where? Do you mean down here?" I asked in disbelief.

Unfortunately, no other car came along and so I did what they advised me to do as I had no reason to doubt them. I drove carefully off the sandy shore and into the water. When the car was half submerged I suddenly felt the front wheels lose their grip and the car began to float. Caught now in the flow of the river, the car started to drift along parallel to the riverbank. I quickly put the gears into reverse and, with no shortage of luck, I managed to get the jeep to crawl back up onto the riverbank. The girls were astonished, and by the look on their faces I could see that they did not understand why it hadn't worked. Then an old man with a tanned and wrinkled face appeared out of nowhere on the riverbank. In a soft voice he said to me, "*Signor, sigua me*, follow me, I know a shallow place where you can cross, it is too deep here, only good for big trucks."

I invited him to step into the car and we drove cautiously along the sandy shore until we came to a small village with muddy sheds and a few brick cottages.

"*Pare aqui*, stop here," he said and stepped out again. Keeping his old worn-out shoes on, he walked into the water and signaled me to follow him. Driving in first gear and with the four-wheel drive engaged I drove into the river after him. It was wonderfully simple. A few minutes later I was safely on the other side of the river. What a relief. However, my aquatic adventure had cost me precious time and it was now getting dark.

The last of the Bolivian carniceros (meat haulers) that flew from La Paz to the cattle ranchos at the Beni River in NE Bolivia. I had many exciting flights on board this aircraft with Captain Antonio, with the ladies always waiting patiently for his return. The captain died in an airplane crash years ago and this plane crashed in September 2012 in an incident that would see the permanent grounding of all C-46 flights from La Paz.

I was very grateful to the old man and handed him an American ten-dollar bill as a reward. Overwhelmed by my gift, the shy Inca peasant said in a broken and subdued voice that he had never before in his life held such a magic bill between his fingers. He muttered something about the blessings of the gods who would protect me on my journey and we said our goodbyes. He had made my day; I had probably made his week.

The bad news, however, he had saved for the last part of our conversation: from here on the road would consist of nothing but desert sand for the remaining 100 kilometers to Uyuni.

Even with the four-wheel drive engaged, I had great difficulty getting the jeep off the sandy riverbank, a harbinger of what was to come. This was going to be a trip I was unlikely to forget in a hurry.

I wrestled with the jeep for the next few hours in the dark across the endless sandy desert without seeing one light, farmhouse, or other human being. I didn't really mind the bumping of the car over large boulders, loose sand, hills, and dry gullies in a pitch-black night over an unknown desert. What did unnerve me, however, was the thought that I might hit a boulder that would do enough damage to leave me with a flat tire. In such a scenario I would be stuck here until the following morning, because it would be impossible to jack up the car in the dry, loose sand and change the wheel in the dark. Not life-threatening perhaps, but not a pleasant prospect either at an altitude of nearly 4,000 meters in the severe cold and in the pitch-dark night.

So I just kept driving doggedly on through the eerie desert with a zillion stars overhead, as if on some kind of space odyssey.

Suddenly I saw two faint lights on the distant horizon: that had to be Uyuni—what a relief. With only fifteen or twenty kilometers more to go I felt I was going to make it, even if I had to walk the last few kilometers. At least I now had a beacon, which gave me a sense of direction. Without that point of light I could have been consumed by the worry of driving around in circles or even in the wrong direction entirely.

An hour later, at 10:00 p.m., I finally drove into the village. It had taken me ten hours to cover a distance of 500 kilometers from north to south across the highlands of the Andes.

Tired and hungry, I went looking for a hotel in this odd-looking village, which looked like an outpost in an old Clint Eastwood movie. On the main street, I stopped in front of the door of a building that looked faintly twentieth century but that still had a wooden veranda and an old-fashioned porch at the entrance. "Hotel," was written in faded letters on the window.

Filled with a strange euphoria that I had made it, this rather dismal-looking little hotel now seemed infinitely more pleasant to me than any of the expensive Sheraton Hotels in Miami, Paris, or Madrid that I had stayed in during my career as a corporate executive. Back then I had found that slick corporate life very fascinating, but twenty-four years of it had eventually proven more than enough. My destiny, I felt, lay elsewhere.

Here in this weird and exotic desert hotel you could smell adventure in every corner. My veins were still pumping with the adrenaline of my crazy drive across the desert when I waddled onto the veranda with my bag over my shoulder. There was a group of Western tourists sitting there, including a conspicuous-looking woman whose eyes latched onto me with a little more than normal interest. I walked past the group, throwing them a polite smile, opened the door of the hotel, and went to check in. The girl at the reception desk asked me where I had come from at such a late hour. Coach, train, or plane were all run-of-the-mill, but all alone in a rental car, without a guide, that was sure to raise a few eyebrows. I understood her suspicion, but I was not in the mood to explain it all to her. I was hungry and in need of a beer or two.

It wasn't the first time I had gambled with my travel arrangements, but I already had a hell of a story out of my trip and the best was yet to come.

As I stood at the desk, the group that had been sitting outside on the veranda came inside. They turned out to be Italians—an older couple, both in their early seventies, accompanied by their daughter in her early forties and her boyfriend. The older man was staring at me with a rather surprised look, obviously wondering where the heck I had come from at this time of the night. I asked them if they knew where I might be able to get something to eat. No problem, the man said, he would show me the way to a nearby restaurant on the main street. It seemed to me that they were a

With the Catalina PBY-5A we visited El Alto airport in 1994 en route from Rio, Brazil to Lima, Peru as part of the Catalina Odyssey trip. We had planned to make a water landing on the highest navigable lake in the world: Lake Titicaca. Flying in an empty plane, we arrived at the landing site in front of the Lakeside Hotel, but just before we were about to touch down, a micro burst with a strong downdraft coming in from over the High Andes mountains forced us down and the Catalina was slammed hard onto the chilly water. Luckily, our expert pilot, Captain Paul Warren Wilson, saved the day: he instantly aborted the landing and the Cat was able to climb out from under the invisible hand of the perturbed Mountain Gods. Strangely, this mishap had been predicted by the local Shaman. Seconds after that harrowing experience, this picture was taken by the Hotel director who did not understand why we had not landed on the water to pick him up for the promised tour.

bit bored and were looking for some distraction and a chance to quiz me. It was clear to them that I wasn't part of their luxury travel club of wealthy tourists, the kind that go looking for something different from their usual top-class but boring destinations like Capri, Monte Carlo, Cannes, and Villa d'Este in Como. And they were very curious as to what I was doing out here *solemente*—all on my own.

We ended up in a very cozy Italian pizzeria packed with affluent Western tourists all in their forties or older and mostly Spaniards, Italians, and Brazilians.

The Italian group who had brought me here turned out to know the other Italians, who were part of the same classy touring group from Milan. I was introduced to all their friends and family. The beautiful Milanese lady from the veranda spoke to me in French. She also wanted to know what I was doing here and what my plans were for the next few days. She was wearing expensive-looking earrings and her dark hair and lavish attire gave her the look of a classic Mediterranean beauty, a bit like an Italian movie diva from the distant past. Gina, maybe, or even Sophia. I told her that I intended to visit the salt flats and then to continue on to one of the Lagunas Verdes to see the flamingos. She and her companions had also planned a trip to the salt flats the next day, so I remarked that maybe we would see each other again. She introduced herself as

At the El Alto "underground airport," quasi derelict aircraft were kept operational. With no FAA in sight, things could go wrong BIG time around here. This DC-6 had been converted a year previously for a new career in cargo. On the day of the test flight the engines fired up all right, but suddenly engine no.2 burst into flames after switch-off. While the pilots frantically tried to restart and kill the flames, the ground crew ran around looking for a fire extinguisher. There was none to be found and the fire brigade from the airport was alerted. It took them 20 minutes to arrive on the scene, a Bolivian ground speed record, but they were too late. The pilots jumped out and ten minutes later, the proud aircraft in its new livery was on its knees awaiting the fatal blow. We stood there watching with 20 other people helpless to ease the agony of this majestic airliner. It was so sad, the crew all prayed and cried as months of investment and hard work went up in smoke in a matter of minutes!

Daniela, daughter of the elderly couple. The man with her was her new boyfriend and she was on vacation with her family for the first time to this remote resort.

It was immediately obvious to me that she was bored with her touring companions and that she was looking for something more exciting than just sitting in a coach all day with a bunch of tourists, even in such exotic surroundings. Slightly overdressed and rather restless, the signals were obvious to me: here was a spoilt lady who had her heart set on having some "quality time" of a different sort, rather than spending all her time sightseeing with her family.

The next morning I decided to drive out to the airport, but that proved to be a disappointment, as it only had a few smaller planes like Cessnas and Pipers, which had probably flown in all the luxury tourists. There were no traces of any abandoned aircraft, much to my chagrin.

I was soon on my way again under a rapidly warming sun to the Uyuni salt flats,

The village of Uyuni is a fantastic Wild West outpost that attracts avant-garde tourists looking for the complete opposite of fancy luxury resorts. Well worth a visit are the Salar (salt) lake, the vapores (Steam locs) graveyard, the Lagunas Verdes and its flamencos, the high Andes Mountains, Potosi and the Atacama desert. All offer more scenic beauty than a curious tourist could handle in a week!

a place that would provide me with one of the most enchanting views that I have ever seen in all my travels around the world. Twelve thousand square kilometers of white flat ground covered with crystal white salt. Sometimes bone-dry, sometimes topped by a thin layer of water and extending far beyond the horizon under a sleek steel-blue sky with an intensity of light the likes of which I had never seen before. It probably has something to do with the high altitude, its proximity to the equator, and the reflection off the salt surface, which acts like a mirror bowl.

After an hour's drive across a partially submerged salt floor, the ground became drier and I was able to follow a trail that led in a westerly direction across the plains to the distant horizon with the ubiquitous mountain ridges of the Andes and their huge snow caps rising up into the sky off in the far blue yonder. Occasionally, I passed a small coach with tourists or a fully loaded salt truck.

Suddenly, a dome-shaped bump loomed up in the landscape. Even from a distance through the fata morgana–like tremble of the hot air, it looked spectacular. I had a blurred view of an island in the middle of all this flatness with the biggest cacti I have ever seen, at least ten meters tall and rising vertically from the flat like a collection of smokestacks. I stopped for lunch at a primitive but tastefully appointed restaurant and found the entire Italian group sitting there, including Daniela, who invited me to come and sit at their table. The view from this elevated height was truly unreal, almost alien-like. After lunch, I walked outside to photograph the cacti and the surrounding area. Daniela came with me, armed with her expensive camera, and surprised me by saying that she would love to accompany me on my trip back to La Paz, or even just to Uyuni. She had had enough of her traveling companions—"sooooo boring."

"Oh, okay, I see . . . but how are you going to explain that to your parents and your boyfriend?" I asked her, feigning complete innocence.

She replied, "He is almost qualified as a professor at the University of Milan and spends too much time working on his academic projects and not enough on 'my project.'"

"Is that so?" I replied. I began to suspect where she might be going with this and so decided it would be wiser not to offer her a lift back to the hotel. The Italian group had all been so nice to me that I didn't want to stir up any trouble. So I told Daniela that it was not such a good idea accompanying me, either to Uyuni or to La Paz, and graciously turned down her proposal.

She looked glum but I figured that she wouldn't give up that easily. This was a woman who was used to getting her own way with everyone, especially with *la Mamma e Pappa*, who obviously adored their princess.

After lunch I drove back across the plains, taking a huge detour so as to immerse myself properly in this unique wonder of nature, a place I would love to visit again some day.

With the afternoon drawing to a close, I decided to check out the mysterious locomotive cemetery situated between the town and the lake before heading back to the hotel. Approaching the spot, I could pick out the shapes of a large number of rusty steamers with tenders and wagons standing out sharply against the huge yellow disk on the horizon.

The mellow yellow rays of the sun setting behind the mountains were reflected in the salt lake, producing a very strange effect not unlike the Northern Lights. This formed a fantastic backdrop to the rusty old iron dinosaurs standing there in complete silence, like they were participants in some ghostly Remembrance Day ceremony.

I was mesmerized by the light show and I immediately climbed onboard the first steam train I came across. The machines were stripped completely bare inside but I could pick out the letters saying "Made in USA" and "Made in Germany." These were early industrial giants, the rolling steam engines that first set the world in motion; fascinating technology that provided man with the first means of mechanically powered transport, over 150 years ago, before the steamship, the automobile, and the airplane came along. The ingenious open mechanics of the long pushrods and the immense steel wheels driven by steam power had long been a source of fascination to me—ever since I had seen my first big locomotive as a child in Surabaya on Java and been flabbergasted by its sheer dimensions and the sizzling hiss of steam.

With the light fading slowly and the darkness beginning to envelop these static monsters, I realized that I was looking at a unique slice of transport history, a time when Bolivia stepped into the twentieth century by unveiling a railroad network that cut a path right through the mysterious Inca Empire, an unprecedented event in these mountainous regions. For the primitive and superstitious people living in remote

The Uyuni Salt lake covers more than 10,000 square km at an altitude of 3,600m. Partly dry and partly covered with a thin layer of water, no photo can do justice to the beauty of this place and its unrivaled cobalt blue sky. This cactus island is a huge mushroom-shaped dome with cactus stacks of up to 8 meters in height that are not found anywhere else in the world.

communities, the arrival of the locomotives must have seemed like the advent of Armageddon.

This place was a dazzling open-air museum with no entrance, no guide, and no visitors. Perhaps that is what made it all the more astonishing.

In total darkness, I drove back to the hotel. When I walked in the door the director came rushing over to me, a look of deep concern on his face. It seemed that Daniela was suffering from a sudden bout of altitude sickness and was insisting that she needed to return immediately to the lower altitude of La Paz.

She had asked the hotel director how she could get back to La Paz the next day, Sunday. The man knew that there was no transport possible on Sunday, except maybe with a man who would be driving back on that day: me. She knew this, of course, as I had already told her my plans. Her parents were in an awful state and they begged me to give Daniela a lift back to La Paz. I was taken up to their room where I found Daniela sitting in a chair sighing like an opera star.

I told her that I could take her in my car, no problem. As a sign of her gratitude she gave me a bold wink and instantly felt a lot better. Her parents showered me with thanks and drinks, but what about her friend? He wasn't anywhere to be seen. Though maybe a nerd, as she had said, I figured he was no fool. Daniela's cunning plan to escape from the group had succeeded. I had seen this plan brewing in her mind on the cactus island earlier that day. But to be honest, her feigning altitude sickness was a clever move; if ever they are looking for a new actress for the famous

The steam locomotive cemetery is a unique open-air train museum. Arriving there just before sunset, I witnessed a sort of Northern Lights effect caused by the reflection of the low sun light on the nearby Salt Lake. Spooky silhouettes of ancient locomotives—the first ever machine-driven transport in the world. Impressive rusty old relics made in the USA and Germany.

La Divina Commedia, they need look no further. No audition required for this diva!

We left for La Paz early the next morning, this time not over the sandy desert route but via a detour that would take in Potosi and some mountain lakes along the way, if all that were possible in a single day. Daniela had to keep up her role of "sick little birdie" for a little longer, while her Mama showered her with kisses and hugs, her Papa looked on anxiously, and her boyfriend glowered in the background. She played the role of altitude victim perfectly. Papa and Mama were overwhelmed with emotion but also very impressed; their sick princess was being rescued by a real-life Indiana Jones character; could it be any cooler? This was the ultimate adventure holiday story and they made sure they got the photos to prove it to the rest of the family back home before we set off. None of their previous trips over the past twenty years to Monte Carlo and other exotic destinations had ever yielded such a thrilling story!

After we left the village the road wound its way straight up into the mountains to the east towards Potosi. En route we saw huge lakes shimmering in an impressively desolate landscape and we had the feeling that we were driving through the set of a sci-fi film. After the harsh colors and light of the Uyuni salt lake, the color palette here was more pastel-like and offered a sense of staggering purity and abandonment, which I actually found a little intimidating. I got out every now and then to admire the scenery and gaze in awe at the beauty of creation. Stunning views but, frankly, not the easiest place in the world to get to.

I stopped at one of the turquoise lakes when I spotted a huge flock of pink flamingos feeding, their beaks dredging the shallow lake bottom. The elegant birds provided a stunning contrast to the blue-green waters; it was a scene straight out of a National Geographic film. By now, Daniela had completely shaken off her "illness" and she jumped out of the car with her camera in hand and followed me over to the lake in order to get a better look. The birds were very timid and would fly away at the slightest sign of danger. When we had gotten to within one hundred meters of the flock and I was lying in the tall reed grass along the shore, she tried to crawl closer to get a good shot. But with that she blew our cover and the whole swarm flew off with much shrieking and flapping of wings, like a huge pink cloud rising out of the lake. "Shit," I thought to myself, "that's them gone for good." Daniela didn't seem to care all that much, however, as she obviously had other plans in mind as we lay there in the reeds—plans that didn't involve staring at a bunch of pink birds. All part of her little "project," no doubt.

We arrived in Potosi at around lunchtime and first took a drive through the old center of that beautiful city, which was founded by the Spanish conquistadores in 1545 after they had discovered the world's largest silver deposits nearby. That discovery resulted in the biggest silver mining operation ever carried out at one single location anywhere in the world, one that would continue for over 200 years. The famous Spanish silver fleets were loaded up in Cartagena, Colombia, with the loot from Potosi before setting sail for Spain. The empire flourished on this colonial wealth, but the silver also attracted others, too, like vultures to a dead buffalo. Once the armada had set sail from Cuba, Colombia, or Mexico to Spain, English, French, and Dutch buccaneers, such as Sir Francis Drake and Captain Morgan, were lying in wait ready to grab a piece of this overseas treasure. The Flying Dutchman, Piet Hein, executed the largest robbery in human history in 1628 when he attacked and trashed the Spanish silver fleet off Matanzas, Cuba, and got away with 177,000 pounds of

Laguna Verde: more to the south, in the direction of the Atacama desert, you will find this lake with its unreal colors straight out of a painting. There are more such lakes on the road to the Silver Mine capital, Potosi, with flocks of flamencos in hues I have never seen before or since. I had come looking for planes, not plains, but with the former nowhere to be found the latter more than made up for my trip out here.

silver, 66 pounds of gold, and tons of pearls and furs.

By the time we got to La Paz later that evening, I had driven a total of 1,400 kilometers in the rental jeep in two and a half days through the very impressive mountainous region of the Bolivian Altiplano. During that time I had been treated to magnificent views, ghostly locomotives, elusive flamingos, and the wiles of an attractive Italian lady. Not exactly grueling but not the slightest sign of a Dakota anywhere either!

Shame on me; was it bad preparation or bad luck? A bit of both maybe.

Daniela had a different view on my fortunes during that trip. She had deceived the whole group out there in Uyuni with her altitude sickness story and cunningly figured that I was her ticket out of her dull predicament. Once in La Paz, she invited me to dinner at a luxury hotel on the Plaza de Armas in the heart of the city, the Italian group's HQ in between their luxury excursions into the wild.

In the absence of prying eyes, she now had the place to herself, and one thing I couldn't accuse her of was any reticence in the pursuit of her goals. Soon we were exactly where two days earlier she had planned us to be: in a restaurant in La Paz, 500 kilometers from Mama and Papa. It turned into a memorable evening with Daniela, one in which she left no stone unturned.

She told me that although her boyfriend had a fantastic job and everything that goes with it, she herself had more of a taste for the Bohemian type, the less bourgeois adventurer or artist who could add some excitement to her dull life of luxury. So it wasn't long before she was asking me if she could join me on the trip to El Alto, where I had to load the container, and then maybe even accompany me on my next expedition to Colombia.

Dreams and reality often become easily intertwined in the romantic notions of tourists who embark on such expeditions. What Daniela saw before her was a very exciting adventure, one she could not buy at a travel agency, and she reckoned that if she could tag along with the Dakota Hunter she would surely have the time of her life, minus the permanent company of her sympathetic but boring family and friends.

She craved a wild adventure like the one in prospect here and in her quest to snare it the Dakota Hunter had suddenly become the prey. I, in turn, told her about others who had sometimes come traveling with me and had often suffered physical problems and hefty mood swings, mostly due to the limited level of comfort on offer. The extreme temperatures, the creepy crawlies, like spiders, cockroaches, and mosquitoes, the hotels with no air conditioning, the poor food, the general lack of comfort, the fear of flying in a rattling old barrel—these are the less pleasant aspects of reality during any expedition, aspects that cannot always be planned for in advance.

The jungle is generally not the kind of place that a Westerner can enjoy being in for long periods of time, especially when there is a shortage of even the most basic of necessities, like food, safety, and comfort. In all likelihood, it is probably because of

This derelict Condor-painted DC-3 made me think of the colorful role of these vintage prop liners in the aviation history of Bolivia. The Dakota is no longer operational in this vast country since the infrastructure of roads and local airports has markedly been improved in the new age. The Silver Bird, here disguised as a Condor, has gone "extinct" and I was lucky to have experienced the very last days of its operational history. El Condor pasa no mas! (Photograph from Pima Air & Space Museum, Tucson, AZ)

my burning passion for the Dakota and my jungle youth in Borneo that I have a somewhat different tolerance level for these discomforts compared to those who accompanied me on my trips. Based on those earlier experiences, I knew for sure that a week-long journey into the Colombian Amazon with a pampered lady like Daniela, deprived of luxury resorts and hotels, was simply not a feasible option. Neither for me nor for her.

Not wishing to dash her romantic feelings entirely, I then told her about the other kinds of trips that I sometimes made, ones that involved less hardship. This was the kind of stuff she really wanted to hear and she edged closer to me as I recounted my tales over our cozy dinner for two. After our third glass of wine, I told her about one of the most beautiful "undiscovered" islands in the world, a place I had visited a few times: the archipelago of Fernando de Noronha situated in the Atlantic Ocean between Africa and northeastern Brazil. Hardly anybody in Europe has ever heard of that place and, frankly, I hope it stays that way for a long, long time.

Daniela was flabbergasted by all this bliss, which I drip-fed her against the background of the prospect of sharing the fantasy island of Fernando de Noronha with me. At that moment, the opening lines of the classic Freddie Mercury song "Bohemian Rhapsody" sprang to my mind—"Is this the real life, is this just fantasy?"—which seemed quite appropriate in her case.

There was a long pause in the conversation. It seemed we had both touched a nerve. The fulfillment of her dreams up until now had no doubt cost a lot of money but emotionally it was not quite yet what she desired, despite her parents' good intentions and generous investment. We both had a strong passion for long-distance travel but we each had our own separate motivation: for her it was predominantly to relieve her sense of boredom, while for me it was all part of my quest to relive a childhood dream that probably didn't even exist anymore.

Based on our diverging stimuli, I now found myself considering my options and looking for a reasonable explanation for why it would be best if she did not come along with me the next day; we had a demanding and urgent job to do in loading the container and only one day in which to do it. We said our goodbyes and promised to keep in touch. I never saw her again.

ALL SET FOR TRANSPORT

The next morning, Martin Proctor picked me up from the hotel for the last piece of business on this trip. It turned into a very hectic day. The container had to be picked up from the terminal, transported over the road to El Alto and then loaded up with the DC-3 stuff I had purchased. Once that was done the container was to be sealed in my presence and then taken on a truck over the Andes and across the border to the port city of Arica in Chile on the Pacific Ocean. From there, the container was to be shipped to Rotterdam via the Panama Canal.

It all sounded pretty straightforward, but the reality on the ground made our plans turn into something of a mirage. After days of waiting, whatever could go wrong did go wrong. Nobody seemed to care much about the paralyzing inertia, except for me. And so much so that I was willing to part with another handful of dollars in order to get the container delivered from the terminal when everyone else was having their siesta. After an unnerving journey of only five miles from the depot to the airport, we arrived just before they locked the gate to El Alto's zombie airport at 5:00 p.m. Getting the truck through the chaotic late afternoon traffic cost us a great deal of blood, sweat, and tears. However, we finally got the container to its destination, where six of the captain's men had been waiting for hours to help load her up.

First, the detached cockpit was gently shuffled inside, then our ultimate trophy, the eight DC-3 wingtips, followed by the other parts, rear wings, and last but not least our bonus catch: the delicate radios, meters, instruments, dashboards, racks, pumps, and pilot seats of a complete Dakota cockpit interior, all in vintage style.

These were nerve-racking hours, but at half-past eight in the evening, in the pitch dark, we finally finished our work under the glare of the headlights of Martin's jeep. As a grand finale, we had to struggle desperately to get the doors of the container closed, as it was literally packed to overflowing. Eventually, the truck drove away carrying the sealed twenty-foot container into the chilly night over the Altiplano en route to Chile. After a long day of stress and an exhausting weekend at 4,000 meters above sea level, I was beat and was struck down by altitude sickness once again. Some paranoia may have slipped in and made me imagine that I might never see the contents of that container again, negating all the effort and several trips to gather my precious harvest of wingtips and cockpit instruments.

I decided on a whim to cancel my flight back to Europe and hop on board the truck in order to accompany the container over the moonlit Andes landscape to the Pacific port of Arica. Fortunately, Martin was able to stop me from freaking out entirely and talked some sense back into me. He quickly drove me out to the international airport to catch my flight back to Miami at ten o'clock that same evening. It all turned out fine in the end, though it had been a close enough shave, and our treasure was finally on its way to Europe.

My flights over the High Andes were awe-inspiring. In the non-pressurized C-46, there was no heating or oxygen in the cramped cockpit. At 6,000m, feelings of paranoia and depression slipped into my mind, undoubtedly helped by Captain Antonio's determination to impress this "extranjero" by flying ultra-low over glaciers and snow capped mountain ridges in turbulent conditions. The rest of my photo team and models refused to step aboard for "insurance liability reasons" and instead flew comfortably overhead in a fast Piper Cheyenne, sipping cocktails in their heated cabin seats. This picture was taken from the Piper while, freezing cold and deafened by the noise, I resorted to sipping oxygen from a plastic tube and tried to figure out how we were going to tackle the huge Cordillera barrier looming up ahead of us. The plane was empty on this leg of the journey, but with 4 tons of meat on board the flight would become a nightmare if an engine suddenly quit on you in these conditions. In such a case, the mechanics would open the cargo door and immediately start dumping beef from the plane in order to maintain altitude. The earthbound meat bombs were allegedly like manna from heaven to the impoverished local population below in the valleys, as long as they did not smack into the thatched roofs of their little cabins.

CHAPTER 6

Colombia I

Never a Dull Day

Colombia had long been on my radar as a possible source for Dakota parts. I had first visited the country early in 1994 when I was involved in the production of the TV film *Catalina Odyssey*. On our stay there I took in the capital, Bogota, and the cities of Cartagena and Santa Marta further north. I also visited the tiny paradise-like Caribbean islands of San Andres and Old Providencia, which belong to Colombia.

At the time, Colombia was struggling with the consequences of the terrible drug wars, and I remember well the sight of army tanks positioned on every street corner in Bogota and in front of the government buildings, along with sandbags and machine-gun posts to thwart any attempted attacks by the drug barons. Only a few months earlier, in December 1993, the legendary drug lord Pablo Escobar had been shot dead during an attempt to arrest him. The drug war, terrorist attacks, and kidnappings had shocked the nation and had turned Colombia into one of the most dangerous countries in the world. After Escobar's death, other narco-gangs from Cali stepped in to fill the vacuum, and the violence continued unabated. In cooperation with the US Drug Enforcement Agency (DEA), the Colombian armed forces succeeded in apprehending most of the drug lords, but the arrests merely served to create space for yet another, even more threatening factor that would soon take center stage in the drug trade.

Since the mid 1960s, FARC (the Revolutionary Armed Forces of Colombia) had been engaged in an ongoing guerrilla war against the regular Colombian army. As the armed wing of the Colombian communist party, they were fighting to take control of this potentially very rich country. The movement allegedly had links with Cuba—not surprising given their shared political ideology—and they enjoyed a certain level of financial and material support from the Soviet Union. However, by the late 1980s, following the collapse of the Soviet Union, those supply lines had dried up and FARC was forced to seek out alternative sources of funding for military activities. The profitable narcotics trade must have seemed like an excellent option.

Colombia's president, Alvaro Uribe Velez, had asked the Americans to come in and help him in his crusade against the gangsters. The DEA entered the arena, and the drug lord soon became an easier target for arrest as his lifestyle, phone calls, and whereabouts, and the movement of large sums of money, began to be monitored with increasing accuracy.

A Colombian Special Forces unit was established that was not subject to the constraints of the regular command structure of the Colombian army and police forces. This elite force went to work in an unprecedented manner, homing in on the drug lords who until then had enjoyed the status of untouchables. They were soon to find that their days of comfort were over, as the old systems of bribing police officers and judges in exchange for early warning signals were quickly disabled. From now on, any raid aimed at making an arrest would come as a complete surprise to them.

In addition, once arrested, the narco-gangsters were immediately extradited to the United States. In this way the authorities were able to circumvent spectacular staged escapes or early releases of drug lords facilitated by their networks and bribes. The habitual recycling of Colombia's gangsters—being repeatedly jailed and freed—came to a sudden halt.

FARC, however, presented a different problem altogether, as they were hidden deep in the jungles of Colombia and could therefore continue their drug trafficking far more easily. Another source of income came from their policy of kidnapping; their most spectacular abduction was that of presidential candidate Ingrid Betancourt in February 2002. She was the well-known French-Colombian daughter of a senator and an intelligent and ambitious woman.

Just two weeks before her PR trip to the southern town of San Vincente, she had a meeting with a number of top-ranking rebels. She may have felt immune to a kidnapping attempt, given her rising stardom, but this was too good an opportunity for FARC to ignore. She was intercepted and taken into captivity while making the trip in a jeep through the rebel-infested jungle. Her overly optimistic appraisal of their

The workhorse of the Colombian outback. The vast plains and endless Amazon and Rio Negro jungles of Southern Colombia are the realm of the 70-year old DC-3. She still survives here in remarkably good condition and in growing numbers!

peaceful intentions were to cost her six long years in a jungle jail, until she was finally rescued by Special Forces in 2008 during a spectacular helicopter assault.

This episode confirmed Colombia's reputation as an extremely dangerous country. In fact, from the year 2000 on it was impossible for foreigners to travel around the country, as FARC had become an extremely serious threat to public safety.

I waited patiently while those years passed, but late in 2006 I finally got the news I had been hoping for. The travel ban had been partially lifted. I could now go there if I wished (or dared to, as the officials at the Foreign Ministry in The Hague neatly put it). Optimistic as always, I decided to go and check out the activities of the country's DC-3 operators in the hope of finding some surplus parts.

I had received some useful information from my good friend Michael Prophet, who had visited the country some eight years earlier, just before certain areas of the country were closed off to foreigners. The world's "Capital of the DC-3," Villavicencio, was the place to be if you wanted to see the legendary Dakota in all its operational glory as well as many C-47s that had crashed, been dismantled, seized, scrapped, or stored, or were in the process of restoration. There seemed to be a limitless supply of DC-3 parts.

The stage for all this action was the region to the south of Bogota: the Colombian Llanos—wide-open plains with green pastures intersected by lush, overgrown mountain ridges and long meandering rivers that flow east into the Orinoco River and south into the dense Amazon jungle. This was where I wanted to be so I could roll up my sleeves and get to work.

However, as well as being the perfect place for sourcing Dakotas, it was also the ideal location for a different kind of beast: FARC. This fertile area was where they grew their coca plants and from where they transported their narcotics to the markets. And what means of transport did they use? No prizes for guessing; the Dakota, of course! The rebels used the DC-3 to transport the drugs out of the jungle to their base in Villavicencio and then on by truck, ship, or airplane to their final destination in the United States and Europe.

The terrain also provided them with the perfect surroundings for fighting a guerrilla war. Whenever the military decided to go after them, they simply pulled back into the mountains or the jungle, both of which gave them excellent cover against detection from the air.

Well-trained and well-equipped, FARC soldiers could hide and survive for years in this environment while their trade flourished and made them richer, year after year. It helped create the illusion of steadily growing support for the movement, but the reality was more akin to that of a shadow economy based on coca plantations and narcotics trading, which had nothing to do with any high-minded political ideology.

The organization did *niente* to create a serious political alternative for the people of Colombia. However, their illegal trade created an adversary with a distinctly different approach and a level of determination and expertise that neither the Colombian army nor the government could ever muster. This new opponent was in a different league and would soon leave an indelible and lethal mark on the skin of FARC's invincible reputation. And I was about to have my first encounter with this new force.

Villavicencio (VVC), 60 miles south of Bogota, is the hub from where most flights to the South take off. The cargo is brought in by vans and trucks with direct delivery to the planes.

COLOMBIA REVISITED. OCTOBER, 2006

I had been itching to visit the country for many years and so, almost the day after receiving the good news that the ban on travel had been lifted, I booked a direct flight from Paris to Bogota with Air France. It was the start of what would prove to be an extremely adventurous trip for the Dakota Hunter.

After boarding in Paris, I immediately noticed that there were only two French people onboard, obviously with diplomatic credentials and sitting in business class, and that the rest of the plane was full of Colombians. No tourists, backpackers, globetrotters, or any other passenger from Western countries on the plane, apart from myself.

We landed at Bogota airport late in the afternoon. As we taxied up to the gate an incredible sight unfolded before my eyes. Parked out on the tarmac were a couple of US Air Force Boeing C-17 Globemasters. The huge military transport jet aircraft were in the process of being unloaded. Dozens of black assault helicopters with folded airscrew blades were being rolled out along the rear cargo ramps and parked in front of an enormous hangar.

I could also see hundreds of blue plastic drums that had obviously also been unloaded from the planes. Uniformed US military personnel were swarming all over the place and helping with the unloading. It had all the telltale signs of a serious small-scale airlift operation. Suddenly I realized I was watching a scene from the war on drugs that the United States had declared on all drug barons and warlords in the Caribbean and beyond.

Since 2003, the United States had been heavily involved in Iraq and later in Afghanistan in its war on terrorism. Those conflicts had taken their toll and the Bush

USAF C-17 Globemasters delivered dozens of helicopters and blue plastic drums by the hundreds directly from USA. In October 2006, I watched them landing at Bogota airport and was impressed by the scale of the airlift. Clearly the war on drugs was not yet over here.

Huey Helicopters patrolled the airport perimeters and the terrain beyond. With machine guns dangling from their doors, they were now the masters in VVC but photographing the soldiers was officially forbidden given their justified fear of FARC reprisals.

administration was the target of heavy public criticism for its two-front war strategy.

One can imagine that under these circumstances the US government was not at all eager to publicize the existence of a third front, one in which American soldiers were to be deployed. With the very limited influx of foreigners and overseas journalists, there was hardly any news about this particular war theater in the international press.

As I had done my homework on the new political situation in Colombia, I had some idea of what I could expect. But what I saw here at the airport was stark evidence of an escalation, not a downgrading, of the war on drugs. I had been under the impression that the hostilities were coming to a close and that that was the reason I was now allowed to come here after many years of waiting. But obviously the war was far from over; the final onslaught had only just begun.

While disembarking, I scanned the airport building trying to find a vantage point from which I might be able to film the scene on the platform. After shooting a couple of minutes' worth of film, I walked out to the main building to pass through customs and collect my luggage. A western businessman with a connecting flight to the south from Bogota was obviously an unusual phenomenon and maybe even a little suspicious. But the immigration officers let me through without too much hassle. I picked up my luggage and headed for the domestic airport hall.

· Suddenly, out of the blue, a tall man appeared before me and stopped me dead in my tracks. He was light-skinned, about 45 years old, short crew-cut hair, neatly dressed in white shirt and dark blue trousers. A small credit-card type ID tag dangled from his belt. He introduced himself as a security agent. He spoke English with a strong American accent. My first thought was that he was a DEA man, posted here in Bogota airport for security reasons.

I was impressed and curious at the same time. Was he really one of those God-fearing DEA agents or just a Colombian customs official? Or maybe he was an impostor trying to make an impression on a traveler from abroad in the hope of earning a fast buck? I couldn't tell and didn't get the time to figure it out either, as this mystery man immediately started to bombard me with questions.

"Sir, may I see your passport? What is the purpose of your trip to Colombia?" As I was rather surprised to encounter an apparently US-manned border patrol post in Colombia, I couldn't help asking him, "May I ask you a question? Have I landed in Miami or in Bogota?"

The man was probably used to a more submissive kind of prey and certainly not some wise guy with an attitude. My question had the effect of a slap in the face. Clearly insulted by my impertinence, he sighed heavily and with a look of disdain replied, "Sir . . . for your information, WE are the ones who decide who comes in and out of here, you got that?"

His answer and demeanor immediately set the tone for what I then realized would not be a friendly chat. Any further inquiry on my part as to WHO those WE

For over half a century the Dakota has been the main means of transport into the impenetrable Amazon jungle. For more remote outposts like Miraflores, where conditions are extremely primitive and a couple of days travel away by boat, the DC-3 can do the trip in 2 hours, flying its passengers into a lost world where local transport is all mules and horses.

VVC is the true DC-3 capital: few places in the world still have so many Dakotas in active service. Five operators are housed next to each other here, all with their own hangars on this "Dakota Boulevard."

actually were would not be a wise move at this stage.

He began to study my passport intently. I tried to explain the situation to him, "I'm here on a business trip."

Flipping through the pages and stamps in my passport, he asked, "Where are you headed?" In all innocence I replied "To Villavicencio."

"Where?!!" he snapped, looking up from my passport. "Villavicencio? Sir . . . you ain't going nowhere!"

His aggressive manner baffled me and the dude had now turned rude. Suddenly it was not my passport he was interested in anymore but its owner. I tried to keep the conversation going: "I have a ticket for this evening's flight. Is there a problem?"

There was a problem all right: I felt intimidated by him and was reluctant to even ask him his name, function, and organization. If I did I would surely only enrage him further. Any indication of a lack of respect or arrogance on my part could trigger a further escalation in this increasingly awkward chat.

Feeling a little alarmed now, I refrained from questioning him any further and the man's true identity remained hidden for the rest of our encounter. It was obvious that this guy had worked hard at creating this mystery identity for himself. If, in fact, he was a DEA agent, he was not going to announce it to the world. He continued in a lower voice, "What are you planning to do there down south?"

Realizing I was now walking on very thin ice, I chose my words carefully in order not to provoke this coke-buster any further and so I played it straight.

"My business is buying and selling DC-3 parts; I'm planning to meet up with the local Dakota operators."

The mere utterance of "DC-3" almost made his eyes pop out of his head and he stuttered, "DC . . . DC-3 parts? Are . . . are you . . . out of your bloody mind? All the DC-3s flying out there are involved in narcotics trafficking. What kind of an idiot do you take me for?"

He was red with rage at this stage but he tried to subdue the anger in his voice and continued, "Foreigners who come to Colombia go no further than Bogota; they do not travel south. This is not a tourist destination, this is the Wild West; do you understand what I'm saying? FARC, kidnappers, drug dealers—that's all you'll find down there, and you think you can just go for a visit? Who the hell do you think you are? Rambo? The goddamn Terminator?"

The raging bull in him wasn't finished yet; the stupidity and naiveté of my plan really stunned him and the F-word started to slip in more frequently. "You listen to me, this is no f…ing joke. If I were you I'd take the same plane back to Paris tonight. Do I make myself clear?"

As the man obviously knew my flight details, I realized now that it was possible that he had been waiting here all along to confront me. He had seen my name and nationality on the passenger list and had gotten it into his head that I posed a potential security risk. He was now trying to talk me back onto the plane using all his powers of theatrical persuasion, a few threats, and a genuine kick-ass attitude.

But I was here on a higher mission, one that didn't involve listening to this dude's negative travel advice. The Dakotas were waiting for me in Villavicencio. I had waited for years for this moment and this buffoon wasn't going to spoil the party. The only thing that stood between Villavicencio and me was this trumped-up sheriff. It was him against me. He had the power, but I had the guile.

By now his temper had gotten the better of him and I sensed that this was all going completely wrong for me. It was time for plan B. Instead of kick-ass, I'd better try kiss ass. Adopting a less confrontational and more humble tone, I stammered, "Excuse me sir, I really didn't realize it was still so dangerous here. It seems I underestimated the actual situation in Colombia. You are quite right to point out the dangers to me, of course."

This more conciliatory tone was exactly what he wanted to hear and it had the desired effect. This was his territory and here his word was the law.

But would he actually have been able to expel me from Colombia? Could he really have sent me back to Paris? I will never know. And frankly, I was in no position to initiate a showdown with this man.

In the end, plan B worked, and after making a long telephone call (to his boss?) he finally said, "Sir, I can let you in on one condition—that you stay in Bogota. You will have to call your clients and tell them to meet you here."

This presented me with another problem: I didn't actually have any clients yet. I still had to find them, down south in Villavicencio. However, I had no choice now but to be diplomatic and keep my cool. There was no more room for negotiation; his decision was final.

He shook my hand and left me standing there somewhat forlorn in that airport building, far from home and with my mission in tatters. All in all, a miserable start to my trip. Little did I know that this was merely a foretaste of many more surprises to come.

With the demise of FARC, true horror stories are starting to emerge. This owner of Aliansa was killed in a drugs smuggling related transport using his aircraft. He refused to cooperate and was killed trying to escape, leaving his family and Aliansa behind in utter distress.

TAXI RIDE TO A FORBIDDEN CITY

So there I stood with a ticket for a flight to Villavicencio in my hand, not knowing what to do next. If I wasn't going to be able to board the flight I might as well at least go to the check-in desk and see whether I could get a refund. I walked over to the desk and straight into the next twist in the tale. The flight to Villavicencio had just been cancelled due to technical problems with the thirty-seater turbo prop plane and the next flight would not be leaving until the following morning.

I joined the queue of disgruntled passengers at the check-in counter waiting to get their new tickets. I waited for thirty minutes, last in line and a full head taller than all the other passengers in front of me.

It was almost my turn when I spotted the captain of the stricken airplane coming through the gate sauntering along in the company of a younger-looking flight attendant, both in neatly pressed airline uniforms. He stopped, looked at me with a curious expression on his face, and came over and asked me in English what my plans were now that the flight had been cancelled. I told him about my encounter with the mystery man who had strongly advised, or rather warned, me not to go to Villavicencio.

The captain came closer to me and whispered in a conspiratorial voice, "You must not believe everything you hear about Colombia. Some foreigners are very paranoid about the situation here, but it's a lot safer than it was a year ago." He then proceeded to make me an interesting offer. "We are taking a taxi to Villavicencio because we have an early morning flight there tomorrow. If you like, you can join us and we can share the taxi fare. Deal?"

Always game for a bit of adventure and blatantly ignoring the advice of the security man, I whispered back, "It's a deal; I'll come with you to Villavicencio."

It was turning dark by the time we walked out to the taxi stand. I looked around anxiously for any sign of the security agent; he wouldn't be at all pleased with this turn of events. After all, I wasn't getting into a taxi headed for downtown Bogota but rather into one that would take me on a three-hour night ride down south across the mountains to Villavicencio in the company of a stranded flight crew. A scenario even I could not have envisaged only fifteen minutes earlier.

I sat in the front seat next to the driver and chatted with the captain in the back. He was very open about the situation in his country and quite optimistic about the future. He believed that the worst was behind them, given that the number of kidnappings and assaults by FARC and drug lords was decreasing steadily. He still saw a number of obstacles, but the chances of a peace settlement were better now than they had been at any point in last ten to fifteen years.

I asked him what he thought of my strange encounter earlier that day. He said, "There are so many secret contracts between our country and the United States that he could very well be an agent for an anti-drug or army-related security organization like the DEA, or maybe a private security officer hired by the airport."

The road we were on snaked its way into a very mountainous region with deep ravines falling off into the dark abyss. We passed small, muddy towns and primitive-looking villages. There were trucks parked everywhere alongside the narrow, winding road.

We were all feeling hungry, so we stopped at a service station for a quick bite to eat. When we walked into the crowded trucker's bar, the joint suddenly went silent and everybody stared at us. An airline captain and a drop-dead gorgeous flight attendant in a tight uniform with a blonde-haired *extranjero* in tow were obviously not a common sight around these parts.

High society had entered the building. The captain was in his element and he strode into the bar smiling broadly, well aware of the attention he and his two "trophies" were attracting.

The hum in the place soon started up again and the truckers forgot their initial shyness and came over to talk with us. They were eager to get me to join in a local game, a kind of *jeu de boules*, the object of the game being to hit an egg positioned on top of a beer crate with three steel balls from a distance of six meters. Not as easy as it looked, as I soon found out.

After they had watched, with great hilarity, my pitiful attempts at hitting the egg, I bought the winner a bottle of beer, which signaled party time for them and their newfound airline friends and their alien amigo. They ordered bottles of beer for our table and set about trying to impress the lady by challenging us to a beer-drinking contest.

DC-3 Mud Ride: this picture explains the remarkable survival of the DC-3 out here. When the rains come, all outpost landing strips are instantly transformed into muddy lanes. Only the DC-3, with its big balloon wheels and its tail-dragger configuration, can handle the soaked ground. The plane's relatively low landing speed enables it to touch down on short strips without the need for a clean and flat surface.

Their work was done for the day, but we had to press on. However, we were not allowed to leave before we had shaken hands with everyone in the bar.

We hopped back into the taxi and rode out of town. But we were barely ten minutes further down the road when we had to stop for a ghostly looking roadblock that suddenly appeared in front of us out of the pitch-black night.

Our hilarity regarding the events in the truck-stop bar evaporated instantly. Soldiers in full uniform and bulletproof jackets with high collars and low helmets gathered around the taxi, shining their flashlights inside. No one said a word.

Suddenly, their commander shouted, "Stay where you are, hands behind your head! You there in the front, hand over your passport, right now!"

A flashlight was pointed straight at my face. A soldier armed with an M-16 opened the door and ordered me to step out. The officer in charge took my passport and started flipping through it. He said to the pilot, "*Que pasa aqui?*" What's going on here?

The tension in the air was palpable. Again the officer barked a few short commands that this time I could not understand. All of a sudden, the soldiers seemed to go on high alert. It then dawned on me that they probably figured that I was the victim of a kidnapping orchestrated by some crazy in a captain's uniform and his mistress in matching airline attire: an unthinkable scenario in Europe but a very feasible one here in Colombia. Stranger things had happened in this country down through the years.

They took me over to a big US-built military truck and ordered the pilot to step out of the taxi. I reckoned to myself that all of the available M-16 automatic rifles were now being pointed at the car. Everything went eerily silent.

The flight attendant was now alone in the taxi, along with the driver. She seemed to sink slowly into a kind of trance and started sobbing quietly. I figured that it would all turn out okay as long as nobody freaked out. But there were a lot of nervous fingers glued to M-16 triggers around.

Five minutes later all the confusion had been resolved. The army captain shook hands with the airline captain and we were allowed to continue on our way. I breathed a deep sigh of relief and dried the sweat from my palms.

Before we left, however, our flight attendant needed to make a bathroom stop. Out of sheer terror she had wet herself, quite normal after such a terrifying experience. She had probably thought that her final hour had come when she had seen all those flashlights and guns trained on her. Later she told us that at the time she had been convinced that the soldiers were actually FARC rebels in disguise who had set up an ambush for us. Whatever the case, she had managed to keep herself more or less under control when the going got tough. Her composure and the soldiers' discipline had probably prevented the situation from escalating into a full-blown tragedy.

She got out of the cab and took her black luggage trolley to the army truck, where she changed her dress and powdered her puffed-up face. Fifteen minutes later she was back, splendid in jeans and makeup and looking very attractive indeed. We were just about to leave when the commander stepped forward and complimented her on her self-control and extended a hand in apology. All the soldiers involved in the incident also came over and shook hands with her, out of respect as well as guilt. The tears began to well up in her eyes again, blotching her newly applied makeup. She bowed her head and hid her face behind her hands. She started to sob and shake as her emotions got the better of her. All of the soldiers were deeply moved, not to mention embarrassed. They stood there, staring at their boots, not knowing what to do. Nobody said a word.

Sadly, this was typical of the frightening level of insecurity to which Colombian public life had descended. It was as if all of us at that scene felt the same kind of shame and sorrow toward the young lady. Fortunately, this most bizarre encounter had had a happy ending.

Back on the road, we complimented her on her courage. But, truth be told, the army captain had been quite right to be suspicious about what he saw inside the cab. As part of their normal duties, they had set up a roadblock to check all the trucks driving up north to Bogota. Just as the last trucks had passed through, and with no more cars on the road, they were about to close the road for the night. Suddenly, out of nowhere a suspicious taxi emerges from the dark going, surprisingly, in the opposite direction, to the south. Not a normal time, not a normal car; instead a cab with a gringo in the front seat and two fancily dressed characters in the rear. This must have alarmed the soldiers. In the middle of a terrorist-infested jungle and on

Wherever you fly in Colombia, the military are omnipresent at every corner of every airstrip. Disciplined and vigilant, they are the safety factor for all passengers and the control factor for all cargo.

high alert for anything out of the ordinary, their suspicions were more than understandable.

After the incident, we drove further into the dark jungle over the mountain road. The girl snuggled up against the pilot's shoulder and fell into a deep sleep, not surprising given what she had just been through. I felt sorry for her; she had probably had entirely different expectations when setting out. Maybe a romantic trip with the captain, no doubt her lover, to spend the night together in a nice little hotel in Villavicencio.

Unfortunately, her dream night had been shattered by the captain's sudden interest in a stranger waiting at the gate at Bogota airport. He had been intrigued by

Dakota flight with passengers into the jungle. Cargo being loaded first into the cabin; passengers come next and fill any leftover space. Some occupy the few canvas folding seats while others find a spot on their own trunk or stretch out on the floor for a nap. It is cold up there at 6,000 feet when the flight takes more than an hour due to the strong and chilly draft inside the cabin.

my presence there. Perhaps he thought I might be an interesting contact and so he had invited me to come along to Villavicencio. Neither they nor I had realized at that point that my appearance in this country would prove to be very conspicuous, up to the point of creating havoc and making some people feel extremely uncomfortable.

The girl probably wished that they had not run into me at the airport and quite possibly hated me for that at this stage. Now here she was trying to recover from a harrowing experience, one that probably would stay in her memory for a very long time.

VILLAVICENCIO, AT LAST.

Exhausted, but relieved that we had made it, we arrived in the city of Villavicencio around 9:30 p.m. We stopped at the hotel near the airport, which I had booked in Holland on the Internet.

The hotel manager walked out of the restaurant and greeted me warmly. "Welcome Signor Wiesman! You are our first visitor from overseas in six years. We have been closed for almost three years due to the war on drugs and FARC activities but we reopened half the hotel four months ago."

He then took me aside briefly and said, "A few house rules; you never stop a taxi yourself, we call one for you, *comprende*? And after 7:00 p.m. no walk out into the streets, please."

I said goodbye to my new friends, the captain and the flight attendant, and they vanished into the dark on their way to another hotel, clearly with other plans for the night. They deserved it after the nerve-racking experience they had just been through.

Perplexed and exhausted by everything that had happened in the last six hours, I did not need much of a nightcap to help me fall into a long, deep sleep in that strange and mysterious town of Villavicencio.

When I woke up the next morning, I had my first view of my new whereabouts. A magnificent mountain massif dominated the background and the wide, open plains of the Meta district stretched out before me.

What a view! And a pleasant temperature to go with it. There were flowers growing everywhere you looked. It reminded me of the south of France with the scent of mimosas and bougainvillea in the air and the lush green hills; a most amazing landscape with an abundance of nature's goodies. The tropical rainfall makes it very green out here in the pastures where livestock breeding is an important source of employment and income.

I dressed and got ready to go to the airport, just fifteen minutes down the road. The hotel taxi drove me out over a very long one-lane bridge that crossed the extremely wide river. As I had come in the dry season, there was hardly any river to speak of. But in the rainy season the river swells and turns into a torrential muddy maelstrom that frequently devastates villages, bridges, and roads and takes many victims.

Here in Villavicencio, all the water from the nearby mountains comes down into the plains to commence a free run of over a thousand miles all the way to the mighty Orinoco River that crosses the continent via Venezuela to the Atlantic Ocean. And when it rains here, it *really* rains. Unlike anything we are used to in Europe. The resulting deluge is akin to a broken dam on a river, with millions of gallons of water being released in a matter of seconds. Streets, canals, valleys—they all turn into huge gutters that drain away the rainwater from the mountains. But right now the river was no more than a mere trickle.

At the far end of the bridge I noticed a small memorial with a crucifix that was covered with flowers and photos. I asked the driver what it was. He told me it was a monument for a police brigade ambushed by FARC some years earlier as the conflict began to take on the sinister form of outright civil war. Eight police officers were killed in the ensuing shootout.

The bridge was the perfect place for an ambush. As the police trucks crossed the river the first car was attacked, killing the driver just before he arrived on the other side. That stopped the convoy, which then became a sitting duck for the terrorists as the trucks and police officers could move neither forward nor backward and were left completely exposed.

Before arriving at the airport we encountered a military roadblock, this time with sniffer dogs and mirrors on wheels for looking under cars. Though he was long dead, Escobar's bombing of civilian aircraft had obviously not been forgotten. Every car was thoroughly checked before being allowed to enter the airport. Eventually, we arrived at the main building and I got out of the cab.

This was the moment I had been waiting for. After all the trials and tribulations of the previous twenty-four hours, I had finally made it to Villavicencio airport! Here I was, all alone on the other side of the world in what many would see only as hostile and perilous territory and certainly no place for a Westerner like me. I felt absolutely elated, as if the gates to DC-3 heaven were about to open up before me. From where

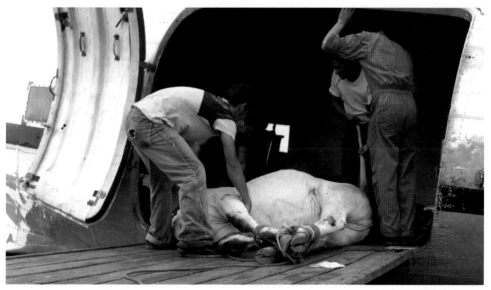

Even a young bull is allowed on board, albeit heavily sedated with tranquilizers. How to get the immobilized bull inside? "Push & Pull the Bull" is the name of the game, with the bull's tail being your most important tool. And you certainly do not want the beast to wake up mid-flight in a cramped cabin so cuffing his legs is a necessary precaution—just in case.

I stood I could hear and see Dakotas being loaded, their engines running. I counted at least half a dozen of them. This was my Holy Grail and I felt the hairs rise on the back of my neck.

It was like a reunion, one that brought my fond memories of Borneo back to the surface; a tropical theater with a leading role for the Dakota—my hero and my lifeline to the outside world against the backdrop of what I associated most with that plane: the jungle. I had waited for years for this opportunity and it had finally arrived despite the best efforts of a paranoid drug agent to snatch it away from me. When I had finally managed to escape his clutches, a bunch of truckers had tried to get us drunk and then a military roadblock had almost put an end to our fancy-dress gallop across the mountains.

With all those hurdles now behind me, here I was at the Mecca of Dakota— Villavicencio, the last remaining DC-3 airport in the world, with five different operators flying to remote camps deep inside the jungle where primitive conditions prevailed. This was the antithesis of the airline world elsewhere. No slick hissing turbo engines here, but instead only the "putt-putt" sound of a radial piston engine as it comes to life, barking a trail of white smoke from its exhaust pipes. Here the Dakota was the leading player in the daily transport of goods to the eastern and southern regions of Orinoco and Amazonas. And, just like in her glory days, the vintage aircraft was treated with respect, not as a greasy, second-hand cast-off rudely dismissed by overpaid jetliner pilots as a flying trashcan.

The airport perimeter was well fenced and guarded by dogs and armed military guards. This was certainly no Opa-locka airfield situation; it was not at all like what I had encountered in Miami. Down here, if I wanted to meet the operators and see their planes, I needed a visitor's permit to get inside. That wasn't easy to accomplish on my own, since my Spanish was not up to the task of dealing with complex safety regulations.

I walked along the airport road, the Avenida del Aeropuerto, so as to acquaint myself with the airfield and I soon spotted a little bar that served food. It obviously wasn't a joint for passengers but a hangout for the mechanics, cab drivers, and baggage personnel who worked here. It looked all right from the outside, but once inside I saw a shabby interior with plastic furniture and tablecloths. However, at the far end there was a clear view of all the activity out on the airfield, with the only thing separating me from the apron being a low brick wall at the rear of the restaurant.

I decided to try and get a closer look, but my attention was immediately diverted to a tall man sitting at a table in the corner. My blonde hair and western complexion had obviously attracted his attention. Though we had never met before, he was gazing intently at me. He then stood up and spoke to me in a quiet voice, as if he felt I needed some help. He introduced himself in English and invited me to sit and have a coffee. I told him about my plans and that I needed to arrange a permit pretty quickly in order to get access to the Dakota operators for a couple of days.

It was still fairly early in the morning and the man, Juan, figured he could help me, as he knew most of the people around here. As we talked, he told me a few hair-

Derelict PBY-5A Catalina and Douglas DC-6 standing here somewhat forlorn looking. I flew in both aircraft in the 1950's and they have a very special place in my memory.

raising stories and also offered me a few survival tips. He stressed the importance of keeping a low profile and said I should run at even the slightest hint of trouble.

"The FARC may be thin on the ground here now but they are still around. You're the only outsider in town and an attractive target for kidnappers."

He advised me to stay no longer than two days and then to fly back to Bogota, and never to take that jungle road again. According to his information, the road we had been on the night before was nothing more than a narrow corridor protected by the military, and all of the surrounding jungle was rebel-controlled territory.

If someone at Bogota airport had become aware of my final destination, Juan told me, he could have made a phone call to a friend and FARC could have staged an ambush on the road, despite the military presence. His words underlined exactly what the flight attendant had been thinking when we were stopped: an ambush and kidnapping. "Not the sort of information that will make you very happy, I'll admit," he said. "So, shall we get to work on that permit?"

Juan taught me a useful lesson or two. "Take your time; it pays to be patient here. And never raise your voice." Being deaf in one ear and half deaf in the other, that was not going to be easy for me.

"Just walk around and try to make friends but do not talk openly about your mission to purchase parts. Forget about trying to do any kind of deal straight away; the war has made these people very suspicious and they will only deal with people they trust. So, if you are serious about doing business here, you will have to come back again at a later date."

His words of caution would govern my every action for the next two days. We stood up and walked to the airport building down the road at a pace slower than I had ever walked before in my life. To him I must have seemed like some kind of hyperactive lunatic with a worrisome obsession for making haste.

Juan was a shy and guarded character and, according to what he told me, had lived through the war years here constantly looking over his shoulder for any hint of danger. His advice was plain and simple: "If they plan to abduct you, it is usually with a car or a taxi. They'll just happen to be getting into the same taxi as you. Your first thought will be that they have made a mistake by hopping into the same car as you. Not so. It is a well-planned and well-timed trick, and they prepare everything a few days in advance. After innocently stepping into the 'wrong' taxi, you will quickly find yourself looking down the barrel of a gun sticking out from under a magazine or a newspaper carried by the man who got in on the other side. Stepping out again is not an option any more. No use in trying to make excuses like, 'Sorry sir, the taxi is all yours, I'll take the next one.' Instead, you will be pinned to your seat, the victim of a kidnapping before you can even blink.

"Without any fuss, they will then drive off and nobody will have noticed that you have just been abducted. They'll stop far out of town and take you deep into the jungle. To them, your passport is a kind of business card, and within a few days they'll make a phone call to your embassy in Bogota. There is no standard ransom for foreigners; it will be higher if you are with the military, DEA, or the diplomatic corps. Your embassy will take all the time in the world to negotiate, but in the end they will probably pay the ransom and your kidnappers will eventually set you free. That can take anywhere from six months to six years, but regardless of how long that is you will always return a mere shadow of your former self."

His advice couldn't have been any clearer.

Now, would that make you want to extend your holiday here for two more weeks?

We walked over to the terminal building and met the airport manager, who turned out to be a friend of my guide. My access permit was quickly arranged. Time to get down to some real work; soon I would be seeing the Dakotas "in the flesh."

Before we could leave, however, the manager came up to me and offered me some advice in broken English: "Signor Wiesman, please remember, there are here more than a thousand eyes on you. If only two eyes have bad intentions and they see you as a walking check, you are in grave danger. Your permit is for two days only. Tomorrow in the afternoon you must fly back to Bogota, *claro*?"

All very *claro* indeed. I would have to try to do everything in just two days.

Juan came with me to see the Dakota operators on my initial charm offensive and we started at the southern end of the airport, near the river I had crossed by taxi earlier that morning. From there I could see the city center of Villavicencio against the backdrop of the mountains on the other side of the river. This was as close as I would get to that city during this trip, however, as time was now at a premium.

View of an upgraded DC-3 cockpit interior with "modern" instrument layout and avionics. Very neat finish for a 70-year old Sky Truck that has flown longer in time than any other plane still currently commercially operational.

THE DC-3 OPERATORS OF VILLAVICENCIO

Our first prospect was Aliansa, a company that had four Dakotas; one parked outside and three under corrugated roofing. The aircraft and workshop all looked very neat and tidy, but there was very little activity. In the office we met a charming woman in her mid-forties who turned out to be the sister of the former owner of the company, a certain Captain Jorge Luis Alvarez Rodriguez.

He had been shot dead a few years earlier in a violent incident out on a jungle strip after, allegedly, a dispute had arisen over the trafficking of drugs. He was lured in on the pretext of picking up some fruit, but when he saw what the goods actually were, he refused to take them and he was killed while trying to get away with his airplane.

At that time, it was FARC and not the regular Colombian army who ruled this part of the country, and many Dakotas were indeed used for the transport of narcotics. The rebels could enforce their own laws as they themselves saw fit.

It was this situation that the DEA man at Bogota airport had been referring to when he told me that most Dakotas flying out here were involved in the transport of narcotics. But, as it turned out, not all pilots meekly accepted FARC law. The Aliansa owner and captain was one of the few who were either courageous enough to challenge them or simply unfortunate enough to be in the wrong place at the wrong time, and he had paid for it with his life. Large framed portraits of the captain posing proudly in front of one of his shiny Dakotas with his two young sons hung on the walls of the office.

The horror of war suddenly seemed very present and we felt it very strongly as we stood there. It all had the effect of an ice-cold wind on our faces, while the lady continued to produce more photos showing her once happy family and company. We looked at the photos and listened to her stories.

Miraflores Main Street has a second important function: as a landing strip. When the rain falls the street turns into a slushy mud track. No problem for the Dakota and, luckily, no problem either for the residents on main street. They simply close their window shutters to keep the splashing mud out.

Then, in mid-sentence, she stopped. The burden of the past distorted her face, embittered by the injustice of the fact that the killers of her brother were still free to roam wherever they pleased. She slowly cracked under the burden of all those memories. It all became very sad, and even more so when she told us that the company was now struggling to survive. Since her brother's death there had not been much of the old glory and joviality around the place. We were very moved and when we were leaving we promised her we would be back in the morning. Shocked by her story, we decided to take a break for a coffee before going on to see the other Dakota operators.

The airport was a hive of activity now with an older Boeing 737 coming in from Bogota, an array of Pipers and Cessnas that operated as air taxis, and an Antonov AN-26 and three Dakotas being prepared for takeoff. Not to mention the many military helicopters flying their training missions and patrols around the area.

A number of crop-dusting planes, all brand new, also caught my attention. These small, single-prop, single-seat, low-wing aircraft with their characteristic bubble canopy are used all over the United States and Canada for agricultural and forest pest control.

Heavily armed soldiers with sniffer dogs patrolled the entire area, while jeeps with machine guns guarded the perimeters of the airfield. Though the worst of the war may have been behind them by now, it was far from over. Filming was strictly forbidden, but I was able to sneak a few snapshots by shooting discretely from the hip with my pocket camera.

We walked up to one of the Dakotas that was being loaded. An old Chevy pickup truck was parked next to the cargo door. Inside the plane, a soldier with a dog was inspecting everything being loaded onto the plane. Two other soldiers were examining the cargo as it came off the truck. I asked their permission to take a photo and they hesitantly agreed, on one stringent condition: no faces in the photo, just in case the snapshot might somehow end up in the wrong hands.

This kind of fear was widespread. The terror caused by the rebel's actions in the past had not been forgotten. To me, this seemed like a form of national paranoia, but Juan was quick to set me straight. FARC has been terrorizing this area for a long time

AeroVanguardia has also redesigned their livery as a sign of confidence in the future of aerial transport from VVC. Maintenance of the radial piston engines is very demanding and requires the full attention of mechanics. The safety record of this vintage fleet is exceptionally high.

now. Over the years, they often withdrew completely in the face of the advancing army, only to appear back on the scene a month later killing police officers or the local mayor and a large number of civilians, and that continued off and on for six years.

The next plane we encountered was the Antonov AN-26 cargo plane. Many operators had turned to this airplane as a possible replacement for the Dakota. However, the Antonov's engines are very vulnerable to the dust and debris that gets kicked up from muddy, uneven runways when landing and taking off, sometimes with disastrous consequences for the engine's innards. And Russian-made spares are very hard to find around here.

So the Dakota remains unchallenged as the dominant form of transport in these areas. It reigns supreme in the Colombian Amazon region because it can fly out and land in jungle settlements, gold camps, and fisherman's villages without any trouble. It is the region's umbilical cord when it comes to the transport of food, beer, fuel, livestock, satellite discs, construction materials, jeeps, scooters, and household equipment. And when the Dakotas fly back to Villavicencio, they take precious loads of fish, fruit, gold, and timber with them.

Passengers are also taken along, filling the vacant spaces in the cargo hold. There are no seats, however; only the occasional foldable canvas jump seat if you're lucky. The passengers sit wherever they can with their backs to the windows. Comfort is not an issue here. The primary concern of these 70-year-old workhorses is in getting their cargo safely and quickly to remote locations; passenger comfort comes a distant second.

For many of these isolated areas, the Dakota is their one and only lifeline to the outside world. Any other means of transport to their remote jungle villages is out of the question. Making the same journey by boat would take at least three or four days.

We walked further down the perimeter road in the scorching sun and came across a decrepit-looking amphibian aircraft of World War II fame, a Consolidated PBY-5A Catalina. She was standing forlorn in the corner of the airfield with a greenish-grey moss growing all over the upper fuselage. This airplane bore all the hallmarks of complete decay. The canvas-clad control surfaces on the wings and on the rudder were badly torn and flapping about wildly in the wind. The tires were flat and the engines were in an advanced state of disrepair.

Yet, despite all that deterioration and corrosion, to me the plane looked simply awesome. The memories of magic flights that I had made with this plane resurfaced from deep down inside me. In my mind's eye, I saw the crocodile-infested Mahakam River in Borneo from which I used to take off with my dad in exactly the same kind of aircraft.

Landings on the river in our jungle settlement at Sanga Sanga were preceded by a siren that warned any small boats still out on the river. I can still recall the sound of that siren; it made me run to the river to watch in wonder as the aircraft first flew over low and slow to inspect and clear the landing area. With all boats safely out of the way, she then came back on a low approach to touch down on the water. The splash created by the bow made the water shoot up in twin fountains that reached up to the parasol wing-mounted piston prop engines, the same as those found on most DC-3s/C-47s. Both types, the Catalina and the Dakota, were designed in the early to mid-1930s and mass-produced from 1941 to 1945. But by war's end they were outdated and both their production stopped overnight.

Now, however, the sight of this Catalina, which I had dubbed "The Queen of the Amazon," was a sorry one indeed. There had been several efforts to save the plane from further deterioration, including an attempt by a team from New Zealand, none of which were successful. I sincerely hope someone will one day find a suitable final resting place for this WWII vintage beauty.

After taking some photos, we moved on until we came to another big hangar with two Dakotas parked outside and two inside in various stages of overhaul. The planes' fuselages and wings were pristinely mirror-polished, their sheen broken only by a blue cheat line along the windows and the company logo—Air Colombia.

It all looked very professional, even by our western standards, with a tidy ramp, clean planes, and a well-maintained workshop. We went upstairs to meet the boss, a friendly man in his early forties with a Latino tint, dark eyes, and stocky build. His name was John Montoya, an engineer who had been running this small airline operation for a couple of years. He spoke a little English, I had a few words of

Seized drug runner found. I came across many derelict drug runners that had been confiscated by the authorities and put up for sale. Here I have just inspected the cockpit interior looking for old instruments, an interesting sideline for my business.

Spanish, and so we managed to strike up a conversation in "Spanglish" about his business. I made up a story about writing an article on the Dakota for a magazine and asked him what flights he had planned for the next day.

He showed me the flight plan chart and I spotted the name Miraflores, a jungle camp out in the Amazon, a couple hours' flight to the south from Villavicencio. It would depart early in the morning, deliver its cargo, load up with fish, and turn straight around to be back by 4:00 p.m. This was my chance to catch a flight into the jungle, in and out in one day and back in time to catch the last flight to Bogota at 7:00 p.m. "John, any chance of a seat on the flight to Miraflores? It would be great for my article."

"Well, I don't know, Westerners are generally advised not to go that far into the jungle."

"But you take passengers on your flights, don't you?"

"Yes, but they are all locals. As a foreigner you would attract too much attention out there."

The truth of the matter, we quickly found out, was that there was no military presence in Miraflores. There was still a power vacuum out there, which made it too dangerous for a conspicuously non-Colombian *extranjero* like me.

"Rumors will spread quickly, even if you stay onboard. They will come from all around to catch a glimpse of you. After all, it's been a long time since any foreigners were seen in those parts. Not a good idea with no army on the ground."

He wanted to be helpful, but there was no way he was taking me on the flight. I had to forget about Miraflores for the time being, and maybe that was just as well. It was still very much the Wild West out there.

I had heard some crazy stories about this jungle settlement and I would have given my right arm to go there. First of all, the landing strip splits the settlement in two. It is actually the main street of the village, which is temporarily closed off whenever a DC-3 is landing or taking off. In the rainy season the street is nothing more than a strip of mud, which the Dakota has to try to plough through to get its wheels off the ground.

On the weekends, hookers are flown in from Villavicencio to ply their trade, and it must be a strange sight to watch them disembark and try to negotiate the mud strip in their stiletto pumps. It may sound to the outsider like a scene from an Indiana Jones film, but here, deep in the Colombian Amazon, it's simply part of the reality of this remote place.

And the means of transport without which the whole economy around here would grind to a halt—a pristine Dakota—was standing here right in front of me at John Montoya's hangar at La Vanguardia Airport, Villavicencio.

John showed me around the workshop where his fitters were carrying out a complete main wing reskinning job on one of the Dakotas. As we were walking through the depot, I suddenly spotted six wingtips stacked in open crates in the back. I was stopped dead in my tracks; this was the very treasure I had come looking for. But I was under strict instructions from Juan not to display any overt interest in them.

I was literally bursting to ask the question "Are they surplus?" but I had promised I would be patient and say nothing about the true nature of my visit. I felt like a kid in a candy shop with his hands tied behind his back.

By the end of that first day in Villavicencio airport, I had seen plenty of evidence of what I had come looking for—a wealth of spare parts.

AGENT ORANGE SPOTTED IN COLOMBIA

Later on that evening, over dinner, Juan recounted a number of remarkable tales. It seemed that the war on drugs had turned in favor of the government troops. The Colombian president, Uribe, had shown no mercy whatsoever toward FARC, and the Americans were willing to provide military hardware, advisers, spy satellite coverage, training for pilots, Special Forces and intelligence agents, and most probably the support of spy drones.

Their efforts were now starting to bear fruit, but the war still had some dubious aspects to it in the form of those blue plastic drums I had seen lined up by the hundreds at Bogota airport. Juan suspected they contained Roundup Ultra, a new version of the infamous Agent Orange, the defoliant used extensively in Vietnam from the mid-1960s on to literally lay bare the Viet Cong supply lines that carried weapons and soldiers into South Vietnam.

In Colombia, they used it to eradicate the coca crops in the fields identified by satellite imaging. But the widespread use of the chemical was subject to much public criticism. It could have some pretty nasty and long-lasting side effects, as had been the case in Vietnam where they used the venomous stuff for almost ten years. Some considered it a form of illegal chemical warfare and it was widely feared that the poisonous fluid could have an extremely destructive effect on the environment and on the poor peasants involved in the cropping.

Once the coca fields have been located by satellite color imaging, the crop dusters that I had seen at the airport were sent in to destroy the coca crop. One can imagine the average drug lord's dismay at the sight of these little planes coming in and spraying his beloved coca plants. The devastating effect of their chemical payload is worse than a locust plague of biblical proportions.

Roundup Ultra can obliterate an entire crop in thirty minutes and, consequently, the drug baron's income. The plantation owners were obviously not very amused and decided to take some counter action in anticipation of the next flyover by that mechanical locust. They went as far as to install big AA machine guns, as deterrents and to shoot these coca killers out of the sky.

The crop duster strategy initially proved successful but later on a number of aircraft went missing, probably shot down. The sprayer pilots then decided they would only continue with their flights if they got better protection by armored cockpits and cover from more powerful airborne friends.

Enter the cavalry in the shape of armed helicopters that followed on crop dusters' tails during their coca killer missions. Whenever the small sprayer airplane came under

Coca Crop sprayers in Colombia: used for many years, but aerial crop eradication as part of the war on drugs remains controversial. The slow and low flying aircraft often came under FARC fire so are now provided with bullet-proof cockpits and windows. (Note the smaller windows). For more info see www.whitehouse.gov/ondcp/targeting-cocaine-at-the-source and the report "The effects of Coca Eradication in Colombia" on www.stanford.edu

fire, the attack helicopters equipped with their impressive side pods would take over. They were able to shoot the hell out of the drug lords' nests with their hefty rockets, which could dish out a real "Kill-em-all, let God sort it out" kind of treatment.

One can only assume that when these rockets were fired they created major havoc on the ground and that both the gun and the gunners below would be annihilated, leaving others much less inclined to initiate any counter action or to otherwise attract the attention of the killer choppers.

Mr. Drug Lord would be completely dumbstruck by the utter destruction of his land, his guns, and his crop. In the best-case scenario he would then simply stop all coke production, given his impotency in the face of such a persuasive show of strength. The next time he considered planting a crop it would more likely (or hopefully) be fields of corn or strawberries. There was only one little snag for him, however, with this "best-case" scenario: the profitability of strawberries is not exactly in the same league as that of coca plants.

Whereas the normal drug lord would think twice before squaring up to the destructive power of this armada, with FARC it was a whole different ballgame. They have powerful friends overseas and their agenda and level of determination are on a more professional level.

Strawberries and corn are of no interest to them as a business model and their efforts to take over the country gave them a totally warped sort of motivation to fight back against the crop duster plague. In the end, the smaller coke plantation owners and dealers stepped back from this confrontation and FARC became by far the most dominant, if not the only, player in the (coca) field. The law of survival of the fittest gave rise to a new kind of enemy for the United States.

In this increasingly lethal game of cat and mouse, the military soon needed more helicopters and extra pilots, and, evidently, a plentiful supply of the blue drums I had seen two days earlier in Bogota. Without these goodies to keep the FARC activities at bay, they would have sufficient time to acquire the capital needed to purchase RPG (Rocket Propelled Grenade) systems. These shoulder-fired anti-tank weapons launch rockets with explosive warheads. The relatively easy-to-use (Russian-designed) RPG-7 does not possess heat-seeking or infrared-homing capabilities but handled by a well-trained operator, it can be an effective weapon, even against low and slow flying aircraft at very short range. The Russians, to their dismay, had experienced the devastating power of this cheap weapon in their wars against Afghanistan (1979-1989) and Chechnya (1994-1996). Allegedly, the Americans had stealthily delivered those weapons to the Afghan Mujahedin Guerillas as from summer 1979. They ambushed and knocked out many a road transport and the giant MIL helicopters turned out to be very vulnerable at low altitude during takeoffs and landings for this RPG.

Putin c.s. are reputed for having good memories, in particular when it comes to defeats, so any opportunity offered for retaliation of their shameful Afghan retreat, would be eagerly considered under their motto: "The Empire strikes back".

Despite the limitations of range and accuracy of the RPG-7, one has no difficulty imagining the kind of hell that would break loose on this new battlefield in the coca plantations of southern Colombia if the RPG made its entrance in anything like significant numbers. Evidently, the manufacturer of this weapon seemed utterly motivated to deliver. Only little hurdle to solve, was how to get the RPG's from the Black Sea to the Green Hell?

Strong sentiments of revenge are sometimes bringing creative solutions and in this case, the Russians played their Joker. The follow up can be read in the Chapter Colombia II.

BACK TO BOGOTA

Early the next day, my last in Villavicencio, I headed back to the airport to meet Juan for coffee. We discussed our options for the day at the airport.

At the north end of the airfield, we found three more operators with Dakotas—one beautiful De Havilland Canada DHC-3 Otter and a huge, fabulous-looking DC-6. Though this four-engine prop liner looked to be in good condition, it was out of service. Its size made it incapable of landing on the remote muddy airstrips in the jungle, while on the tarmac runways it had lost out in the face of competition from jetliners and turbo prop liners. DC-4s and DC-6s were unable to generate the same revenues as the jetliners when operating on an even playing field with modern airfields and extended asphalt runways.

The DC-3s/Dakotas are in a different league here; they will probably continue in operation for at least another decade or so. The number of DC-3s on the airfield, in every shape and size and from operational to derelict, was overwhelming. I had never seen so many of the same type together at one airport at any time in the previous thirty years.

The sheer number of Dakotas all around and their long history in this region meant that there were also many junkyards and hangars piled high with airframe parts and wings. Sixty years of Dakota flights had left their mark—and their parts—out here.

However, I could not do any direct business for the moment and was forced to keep my eagerness on ice. But it was clear that I would have to come back here sooner or later, back to this Dakota Hunter paradise. I would be going home empty-handed again. However, the things I had seen and the contacts I had made in only two days in Villavicencio would prove invaluable to me in the near future.

Sometimes you have days that seem to drag on forever. Boring and endless. And sometimes you feel like there are simply not enough hours in the day. Here in Colombia, from the minute I stepped off the plane at Bogota airport up to the end of my second day in Villavicencio, I felt like I had crammed two weeks' worth of wild adventure into less than forty-eight hours. It made an overwhelming impression on me to see this region struggling to its feet in the aftermath of a six-year jungle war.

Vintage planes fly in and out of here as if in some kind of time warp, military roadblocks

*Blackhawk AH-90 Helicopter Arpia III
Originally built as a utility helicopter for trooper
transport, the AH-90 is a modified Gunship
version, fitted with impressive outriggers and
rocket pods on either side.*

appear around every corner, wild stories abound about kidnappings, helicopters, sprayer planes, and Dakotas. What a goofy world this was, but not everybody's cup of tea, admittedly. For me though, this had been one of the most memorable (and bizarre) trips I had ever made.

That same evening I flew back to Bogota, returning to a relatively normal world. Bogota actually seemed kind of dull to me now in comparison. It felt like a pleasant tourist destination, only there wasn't a single foreign tourist to be found anywhere.

I stayed for three more days, time that I had initially planned to spend in Villavicencio. I went sightseeing in the Old Spanish quarter of Bogota, once the home of Simon Bolivar. He had cherished the dream of liberating Panama, Colombia, Venezuela, Ecuador, Peru, and Bolivia from their Spanish colonial masters and bringing them together in a United States of South America, with Bogota as the capital.

The dream did not last long, however, as the idea of a greater republic had been abandoned by the end of his eventful life in 1830. It had fallen apart when the common goal that had once united them had been accomplished: to be freed from colonial Spanish rule.

I visited the huge white church of the Morena Virgin on top of the famous Monserrate Mountain, which overlooks Bogota so magnificently. It felt like the perfect setting in which to take some time out in order to reflect upon the events of the past few days.

I had to admit, in hindsight, that the DEA man at Bogota airport might have been right after all. But his manner had been too aggressive, his identity too vague. His attempts at stopping me from going south just served to make Villavicencio even more mysterious and attractive to me, a kind of forbidden city hidden behind a fence, pulling me like a magnet. My tendency to embrace the unknown simply took over, partly, of course, because of my unbridled desire to meet my beloved Dakota again.

*In spite of the crop duster's "armoring" preps, in
October 2013 two crop dusters piloted by
Americans were shot down. Sadly, one of them was
killed in action and all crop eradication flights in
Colombia were immediately suspended. It is now a
matter of search, landing and destruction of coca
plantations " by hand" with armed forces.*

The warnings given by the people I met in Villavicencio made more sense to me. No wonder, either, now that I had seen for myself the very serious military presence that left me in no doubt as to the nature of the hostilities in that region. I followed their advice and I returned unharmed.

Was I lucky? Yes, but I must admit that my internal alarm system for danger and my risk-avoiding attitude sometimes failed to function as normal. I had had previous experiences of this failure in Borneo, where I frequently fell out of trees or found myself being attacked by ferocious animals. Later on in life, the inner urge for thrill seeking and pushing the boundaries kept on resurfacing, at times resulting in broken legs, nose, rib, shoulder and other temporary discomforts.

Never a dull day—that's a motto that fits me just fine. I could have stayed at home or in a hotel in Bogota, but I didn't. I decided to pursue my journey on to the Llanos of southern Colombia. It proved to be the trip of a lifetime. I got to see the Dakota in all its glory against the backdrop of the jungle and, of course, in the theater of the war on drugs. And I also found myself a treasure trove of surplus wings and spare parts.

I left with the words of the Hollywood Terminator fixed firmly in my mind: "I'll be back."

Russians learned to their dismay the devastating power of destruction that the simple RPG could inflict. This photo is not a Hollywood movie scene but the hard reality of life in Dagestan near the Chechen border in summer 1999. A huge MI-26 Helicopter crashed just before landing, most probably hit by an RPG, launched from the nearby mountains. The same weapon entered high on the FARC wish list for flushing out the Colombian Army Helicopters and we can presume that the Russians were more than eager to deliver the weapons to keep the armada of man hunters at bay.
(Photo courtesy The Examiner, Sept 28, 1999)

CHAPTER 7

Madagascar
Dancing with Colonels

One day in 2007, completely out of the blue, I received an email from a man living in Madagascar, the huge island southeast of the African continent, some 500 kilometers east of Mozambique in the Indian Ocean. The man, named Daniry, sent me a most interesting story. His father, now retired, had been the chief mechanic of the Malagasy Air Force (MAF) in the years right after the island had achieved independence. Freed from French rule in 1960, the new emerging nation was presented with a number of military aircraft by France, including some Dakotas from the French Air Force. A birthday present, and a very practical gift for both the fledgling country's civilian and military transport requirements.

At the Ivato Air Force Base just outside the capital of the Malagasy Republic, Antananarivo, Daniry's father had spent a lifetime keeping the Dakotas operational, from 1955 until the early 1990s. Now, fifteen years on, those Dakotas were all parked out in a field, no more than a heap of trash for the authorities but fond tokens of

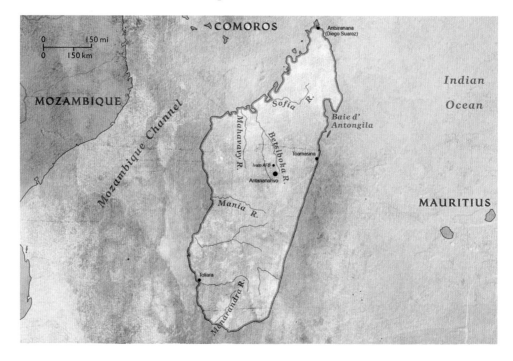

remembrance for him.

He asked me to come to Madagascar as quickly as I could, as he had been informed that the local boneyard at Ivato was to be cleared to make room for an extension of the runway at the international airport. He had found our website when surfing the Internet and figured it wise to inform me of the prospect of salvaging parts from that airplane cemetery. It was clear that he was trying to save whatever he could of the Dakotas before the scrappers came and chopped up all the vintage aircraft out there. Given their glorious past first with the French Air Force in Indochina and later another thirty years in operational service for the MAF, these vintage planes deserved a better fate than "death by cutting torch." It was an emotional and desperate cry for help and I was his one and only hope of salvaging the five Dakotas standing in an open field in the heart of this tropical island in the Indian Ocean.

Madagascar is almost 1,600 kilometers long and 600 kilometers wide and has a rather primitive road system for such a big island. Covered by mountain ranges over much of its length, one can imagine the importance of having a good air transport system for the armed forces. With the capital located in the very center of the island, the airline connections also play an important role in governmental administration and personnel transport.

When the country gained its independence, it was in dire need of aircraft and maintenance facilities, so the MAF acquired ten Dakotas from the French for their transport requirements.

Tracking down the manufacturing numbers of those MAF Dakotas was, from the outset, an extremely interesting task and I knew I would need professional help to research the records and find out what we could do with these planes. That help came

DC-3 operated by Air Madagascar. This aircraft, along with others, was a gift from the French Government to mark the island's independence in 1960. Its wheel well caps are not standard on the C-47/DC-3.

from a man I had met a few years previously—Bart Nopper, an ex-paratrooper and now a professional filmmaker and photographer. For years he had supplied crucial inside information that had led us to wingtips all over the world. Through the Internet and various books he was able to establish the background of the C-47 registration numbers found in Madagascar.

Every DC-3 and C-47 produced in US factories between 1936 and 1945 had a certification plate riveted inside bearing its manufacturing number, specifications, and year of construction. Most of this information was stored in very detailed records and books that are still available for public viewing. In some cases, logbooks were kept that describe the careers of different types over the many years of their life cycle after the war. Many of the planes were sold to foreign air forces, civilian airlines, and aircraft dealers, or to oil companies, governments, or private owners.

In many of the Dakotas I came across, the original manufacturing plates were still riveted to the rear wall of the cockpit, just aft of the copilot seat. This was particularly interesting for war and aviation museums, as a Dakota or a cockpit with a documented war history adds considerable value to their display. An aircraft with a fully documented and glorious past transforms the exhibit from that of an anonymous aircraft to one with a unique war hero.

From our preliminary research we found out that one of the DC-3s in that field in Madagascar was an ex-KLM Dakota, while another one was ex-French Air Force and had served in Indochina. We decided it would be worth taking a trip out there to try and save these MAF Dakotas from obliteration. Even if we were only able to salvage some of the parts, we would at least be keeping the souls of these war-weary aircraft alive in some fashion or other.

The affordable option was to separate the most valuable components from the fuselages and leave the rest for the local scrapper. Wingtips, propellers, cockpit sections, and interiors, instruments, engines, horizontal stabilizers, fins—those are the parts that were valuable to our trade and small enough to fit in a sea container. Larger parts, like the fuselage or central wing section, could only be shipped in one piece as a wide deck load and needed special deep loaders for road transport. With the nearest port over 250 kilometers from the airport, the cost of transporting such large pieces was simply prohibitive.

The exotic location of the airport's boneyard worked against us; if this collection had been found in Europe or in the United States, the budget for dismantling and transporting the complete airframes to museums would have been manageable. Sadly, our preferred option was simply not affordable and could realistically harbor the risk of surpassing the economic value for museums.

Bart and I quickly decided to fly to the island to see what could be done. My local contact, Daniry, and his father were on friendly terms with an Air Force colonel who was the commander of the Ivato Air Force Base. They felt confident they could introduce us to the colonel and the ministry of defense in order to commence direct

Aerial overview of part of the aircraft scrap yard at Ivato Air Force base in the center of the Island, close to the capital Antananarivo.

negotiations regarding the purchase of the abandoned aircraft. And so began a very special trip to Africa—one in which we would learn to dance with and around the military and that would provide us with a glimpse of how military commanders operate in a country with a relatively unstable political structure.

For the serious job of cutting up a cockpit hanging fifteen feet above the ground you need some serious power tools and a hoist or large forklift to support the cockpit as soon as it comes loose from the fuselage. You also need an electric generator and a sea container to stow everything in.

Our chances of success seemed good, as I had already found a few prospective buyers for the cockpits, including three museums. That certainly made it even more worth our while to pursue the project, as the museums would be prepared to cover some of the expensive transportation costs to Holland.

Our intention was to reach an agreement with the military as quickly as possible upon arrival so that we would have enough time to salvage the aircraft components, load the parts into a container, and arrange their export to Rotterdam. I had pulled this off successfully before in Bolivia, but I had the help of a crew of very experienced mechanics, a makeshift crane, and an English agent who had taken care of all the transport and export documents and organized the container.

A week before Bart and I left for Madagascar, I contacted a filmmaker, Axel, in New York whose name I had picked up from a television documentary series on the Discovery Channel. His company produces films and series for international TV networks. He was a producer and director at their New York branch and he said that he would love to accompany us and catch our mission on film.

It quickly became apparent that he was the right man for the job, which required filming in hot and unfamiliar conditions with one single camera. All in one: sound and camera work, no script to speak of, no retakes, filming everything as it happens, and in some cases being required to film "undercover." Axel had done all of this many times before and felt very confident about our mission to that African island, a place none of us had ever visited before.

Well packed and fully prepared, the three of us took a flight to Paris, and then caught a connection to Antananarivo. After arriving late that evening, we took a taxi to a small hotel near the airport owned by a German-French couple.

The next day we met up with Daniry at the entrance to the Ivato Air Force Base, just a mile down the road from the international airport. His father was with him and the five of us walked up to the gate where the guard announced our arrival by telephone to the base commander.

We had to wait for the commander to pick us up at the gate before we could enter the base. We sat under a huge tree in front of the gate on a stone bench in the shade and I talked for the first time with Daniry's father, in French. He had come dressed to the nines in a suit jacket and tie for the prearranged meeting with "Le

First encounter with the Dakotas at the Ivato base. Accompanied by the Chief in Command of the base, we were finally allowed to enter this swampy area to view their collection of derelict aircraft.

This scrap yard is quite unique in the world and reflects the switch that Madagascar made in its political preferences. Aircraft from both the Western and the Eastern military camps are peacefully united here.

Commandant," an officer and a gentleman with the rank of a colonel as it turned out. Daniry's old man had huge respect for his ex-employer, yet on a few occasions he let slip his frustration concerning a number of recent developments in his country.

He didn't hesitate to fill me in on some remarkable facts regarding the political and military situation on the island. Frequent military coups against democratically elected presidents had had a devastating effect on the status of the military, and their relations with the government had reached such an all-time low that for many years now the air force had not received sufficient funds to safeguard their status as an efficient military entity.

The situation had progressed so far that there was not a single operational aircraft left in the MAF! This left me wondering what the actual purpose of this air force base was now, but it wasn't long before we found out; and in a way that we could never have imagined as we sat there waiting outside the gate.

Finally, after we had waited in the shade for more than an hour, the colonel showed up, a tall and slim man looking very prim and proper in his neat blue uniform. He arrived in a faded, grey-colored vintage Volkswagen Golf, which contrasted sharply with his own appearance. We managed to cram ourselves into the Golf and drove like a tin of sardines at a snail's pace to the main building where he had his office. There was a complete absence of military discipline. No saluting, no flag, and no personnel engaged in aircraft-related activities. All of the hangars were closed and there wasn't an airplane, or even another vehicle, in sight. The place looked like a ghost town.

The main building was ramshackle inside, with cracked paint on the walls, loose ceiling panels, rainwater leaking along the walls, and long dripping stains of wet moss.

And, of course, that typically third-world phenomenon: loose telephone and electricity wires that ran everywhere along ceilings and walls and down the marble stairways in the hall. It was as if the place hadn't been touched since the French left in the 1960s.

We went up to the commander's office on the first floor. It was very spacious and filled with vintage wooden furniture, including a huge classic wooden desk that was painfully bare—no computer, no mailbox, no nothing. Only the scent of total decay.

Monsieur le Colonel was a very soft-spoken character. We talked in French about our mission. Axel sat across from me with his camera running, filming our conversation. Daniry and his father were sitting on the opposite side, looking very humble. They hardly even dared to speak or look at the colonel. Bart, as always very outspoken and direct, sat on my left and contributed eagerly to the conversation.

From his body language it was clear that this officer was not at all at ease. Was it the camera or was he ashamed of the state of decline of his office and the base in general? As the conversation went on, and with the camera eventually switched off, he became more relaxed and we slowly came to the subject of our business proposal. I told him we would like to see the abandoned aircraft first in order to assess their current state and value. But the Colonel had a better idea; he made me a blind offer.

He was determined to dictate the course of events before we even had a chance to go out and have a look around. Monsieur le Colonel wanted to impress us and seal the deal straightaway, as if the inspection tour was only a formality for later. It wasn't long before he was offering the whole scrap yard for sale as one package: twenty aircraft of various types, including the five C-47s, the MIG-21s, the Antonovs, and the Mill helicopters.

In order not to frustrate proceedings at this pre-negotiation stage, I asked him to name his price for the whole lot, even though I had no real interest in all those Russian aircraft, often dubbed derogatorily by the Americans as "Ruble Rubbish." He stood up from his chief's chair, took me by the arm, away from the camera and the others, and ushered me out to the stately Mediterranean-style balcony.

We stepped outside through the door behind his desk. The view out over the airport was magnificent. In my mind I could see the last French commanding officer standing here in 1960 making his farewell speech after the declaration of independence. Somewhere out on this huge apron in front of us the Dakotas must have been standing proudly back then, well-polished, with a band corps playing and the champagne flowing. A *ceremonie protocollaire* as only the French know how to throw them.

But now, almost half a century on from that day, the place was deserted; the concrete was cracked everywhere and overgrown with grass. No glory and no pride to be found in this tomb of Malagasy aviation history.

I felt sorry for the man; was he maybe the last remaining officer in the whole of the Malagasy Air Force? Would they allow him to work on until retirement and then just close down the place and the Malagasy Air Force along with it? That scenario

Here Axel is filming what is probably the same Dakota (with wheel well caps) as the one referred to as the Air Madagascar DC-3. (Madagascar Photographs Bart Nopper)

must have been very *triste*, especially for a man so proud of the wings on his jacket. The idea must have had a devastating effect on his morale as an officer, as we were about to find out.

I noticed a slight tremor in his hand as he lit up a Gauloises cigarette. A little nervous maybe? He became absorbed in melancholic thoughts and nostalgic recollections of the past and began to tell me about his career. From a wealthy Malagasy family, he had trained as a pilot in France. He hoped to go back there when he retired. His spirits lifted during this conversation and he began to enjoy himself.

But when the reality of his situation hit him again he suddenly looked tired and pale. Exhaling a final puff of smoke, he regained his composure and said softly but in a very decisive tone, "You can have all the aircraft and spare parts out there for one price. What I want in return is a flying Piper Navajo."

His suggestion knocked me completely off my stride.

"A Piper Navajo? Monsieur le Colonel . . . that aircraft would cost me at least $250,000 even before thinking about how to get it out here to Madagascar. Frankly, I think that is far too hefty a price for all the abandoned airplanes out there."

The amiable atmosphere we had been enjoying only a minute previously chilled instantly and I had visions of us having made the whole trip in vain, with this megalomaniacal colonel now asking a humongous price for a pile of scrap metal lying around in a field.

An awkward silence fell between us, probably due to my straightforward but far from diplomatic reply. I quickly weighed up my options and tried to win some time to arrange a meeting with other parties, as Daniry had already suggested to me. I asked him if we could go out to the boneyard ourselves in order to assess the value of the aircraft. He agreed that we could come again the next day to carry out our inspection.

VISIT TO THE GRAVE YARD

The following morning we were there again, exactly on time, at the gate of this out-of-order air force base. And, as on the previous day, the colonel had us wait for more than an hour on the stone bench under the shade of a big old African tree.

He finally arrived in his VW Golf, this time dressed in some kind of golfing outfit and again without any apologies for his late arrival. It seemed that he wanted us to know exactly who the boss was around here.

All squashed into his Golf again, we drove out to the swamp where the planes were parked, passing a huge hangar with a massive lock on it on the way. "*Acces Interdit*," said the sign, and it was immediately clear to us that that would be our next target. Row upon row of buildings followed; a totally abandoned military camp, just like the one I had seen in Fréjus in southern France.

At the very end of the camp, in a desolate backyard location, we finally found ourselves standing face-to-face with the most amazing collection of vintage planes I had ever laid eyes on. It wasn't so much the size as the bewildering variety of the collection that astounded me, all randomly dumped in the tall grass that grew profusely in the marshy ground.

The first thing I saw was a Mill MI-8 Russian-built helicopter acting like some kind of gate guard and directly behind it a Dakota that still looked in pretty good shape, with its engines and props still in place. Further on was a row of MIG-21s, their sharp frontal inlet cones pointing straight at us. A threatening sight initially, but no more dangerous than the teeth of a paper tiger. In the second row of planes, right behind the MIGs, we saw a disorderly arrangement of more Dakotas, Mill helicopters, and Antonov cargo planes. What made it all even weirder was the

The swamp is home to snakes and giant spiders whose webs barred all the entry doors to the planes. However, these creepy deterrents had not stopped looters from going inside and stealing the most valuable parts.

The interiors of the Dakotas were stripped to the bone; even the floor plating had been taken out of the cabins. All that was left was 3 paratrooper folding benches; ironically, these are highly desired objects for every war/aviation museum in the world in their efforts to restore their C-47s back to WWII configuration.

mix of types from both sides of the Cold War.

This unreal array of aircraft was a perfect reflection of the bizarre political path the island had wandered in the wake of independence. Since 1960, the island had enjoyed a quiet start that abruptly ended with the first military coup in 1975. The "Red Admiral" Didier Ratsiraka kicked out the old French style of capitalism and proceeded to bring the island straight into the socialist camp. With his newly acquired VIP status in Moscow, he was presented with the obsolete MIG-21s and all the other Russian airplanes we had seen—the usual giveaway toys for Kremlin comrades around the world.

We stumbled from one surprise to the next while inspecting the aircraft. You had to move carefully as the marshlands are home to snakes and big spiders. We didn't encounter any snakes but we did see lots of spiders as big as a mechanic's hand. They had built their webs on and in the planes, and before you could step up onto a wing or through a door you first had to check for the sentry spider and push both him and his web gently aside. When you did so, Spiderman would come rushing over to protect his web and start a feigned attack trying to deter us from entering.

A Pratt and Whitney Radial Engine R-1830, which produced 1200 HP at full throttle. Now a rusty piece of archaic industrial art but still an impressive sight.

Unfortunately, all the snakes and the spiders in the swamp had not had the powers of deterrence required to ward off the many looters around here. The Dakotas, in particular, had been stripped almost completely bare inside.

The colonel was watching us from a safe distance and yelled at us that we should be very careful with those spiders as they were venomous and, according to his information, could even fly. We had traveled a long, long way, however, and the ex-commando and Borneo brat were not going to be stopped here at the door to this first Dakota just because of a bunch of creepy crawlies. Even if they were substantially bigger and meaner than their European brethren.

I could not hear what the Colonel was shouting at us and actually couldn't care less. "Did he say something about flying spiders or tarantulas?" Bart wondered with a grin on his face. We pressed on regardless, and the spiders took fright when they saw the tall intruders and beat a hasty retreat. Of course, we would have shown a lot less bravado had we run into snakes or killer bees.

Once inside, moving around was troublesome, as the aluminum floor plates of the cabins and cockpits had been stripped to the bone, or more accurately to their lower ribs. Most of the instruments, the components that make a cockpit so valuable, were also gone.

A Russian Mil helicopter. Exposed to the scorching sun it reveals its prior identity with the ex-Aeroflot lettering showing as the paint fades away.

The USSR Aircraft Dept. with Mig 21s and Antonov cargo planes. The Mig's main role was its annual low fly-past on Independence Day, giving the military the idea that they were still a factor to be contended with.

This C-47 was still in remarkably good condition, with its wings clearly re-skinned. It turned out that maintenance support was provided by the USA in 1989 for the Malagasy Dakota fleet through a military assistance program. This aircraft is probably final proof of that support.

The most amazing thing we noticed was that a single prop blade had been crudely sawn off six inches from the prop hub on one of the best-preserved Dakotas out here, its engines still mounted. Why on earth would someone do that? For the sake of a few bucks at the metal scrap yard? With floor plates we could imagine their usefulness in the construction of a hut or roof, but what can you do with a seventy-five pound prop blade?

We puzzled over this and a lot of other questions. This aircraft cemetery is part of the military base and is fenced off and officially guarded by the military, all under the command of our host, the colonel. So where had all the spare parts gone? Instruments, engines, props, pilot seats, and even wingtips had been removed, leaving only the near-empty shells of these once proud aircraft.

Removing parts like these takes time. A lot of time. And you also need special tools and tripods to remove props and aero engines. That's half a ton of heavy metal hanging two meters above a field, after all. There was no way casual thieves could have done it. We asked the colonel where all the heavy stuff had gone and he simply said that it had all been stolen by the locals. An amazing answer given that it had all apparently happened under his very own eyes, or at least while he was responsible, as the commander of the camp. Unbelievable that anybody would let things go so far.

The stuff lying around in this graveyard wasn't worth much more than $1,000 per airplane, so Monsieur Le Colonel could forget about his dream of getting a Piper

Navajo in exchange. Though not expressed in so many words, that was more or less the message he got from me *sur place*. We felt like we had been cheated, having been lured into a trap containing nothing but five empty Dakota shells stripped to the bone just waiting for the scrapper to come in to deliver the final chop for a few hundred bucks.

We took a few minutes with our team to deliberate our next step. Daniry and his father were shocked to see the aircraft in such poor condition, and they offered their apologies for the misleading information they had sent to us prior to our trip. I told them not to worry about it. We were still interested in doing the cockpit cutting, but with all instruments missing we had to agree on a different purchase price for the Dakotas, unless we could find the missing parts.

We had our suspicions that the colonel knew more than he wanted to admit and that the missing parts might eventually be found inside that hangar with its big "No Entrance" sign.

MEETING AT THE MINISTRY OF DEFENSE

Daniry had arranged a meeting on the next day with the minister of defense, a civilian female lawyer, who invited us to come over after the news of our arrival had spread around town. The Gold Rush Game had started, and everyone's mission, it seemed, was to get their hands on our money before someone else did. In this oppressive atmosphere we were set to witness a lot of competitive commotion over the coming

Hilarious taxi-ride in the center of Anta. With Bart Nopper and our friends on the rear seat of a 40-year-old Renault 4. Carrying too much weight, the exhaust pipe scratched over the road and worse, the doors popped open at every corner. On our way to Colonel #4, losing sight in a labyrinth.

days. Just as I had experienced in South America, my presence as a Westerner was often interpreted as the arrival of Big Money, attracting a whole lot of racketeers and rakers in the process. Buying a plane, no matter what condition it is in, is a million dollar business for them.

We were left waiting again at the ministry (Le MinDef) before we were informed that our meeting would be with another colonel because, for whatever reason, the minister had other urgent matters to attend to and had changed her schedule at the last minute.

This stand-in turned out to be a crusty colonel who was clearly not amused by the fact that we had contacted the other colonel first. When he asked us what price the commander of the Air Force base had asked for the derelict planes, I told him about the Piper Navajo. His eyes opened wide in surprise and he took a very deep breath, dropped his pen on the desk and scrambled off into the bowels of the building. Bells started going off all over the place, telephone calls were being made, and we sat there for another hour or so waiting. The near empty building, which had shown no signs of activity when we arrived, changed almost instantly into a buzzing hive of industry.

Our friend Daniry deemed it wise to give us a second lecture on the intricate political history of the island. This time it had to do with the more than morbid relationship between the military and the political establishment on the island, a not uncommon phenomenon in quite a number of countries in Africa and, up until a few years ago, in South America too.

Marc Ravalomanana, the once popular mayor of the capital, Antananarivo, had won the 2001 presidential elections against the previous incumbent Didier Ratsiraka, aka the Red Admiral, who had almost ruined the nation some ten years earlier with his experimental socialist paradise ideology. He had leaned heavily on the Soviet Union for help, as they were keen to have a sort of African Cuba next door to South Africa. But with the demise of communism in 1989, Madagascar collapsed in much the same way that Cuba did. With the support of the IMF and some "compulsory financial medication," democracy was restored in 1991, but the military retained their special role. The nature of that role would soon become very apparent in our bid to salvage the last Dakotas of the Malagasy Air Force.

During the democratic rebirth of the nation in 1991 the controversial Red Admiral stayed out of sight for a while. But one day, in the mid 1990s, he stepped forward, simply said sorry to the nation and ran again for president in 1997. Unbelievably, he won the election. A miracle or a disaster?

The right answer is the latter, unfortunately. In 2001, he refused to step down after being defeated by Marc, the former mayor. The Red Admiral forgot all about his public apology and once again tried to stage a coup against democratic rule. A mini civil war broke out between the two rivals. The Admiral was supported by the Army, while his newly elected opponent, Marc, had the support of millions of civilians and

The Mada Dakota Massacre had started one day earlier. I entered the fray online but was too late to save the finer components, such as the cockpits. The total aviation history of the island was shredded to scrap in an instant, like a mid-air collision had just occurred overhead.

of the US government. They were all thoroughly fed up with army involvement in political affairs.

Marc had won power through the ballot box and with the help of some powerful friends overseas, but he did not have many friends left in the Malagasy Armed Forces. True or not, there are allegations that after Didier's defeat the army made a new attempt to restore their previous ruling position. A year after the defeat of the Red Admiral, an Air Force Antonov aircraft was allegedly sent on a bombing run over the presidential palace, where Marc was living. I could find no evidence of this having happened on Google, but our friends were very sure about it and said that it had even happened twice, in 2002 and again in 2004.

No prizes for guessing who was in charge of the Air Force base at the time, from where that plane came. The weird story went on. Though Marc was the nation's president and his life was in danger, he was not in a position to arrest the pilots or officers involved in the assaults as he didn't have sufficient support from the army.

With the "Bad Boy" Red Admiral now exiled to the Seychelles and out of the way, Marc allegedly went after the other military figures responsible for the assault on him. It was the beginning of a dangerous game of chess, with the antagonists trying to predict their opponent's every move.

ENTERING THE LABYRINTH

We got completely lost in the complexities of "Mada's Military Madness," while all we really wanted to know was where we could find the man or woman who could legally sell us the aircraft for a reasonable price and give us a receipt for export.

All our efforts to meet the minister had so far been in vain. Worse still, the ministry was far from happy about the proposal the colonel had made to me. Did they fear that an operational aircraft, even a Piper Navajo, could eventually lead to another attack by the MAF on the presidential palace? Not likely. Others have suggested that the colonel wanted to have a plane that could fly him out of the country if needed. To the Seychelles, maybe, where an old friend would be waiting to welcome him? Whatever his reason might have been, it was made compellingly clear to us that we could not carry on with our deal with the colonel. It would be an illegal act to fly in any aircraft from abroad, they said.

We sat there totally flabbergasted, about to be arrested as suspects of a crime against the state by supplying an illegal aircraft to a suspicious warlord, one who was trying to keep himself out of the reach of justice. Their paranoia was fed by wild rumors that another coup by the military was imminent and that the stealthy arrival of a plane from abroad could be the prelude to this. Though I was completely unaware of all this, they may have actually suspected me of being an " agent provocateur" working for the military conspirators.

Finally, we were allowed to leave the ministry building, much to the relief of Daniry and his dad. I did not feel like anything all that threatening had happened to us, but they acted like they had just barely escaped execution by a firing squad.

On our way to our rendezvous with the next colonel, we hailed another taxi. This time a forty-year-old Renault 4—a tight squeeze for five passengers. Axel installed himself with his camera in the front seat next to the driver, with Bart up against the right rear door, me straining against the other side, and Daniry, with his fragile father on his lap, crammed in between us. The old car seemed to be bulging at the seams and the door on my side refused to close properly. I held on tightly to Bart's hand across the old man's knees for fear of being flung out of the car if we took a right-hand turn a little too enthusiastically. The old French car leaned back heavily on its feeble rear axle springs under our combined weight of 350 kilograms. The midget-size driver, by now perched at a precarious angle in his worn-out canvas foldable chair, strained to see out over the dashboard to no avail. With the help of a cushion he was able to catch an occasional glimpse of where he was going through the side window or out through the spokes of the steering wheel. After a couple of hair-raising maneuvers, we were convinced that all he could see was the blue sky and the birds above and certainly not the traffic on the road. So Axel took it upon himself to give him a running real-time commentary on the actual traffic situation in front of him, pointing out things like red lights and pedestrians. Handy information when you're behind the wheel. Our driver accepted his help without a murmur of complaint.

One colonel had the guts, at the very last minute, to try to save a bit of history for a future museum. This DC-3 standing in the left corner escaped the fires.

However, as if things weren't already ludicrous enough, we then ran out of gas. A plastic cola bottle of jalopy juice solved that problem and our old thunderbolt was soon flying again, complete with its anxious driver doing his best to dodge the oncoming traffic and a rear door with the unnerving habit of springing open without warning. And so we continued our journey, a memorable and hilarious blind ride across downtown Anta.

With the next colonel we discussed the deal at Ivato for the third time. He told us that our problems would soon be resolved because he had arranged for us to see yet another colonel in an old French fortress elsewhere in the old town. How many colonels did they have in this country, I found myself wondering.

The fortress was like a war museum with its sixty-year-old tanks, jeeps, and armored cars, freshly painted for the annual Independence Day parade in which they would all be put on show and up and running, if there was sufficient fuel. At the previous year's celebrations a few of the jeeps and armored trucks had ground to a halt due to mechanical problems or fuel starvation.

I figured that the museum pieces were kept operational only for the purposes of this annual parade, as they did not look very effective as military vehicles. This was colonel number four on our roundabout tour and we felt we had now lost all control over the situation and over "who is who." None of the new contacts provided us with anything in the way of useful information and they all kept us waiting for hours on end. Things got more complicated with each passing day and I wondered whether we

In real time, via our cellphones, I took part in an online auction at the scrap yard. Though we were one day late, we managed to save a few parts from total destruction.

were actually walking ourselves into some kind of psychological ambush.

Four days of travel, back and forth, waiting and lingering, no real progress; all we seemed to do was run around in circles. Was it all part of a cunning plan to lure us into a labyrinth and eventually exhaust us? Whatever their motive, this "Dancing with Colonels" act had a paralyzing effect on our morale. We were simply not up to the job, while they were all expert dancers honed in the skills of this unique military and political survival charade over the past twenty years or so.

We had already lost all hope of walking away from this island with our trophies of Dakota parts and cockpits and taking everything back to Holland. Rather disappointed and increasingly disoriented in this military political landscape, we made another appointment with the colonel of Ivato Air Force Base for the following day. Much to our surprise, this time he arrived on time at the gate. Just as we had gotten used to the idea of having a free hour or two to ponder our strategy, there he was waiting for us. Wow, had he done that on purpose to mess with the pattern of our prior meetings? No idea, but we were impressed by the honor.

The colonel had obviously been in touch with all his colleagues and maybe even with his boss, the minister of defense. He was calm and kept his mouth shut about the contacts, but he did make a remarkable about-face in his dealings with us. First, the price that he now wanted for the purchase of the five Dakotas came down from his initial outrageous idea of acquiring the twin-prop Piper plane. He also understood that he was no longer in control of the funds arising from any eventual deal, which was now in the hands of the ministry. However, in recognition of his help he wanted to have a new computer with a large flat-screen monitor for his desk. In black. Please.

"Finally, Monsieur Le Colonel, now we can talk like friends." I teased him with some sarcasm.

I agreed that this was a reasonable reward for his help. But there remained one little issue that I wanted to address before our departure the next day.

"What's inside the hangar with the big locks and the *Acces interdit*" sign?" I asked him.

He looked at me with a grin on his face, waiting and weighing up his answer. With a conspirator's smile, he finally replied, "Many, many Dakota parts, very much of interest to you."

"OK, are those parts taken from the five Dakotas we saw?"

"Yes, many of the cockpit interiors have been taken out by us in order to prevent them from being stolen by the locals. We have the instruments, radios, seats, engines, propellers, and wingtips." I did not want to make a fuss about the lies he had told us before; I was simply happy to hear that it was all still there. So I carried on.

"Can we go to the hangar now, just to have a look inside?"

"I would like to show to you, but the sergeant who has the keys is out today."

"Okay, can we see it tomorrow morning?"

"Yes, come over and I will show you our hangar tomorrow."

The next day, our final day, we went to see him to say goodbye and to have a quick look in that huge hangar. Would it turn out to be an Aladdin's cave or just another trick by this rogue shark who was at the end of his career in the Air Force anyway? It was clear that he was making a final attempt to earn something for himself out of all this wheeling and dealing, before his retirement.

We waited again for an hour before he showed up, and as he approached he said with a deadly earnest poker face, "The sergeant has not come in today, he is sick. Sorry, we have no key."

Holy shit, no key . . . ? He could hardly have come up with a weaker excuse. We had had enough of the colonel's games by now but we really should have anticipated something like this happening.

"Can we go to his home and pick up the key?" my friend Daniry asked in a final attempt to make our day.

"No, impossible, but when you come back next time to Madagascar I will show you the hangar for sure."

We were all fairly sure, however, that this was the last time we would be seeing him. Though this man was very slick and quite devious, it seemed he had lost control of the trading setup around here. And, according to some locals, there wasn't even much left in the way of spare parts in the hangar anyway, as most of them had been sold to foreigners over the past few years. It was probably half empty at best. We were not the first ones to show up displaying an interest in the derelict planes and their components. It is quite clear that he himself was actually the thief who had looted the aircraft for the best parts. But we had no time to find out, as we were leaving that afternoon on a flight back to Paris, and from there on to Amsterdam.

IN THE WAKE, MORE SURPISES TO COME

We arrived back in Holland empty-handed; we had no wingtips, no cockpits, had done no deals, and had not even found any souvenirs. All we had were a few reels of interesting documentary footage shot by Axel and a ton of photos taken by Bart.

We thought we would be able to go back soon, when the situation was clearer, and do business directly with the minister of defense. It was a simple scenario: strike a deal, get an export permit, cut off the cockpits, have a look inside the hangar for the missing parts to complete the cockpits, and stow everything in a container or two. Short story, major deal. But it was never going to work like that. Madagascar had other surprises in store—ones that surpassed all of our own best and worst scenarios.

I stayed in touch with my friend on the island and, after a few months trying hard to get closer to the minister, a scandal broke out. After counting the total MAF stock, it appeared that there were two aircraft completely missing. They were there in the books, all right, but were nowhere to be found at Ivato. A rumor went around that they had been flown out a year or so earlier and sold to a foreign group. The colonel had a lot to answer for, as he was ultimately responsible.

In 2009 I received the long-awaited message that he had finally been forced into compulsory retirement. Not surprising, given the scandal, but still a rather light reprimand if he was actually guilty of the theft of the aircraft and their parts. The ring of protection around him was still intact, however. Did that have something to do with his alleged role in the palace air raids some years earlier?

However, this was only the prelude to a new "Clash of the Clans," as another surprise came our way a month later, one completely in style with the island's political tradition. The sitting president, Marc, who had been reelected in 2006, started to make some megalomaniacal moves. He bought himself a jet, his own Malagasy Air Force One, believing that it better fitted his presidential status. Whereas his old opponent Didier the Admiral had been given the MIGs almost for free by the Soviet Union in the good old days of the 1970s, Marc had gone to Miami to buy an ex-Disney luxury Boeing 737-700 jet for a whopping $60 million, one half paid by the state and one half out of his own capital. Marc "forgot" to inform parliament about that first half, which the state had coughed up. Okay, that can happen in a busy life, but what about the other half from his personal funds? That raised even more questions. Where and how could he have made such a fortune in the eight years he had spent running one of the poorest countries in Africa?

Sadly, the cockpits were cut in half without any consideration for the nose-art and emblems.

For the first time in his career he was faced with a smoldering scandal, including public allegations of self-enrichment, corruption, and contempt of parliament. Regardless of whether it was orchestrated by the military, they finally had the scandal they could pin on "Big Spender" Marc. They may not have started the fire themselves but they certainly did their very best to poke it. This was the opportunity they had been waiting for to get rid of a hated president who was intent on destroying the power of the army and the air force. Thanks to this colossal political blunder by Mr. President, they were now ready to take over again and restore the levels of influence and budget they believed were more fitting to their status.

Another angry young man, the new and popular mayor of the capital, Andry Rajoelina, challenged the sitting president in 2009, helped in no small part by the public protests in the capital against Marc. The same recipe that had brought Marc to power was now being used against him, this time in the guise of a good-looking, pop star–like civilian supported by the army. It was revolution time again but in a slightly different setting.

As is prescribed in the handbook of revolution, the presidential palace was attacked again by the military, this time with troops and armed vehicles because there were no more planes left to execute the traditional bombing run. The best three of the vintage French armored vehicles that we had seen in the fortress were sent in to crash

The sole surviving DC-3 overlooks the terrible scene of destruction and the makeshift smelting ovens. These dreaded "Pac-man" smelting pots operated non-stop for 6 days in a row and we had to stay ahead of their appetite in our reeling and dealing to buy wanted parts.

the gates of the palace. However, in doing so the vehicles exceeded the limits of their normal once-a-year use for "show parades only." Not surprisingly, therefore, two of the vehicles ground to a halt due to mechanical problems or fuel starvation. It must have been a hilarious incident in what was a deadly serious struggle for power. The third vehicle managed to get inside the palace gardens, but the president had already escaped to a safe house, where he sat watching TV reports of the assault on his own palace.

In order to avoid the chaos and civil unrest that had been a feature of the past forty years, the president was put under such extreme pressure that he eventually went to see the military and handed over all political power to them. The ex-president Marc then fled to South Africa and was later sentenced in absentia to four years in prison and fined $70 million for stealing property and monies from the state. He tried to return in February 2012 to run for president again, but he overplayed his hand. The South African Airways airliner flying him from Johannesburg to Antananarivo was refused permission to land and simply flew back to South Africa, where he has been waiting in exile for another bite at the cherry ever since.

THE MADAGASCAR DAKOTA MASSACRE

So what did all of this have to do with our Dakota purchasing scheme?

Nothing really, or maybe everything. With all the political turmoil going on, we were advised not to return to Madagascar. The dust had not yet settled.

The process of restoring democracy so that the military can take a step back is still underway, though many doubt whether that will ever be possible. With the country's long history of coups, most commentators view the military as no more than a group of silver-tongued devils who try to secure vast development projects and financial aid from the United States for their own benefit by promising a return to democracy.

The military culture, set in place initially by the French army, includes a very strong institutional survival instinct. Unfortunately, members of the military persistently show little or no respect for democratic rule whenever an elected government seems to be turning the tables against them. In hindsight, it appears that Marc drifted too far from the kind of diplomacy needed to keep the army happy. Like it or not, they are a major factor that can never be ignored in emerging states, even by an elected president.

To make matters worse, Marc himself had great difficulty in keeping up any appearance of austerity in his lifestyle. His private ambitions and pursuit of higher status got the better of him. Not a smart thing when you have a reputed enemy in close vicinity always on the lookout for an opportunity to chop your head off.

I had abandoned the idea of ever striking a deal for the Dakotas in that snake pit when, to my complete surprise, I received a message from Daniry at the end of February 2011 telling me that the unthinkable had happened. The entire lot at the

All the aircraft scrap was shredded into strips of aluminum and inserted upright into smelting ovens. The liquid aluminum then dripped out from below in pizza-shaped ingots (right lower corner). The recycled metal was much in demand for the fabrication of simple household utensils like pots, pans, cups etc.

Ivato airfield had been sold overnight to a local metal scrapper. Barely believing the rumor, he had taken a taxi straight out to the airport to check it out.

Instead of arriving on the eve of destruction, however, he found that the nightmare had actually started that morning. All of the airplanes' wings had already been sheared off and cut up into large chunks and pieces, turning everything into junk in a matter of hours. All he could do was send me a few photos of the devastation from his cell phone so that I could make a quick selection of the parts I wanted. There were dramatic photos of the cockpits cut in half and wings ruined by random cutting with grinders and torches. The airfield looked like it had just witnessed a midair collision directly overhead.

I had a real-time view of the butcher's block and the makeshift ovens constructed from red bricks. They simply shredded the aircraft skin and smelted the aluminum strips by stacking the pieces upright in small open charcoal furnaces, which burned around the clock for days. Liquid aluminum poured out from the lower side of the ovens, solidifying in pizza-shaped ingots—a very simple recycling of a much sought after metal on the local markets. I had seen the same process of recycling in Bolivia, where the aluminum tablets they produced were used for the manufacture of kitchen utensils like dippers, pots, pans, forks, and spoons. But the pizza ovens at Ivato did not have an off switch; they were built to consume the aluminum of our beloved airplanes as quickly as possible, like Pac-Man.

Daniry urged us to make an instant selection of the components and wing panels we wanted to reserve and to arrange for a quick money transfer. The scrapper would only keep the selected parts for us if the money was forthcoming before the smelting process was done. Scanning the pictures on my computer screen, I picked out a pair of wingtips, some dash panels, several instruments and an overhead switch panel, a few cockpit doors and, finally, a set of cargo doors.

This was the first time I had ever done any Dakota Hunting online in a kind of weird chopping auction, not bidding against others but against a squadron of hungry ovens. We were running a race against a couple of little smoking smelters out there in the field that would have no trouble eating all that aluminum in a matter of days. With Smokey and the Bandits trying to crank out as many aluminum pizzas as they could, I found myself bidding hard at a distance of 20,000 kilometers from the fires, trying to save some old glory.

In this Madagascar Dakota Massacre, they managed to destroy fifty years of aviation history in a three-day barbeque. Fortunately, one of the colonels at the airfield understood the irreversibility of such a shredding act and ordered that the best of the Ivato collection, including the DC-3 with engines and an AN-26, should be saved from the pyre for preservation in a future museum. Bravo.

It was a chaotic situation out there, with the military taking souvenirs from the scene free of charge amid hundreds of other participants and spectators. They had all been attracted by the prospect of finding a precious gem among all the rubbish and

At the end of the 3-day massacre we were able, via our friend, to save a couple of wingtips and ruptured cockpit parts. During our efforts to export these goods, a new scandal broke out: all "scrap metal" transportation was forbidden overnight and our container is still there today and it is highly unlikely that it will ever be released to us.

debris strewn over the vast terrain. The mob that descended rapidly grew out of control.

The security guards hired by the scrapping company tried their best to ward off these vultures, but they were in danger of losing control over the frenzied and rapidly growing mob. So they resorted to violence, and even my friend Daniry got walloped by a bludgeon, even though he had bought an entry ticket that gave him the right to be on the site. The crowd was finally removed from the premises, but not without incident. Daniry limped back home nursing a sore leg and the even more painful feeling that his father's legacy had been sullied by the military.

Thanks to his rapid intervention, however, he had managed to save four wingtips and several cockpit parts, pilot seats, instruments, and panels. The downside of the story, however, was that the prized cockpits were totally ruined and thus useless as museum grade artifacts.

The parts we had saved remained stored in Madagascar, as we realized that transportation to Rotterdam would be too time consuming and expensive for the moment. The purchase was more complicated than we had foreseen, but that only enriches the history of the rescued Madagascar Dakota wingtips, and, in the end, the desks made from these wingtips have a stunning story to tell.

"Saved by the bell, they escaped from a burning hell."

THE SCRAP METAL SCANDAL

Eventually, just when we thought it was only a matter of time before we would see the container arriving in Rotterdam, we were confronted with another "Megalogasy" surprise. Yet another scandal broke out on the island—one that would torpedo our plans again as if we were destined to remain cursed by a never-ending string of misery.

For many years a well-organized gang had been poaching valuable metals such as copper from telephone and electric wires on the island. Miles and miles of public wiring would simply disappear overnight from over- and underground networks.

Things took a turn for the worse one night when the railway system became a prime target for the thieves. This marked the beginning of the slow but steady destruction of the entire railway infrastructure on the island, with the police, government, and military powerless to do anything about it.

With corruption running rampant in all ranks of society and with very weak central government and law enforcement, rumors soon circulated that high-ranking officials or even the military were behind this criminal act. The professionalism of the thieves and the tools, trucks, and expertise needed to carry out their activities led to widespread suspicion among the public that the conmen involved had close relations with and enjoyed the protection of the almost certainly bribed authorities.

Some customs officers had grown very suspicious about the ever-growing number of containers that were being shipped to China bearing freight that was inevitably registered as scrap metal. Their suspicions were confirmed one day when one smart customs officer in the seaport opened up one of these scrap metal containers to carry out a closer inspection. What he found inside was a surprise to say the least: the container was full of "pre-owned" rails freshly harvested from a public railroad track only a week earlier. That set the alarm bells ringing and the ensuing investigation exposed the participation of a number of top-ranking customs officers in a scandalous smuggling scheme sending metal to China, all under the innocent label of "scrap metal."

This development couldn't have come at a worse time for us. Right in the middle of that hectic period and immediately after the detection of the scandal, our agent went to the customs office bearing the documents required for our export permit. No prizes for guessing what was written on the paperwork: "scrap metal," of course. The customs officers probably went berserk

Ex-French armored Scout Car: we saw dozens of them in a military garage just outside the capital. Due to lack of operational aircraft for bombing the Presidential Palace, a Scout Car was used to bust the gates during the ousting of the sitting president in 2009.

La Merveille de Madagascar. We enjoyed our stay on the island so much, met very amiable people and a wonderful nature and scenery. The contradiction that we encountered in our dealings with the Military can not be fully blamed to them alone. The intricate political reality on this island made it all awkward to ever make a deal. With that the island had more important challenges to handle.

upon reading our documents, believing that the smuggling gang had now found a new route for their illicit trade. Not surprisingly, our request for export was suspended pending an investigation into the true contents of our cargo.

The goods have remained in Madagascar ever since, as legal restrictions have made it nearly impossible to get anything like that out of the country. It now seems quite likely that the stuff will never be released for export. A curse now rests permanently on the words "export of scrap metal" in Madagascar, no small consideration in a very religious country.

L'AVVENTURA CONTINUA

The Madagascar adventure provided us with fantastic insight into a fabulous island, thanks to a number of very helpful and amiable people. The macabre "Dance with Colonels" and the president's antics, however, had tarnished our otherwise splendid memories.

Eventually, we slipped back to Holland, and the Dakotas vanished forever into oblivion, in much the same way as democracy on the island did, for the time being at least. I had to conclude this chapter of my adventures with a poor score showing on the board. The Dancing Colonels and the Pac-Man ovens had won this particular game hands-down.

CHAPTER 8

Thailand

Sinking the Dakotas

In early March of 2008, my friend Bart Nopper emailed me a copy of a press release from Thailand announcing the sinking of five Dakotas in the waters off Phuket Island in the southern part of the country.

It was a most remarkable message and one that immediately grabbed my attention.

I knew that there were Dakotas to be found in Thailand, but why would anyone want to sink them? Through the press release, I soon had a contact name and email address for someone on the island. He turned out to be a German guy, named Rainer, who had been running a scuba diving school there since the beginning of the cheap international tourist flights in the early 1980s.

He told me an interesting story about a deal struck between the Thai Divers Association (TDA) and the Royal Thai Air Force (RTAF). The deal concerned the delivery of five derelict Dakotas and six Sikorsky helicopter airframes from the Lop Buri Air Force Base (60 miles north of Bangkok) to the port of Phuket, over road and sea by deep-loading trailers and barges across a distance of more than five hundred miles.

Upon arrival at their destination, the five C-47 airframes were to be reassembled, as their wings and tails had been removed for the sake of practical transport. The plan was to then winch all eleven airframes onto the platform of a huge barge in the port and ship them to their final sinking position at a depth of twenty-five meters, just a mile offshore from Layan Beach on the northwest side of the island.

I was very impressed by the complexity of this operation, which involved the transport of eleven airframes by land and sea and a sinking operation in the strong currents of the Andaman Sea. It was clear that this would be a costly operation and I asked Rainer about the justification for such enormous expense for the sake of a few old corroded airframes.

He bounced back with a remarkable reply: "It has to do with the infamous tsunami that struck the Phuket coast on December 26, 2004, and literally wiped out the beach resorts and coastline on the west side of the tropical island. The material destruction on land could be repaired in a year or so, but underwater the environmental devastation and ravage was of another dimension altogether," he explained. "Most people are simply not aware of the long-term damage that this disaster caused to the island as an attraction for tourists."

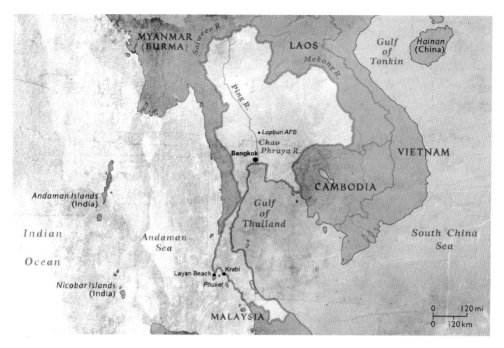

What had happened underwater when the tsunami struck the island soon became clear: "The phenomenal offshore coral reef formations with their lush and colorful fish and other marine population are all gone, destroyed in a single day by that monster wave."

The aftermath of the tsunami had a disastrous effect on high-end tourism to the island. With much of the underwater wonderland and fish population gone, the scuba diving schools experienced a very hard time, with a drop in clients of up to 50%. The more common overseas tourism influx in the lower budget classes managed to recover to a certain degree, but there was a marked loss of income for the local population and for the diving schools in particular. Their top ranking position in the list of "Best Scuba Diving Spots in the World" had disappeared with one blow.

The island had burst onto the stage of luxurious exotic tourism thanks to one of the most legendary James Bond films ever made. In 1974 the movie *The Man with the Golden Gun* was filmed on and around Phuket Island. The tiny isles of Krabi and Phi-Phi in the Sea of Phuket, in particular, became icons of exotic adventure almost overnight. With their peculiar acorn rock shapes and crystal-clear waters, the islands were imprinted on the minds of the millions of people who went to see the movie.

Such dazzling free publicity from one film for a tiny destination like this one, and featuring Roger Moore and Christopher Lee, was unique and paid off big time. Phuket turned into a gold mine, also helped by the revolution in mass tourism taking place at the time. The world was on the eve of a new phenomenon: the globalization of overseas tourism thanks to the genesis of yet another world wonder, the Boeing 747 Jumbo.

With the advent of that mega carrier, people could now fly further and cheaper than ever before. The stream of tourism gold would now begin to flow beyond classic holiday resorts like Greece and Spain to places like southern Thailand. Phuket soon had its own international airport and quickly became a favorite of luxury tourists who wanted to experience its wonderful waters. The influx of tourists continued to grow and grow, especially in the wintertime. Over the years, millions had come to see the fabulous fish in those waters, some of whom were attracted by the prospect of making a living out of the swell, including a few "rogue sharks" drawn by the smell of money.

THE MASTER PLAN

Now, however, with that single giant wave the boom had suddenly come to a standstill. The decline was felt particularly hard in Phuket, where the scuba diving business played such an important role. In an attempt to counteract the downturn, the TDA had come up with an ingenious plan, devised by a member of its board of directors, their financial treasurer, a high ranking ex-officer and part of the old boy's network in the RTAF. He had all the contacts required to execute the plan, which was kicked off with the free donation of old derelict military aircraft by the RTAF to the TDA.

The master plan was to sink the eleven ex-RTAF airframes in the Phuket offshore waters in order to create new breeding grounds for fish through the formation of an artificial reef. Over time, the coral and fish population would be able to find shelter and grow inside the fuselages and wings of the airframes.

A new diver's paradise was to be created, one with the rather unique added attraction of a scuba diving tour to an underwater aircraft museum neatly positioned on the bottom of the Amandan Sea. The sinking of warplanes for the preservation of the natural underwater habitat of marine life would also generate huge amounts of press and television coverage and free publicity for the region.

Not a bad plan at all, so I asked Rainer about the budget for all this and if I could be of any help, given my experience and my interest in possibly snatching a few wingtips in the process.

My contact with Rainer was very warm from the outset, as we shared the same passions and both had an energetic drive to do business to our mutual benefit. A day later, I drew up a proposal in which, after some stiff negotiating, I offered $1,000 for each wingtip we retrieved from the derelict Dakota airframes. I spoke with Rainer on the telephone and he said he would put me in touch with the ex-RTAF officer and CEO of the TDA management board to discuss the details of my proposal.

Rainer was also a member of the TDA board but had only a technical function and was not involved in financial matters. Nevertheless, he found my proposal interesting enough as a financial backup for TDA's operational budget. Five Dakotas could yield ten wingtips for a total of $10,000—not bad in a third-world market where the dollar still retains much of its old value and glory.

The derelict hulks of 5 C-47s and 6 Sikorsky Helicopters were transported from Lopbhuri AFB to Phuket, a tourist island in the south of Thailand, for the creation of a submerged Reef Squadron/Divers Paradise.

It wasn't long before I found myself caught up in a typical third-world game, which would inevitably involve a whole range of parties, including the military. I knew from prior experience that wherever the Green Stuff is involved, the Green Uniform is never far behind.

A classic story of rake-offs, scandals, and intrigue soon began to unfold, with a most surprising end for all involved, including a number of JUSMAG officers from the US Army who did their best to thwart my every effort and whose actions, though strictly according to the book, would have serious implications for me.

My first attempts to contact the ex-RTAF officer from the Thai Divers Association were not encouraging, to say the least. I did not get any reply to my emails

The C-47s were all ex-USAF aircraft acquired by Thailand after the fall of South Vietnam in 1975, with the intention of defending the Kingdom against invasion by Communists as the next victim of their expansion in SE Asia.

and could not get him on the phone either. Finally, I started sending copies of my email correspondence to Rainer asking him for assistance in establishing initial contact. Rainer was helpful, and eventually the ex-officer replied to me with a word of warning; he asked me "not to send any copies of our correspondence to anybody else from TDA." Surprise, surprise.

He wanted to talk with no one except me, and preferably face-to-face as soon as I arrived in Thailand. I was a bit stunned by his reply and it smelled of trouble. But the next day, before I had time to react, I received another email from him rejecting the proposal I had sent earlier to Rainer. I was disappointed, of course, but figured, "Well, that's life." It appeared I had reached the end of this adventure before I had even started.

One week later, however, I received an unexpected telephone call from Rainer. "Hans, what is the situation now with your proposal to TDA. Have you talked to the man?"

After the tsunami in December 2004, tourism badly needed a boost. The arrival of the aircraft for the purposes of creating an artificial reef for scuba diving was a fabulous idea in terms of tourist development. This derelict Dakota and the cruise ship were both instrumental in attaining that goal.

"Yes, he sent me an email stating that my proposal was rejected by you guys."

"Rejected? Are you kidding me?"

Rainer was quite upset that nobody had informed him about the decision and asked me if I could send him a copy of the CFO's email. Yes, of course I could. I had nothing to hide, after all.

The result was total confusion for Rainer and, half an hour later, for the TDA president, who was also unaware that his own CFO had rejected the proposal. It turned out that the man had acted entirely on his own and had not consulted the other members of the TDA board.

Now, the Thai president of TDA urged me to come over to Phuket and talk business directly with him, and he seemed very eager to find out about his CFO's antics. Thanks to my email correspondence with the ex-colonel, I was suddenly a key witness in the complaint against him. The president had correctly reacted by immediately suspending the man, who, in the ensuing investigation, was later admonished and dismissed.

Despite his exit, however, the role of the military in this operation was far from over. On the contrary, they had other tactics for homing in on their prey and in a much smarter way than the Malagasy colonels had ever done. Basically, however, it was the same "Dance with Colonels."

The TDA president was in an awkward position, as removing a member of the old boys' military network could have serious repercussions. And there were a few other snags to overcome as well, mostly to do with safety regulations regarding the sinking operation. He asked me over the telephone, via his secretary, if I had any experience with the sinking of Dakotas. For a split second I wondered how to reply, but by now I was so eager to do business that I boasted, "Yes, of course. I am very experienced with Dakotas."

My reply was correct, if not entirely adequate. Experience and sinking are not synonymous, but hey, this little lie was only a drop in the ocean compared to the suspected swindling and fraud committed by their CFO and his network. I figured that my response would not make much difference to the actual truth of the

The Sikorsky Helicopters and most C-47's were nothing more than empty shells in poor shape. I wondered why the transport over 800 km and the sinking operation were so ridiculously intricate and expensive.

matter. In any event, in a mood of wishful thinking, Mr. President was quickly convinced of my expertise. He became very excited, as he realized that the contract could be doubly beneficial to him, firstly by collecting money for the wingtips and, on top of that, free consultancy from an "expert" for the sinking operation. The perfect deal for him.

I prepared for my trip to Phuket, not worrying too much about the ex-officer's uncertain fate in which I had played a role. But in my relief at finally being rid of him, I had made a mistake; the empire (or the army) always strikes back, a lesson that I should have learned in Madagascar. No matter what I do or who I contact, it is quite impossible to do business in these countries without their involvement, simple as that.

Three days later, I was onboard a plane to Bangkok and from there I had a connecting flight to Phuket. Rainer had promised to pick me up from the airport. He was easy to recognize—a big, bronzed, blonde man wearing a white, open-necked shirt, Bermuda shorts, and flip-flops. He lived in a villa near the airport and had arranged for the rental of a small house next door for me. He was a strong man, an ex-boxer and an expert scuba diver.

A long-time resident of the island, he owned a scuba diving school and some property. Rainer was married to an attractive Thai woman from an upper-class family with a military background. She had a useful network in the Thai military community and it was this network, along with the entrepreneurial activities of Rainer in scuba diving that had brought his family great wealth in the booming era since the early 1990s.

We went to his house for lunch. As I looked around in the garden, everything seemed very familiar to me. Banana trees, a white garden wall, a big roofed terrace with a huge fan turning slowly overhead, the chatter of servants in the kitchen, chickens walking around freely in the yard, and an ever-present guard dog lying in the shadow under a big tree. It brought me back to the exotic world I knew so well from my childhood.

After lunch I was free to do as I pleased, and while everyone else went for a siesta I borrowed a scooter and rode to the beach, three miles to the west. The desire to explore new environments had stayed with me since my youth and I could feel the beach luring me for a swim. On my way there, the similarities with Indonesia became even more striking: same scent, same trees and vegetation, same temperature. Everything reminded me of my Borneo years.

Back in my little villa after some fantastic body surfing in the high swell, I got ready to accompany Rainer on our first appointment with the Dakotas. We planned to drive out to Phuket Port to see the airframes, which were parked up on the quay. Then we would drive out to the TDA headquarters for a meeting with the president. I anticipated a test of my skills as a "sinking expert" during that conversation and the success of my mission would greatly depend on the outcome of that exam.

Before leaving Holland, I had taken a crash course in how to become a Dakota sinking expert in one day, so as not to make a complete fool of myself in front of the president. Down through the years I had learned quite a bit about the structure of wings and fuselages, but that did not make me an expert, by any stretch of the imagination, on how to sink an airplane.

I had found a remarkable film on YouTube about the sinking operation of an old jetliner B-737 in western Canada. That plane was markedly bigger than a DC-3 but the conditions seemed similar for both projects, so I watched the film several times and jotted down any information that seemed crucial to the successful sinking of an airframe with wings still attached.

I also contacted the people who had made that film and got some more valuable information. An aircraft frame complete with wings makes a huge floating body. When stripped of all its heavy equipment, such as engines, wheels, and hydraulic systems, such a hulk can float for hours, even days, mainly due to the buoyancy provided by air pockets in the wings.

What you don't want to see is an aircraft dangling from a hoist on a platform or barge and that then floats on the water, refuses to sink, and starts pulling on the cables. That kind of situation can be very dangerous. Once in or (half) underwater, the airframe comes under the influence of the prevailing tide or water flow. With a DC-3 body length of twenty meters, and under the exertion of lateral current pressure, there is a potential danger of the uneven sinking of the left or right wing, each of which is over twelve meters long. That can cause the airframe to roll over on one side into the water, and if the hoist cables cannot compensate for such a roll then this can exert tremendous strain on the cables. The river current or tide can catch the submerged wing and make the airframe bank even further, eventually snapping the cables or pulling the hoist over the side.

The solution to preventing such a nightmare scenario was not described in full detail in the film, but the information I got from the Canadians would prove to be very useful. It is mainly a matter of achieving the fast and efficient elimination of all buoyancy factors. Once the airframe hits the water, there must be an immediate and evenly distributed flow of water into the hull and, most importantly, into the wings. As water enters from below, air must be able to exit via holes in the upper sides in order to prevent it from becoming trapped in multiple wing cambers. That requires man-made holes for rapid water penetration combined with air escape openings, all to be drilled in a perforation scheme on the upper and lower sides of the fuselage, wings, and stabilizers.

When he had risen after his siesta, Rainer drove me out to the Phuket port facilities, a thirty-minute ride over the island in typical Asian semi-chaotic traffic in a bewildering mix of small cars and vans and with thousands of scooters scrambling to fill the narrow spaces between the cars when they stopped at the traffic lights. The port facility was a weird empty place that looked abandoned, with a huge concrete ramp surrounded by the typical tropical view of palm trees and a crystal-blue sea with

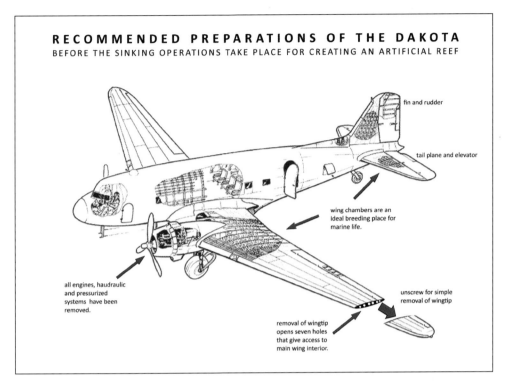

RECOMMENDED PREPARATIONS OF THE DAKOTA
BEFORE THE SINKING OPERATIONS TAKE PLACE FOR CREATING AN ARTIFICIAL REEF

fin and rudder

tail plane and elevator

wing chambers are an
ideal breeding place for
marine life.

all engines, haudraulic
and pressurized
systems have been
removed.

unscrew for simple
removal of wingtip

removal of wingtip
opens seven holes
that give access to
main wing interior.

With so many parties involved, a clear argument was required, on paper, as to what the environmental benefits would be if the wingtips were to be removed from the aircraft before sinking.

small overgrown islands in the background. The high, steep, fertile hills behind were filled with the shells of half-constructed holiday resorts. They too looked abandoned—a sure sign that the high tide of tourism had dried up in the wake of the tsunami.

I stood there with Rainer on the deserted dock looking at the collection of aircraft parked right in front of us. The planes were about to be mounted on five-feet-high concrete cradle constructions. The Sikorsky helicopters were lined up behind the C-47s, already completely stripped of their landing gear, rotor blades, tail rotors, and engines, leaving nothing more than their huge empty shells.

I was awestruck by the sight of these Vietnam War veterans standing there on death row. They had all been stripped to the bone but still had their old uniforms on, displaying their original camouflage colors from their USAF tour of duty in the Vietnam conflict. All of these aircraft had flown on the front line against Viet Cong troops and had surely been witness to many hairy moments.

The C-47s started their career in World War II either in Europe or the Pacific and came to the Korean Peninsula during the 1950–1953 Korean War. After the armistice, they were shipped to Japan, and many were transported from the early 1960's to join the ranks of the South Vietnamese Air Force (VNAF). With the

The C-47's were hoisted on board a barge that would then take them to their final resting place at the bottom of the Andaman Sea.

escalation of the Vietnam conflict, the VNAF faced soon a lack of experienced pilots. An American group of 30 USAF pilots (dubbed the Dirty Thirty) flew C-47's as from April 1962 as the first US 'advisers' or 'combatants' in the service of VNAF until the time that America got fully involved in that war in 1964/65.

In Sept. 2014, I re-visited the National Museum of the US Air Force in Dayton, OH and viewed a most interesting display of this group of volunteering DC-3 pilots.

See also www.nationalmuseum.af.mil

The Paris Peace accords were signed in 1973 and brought an end to the US advisory capacity in South Vietnam but that was not the end of the hostilities Early in 1975 , the North Vietnamese Army started their all out assault and a chaotic collapse of the South Vietnamese defenses was imminent. In the final evacuation, over 100 VNAF aircraft arrived in Thailand.

F-5s. A-37s, A-1s, C-130s, AC-119s, C-7s and thirteen C-47s landed in the peaceful Kingdom. Another 100 VNAF helicopters landed on US ships anchored off the coast as Saigon fell on 30 April 1975

War weary or otherwise, there were by 1975 55 C-47's delivered / flown to

Thailand (including 15 AC-47 Gunships) and served in the RTAF until the mid-1990's. Eventually phased out of active duty, they had survived three conflicts over a period of fifty years. A rather unique military career for these unsung heroes!

There is no other means of transport anywhere in the world that can boast an extended active military career that matches that of the Vietnam Veteran C-47s. A little more respect for these planes would be more than justified, I believe.

As a last salute, they were now dumped here in the Phuket port facility waiting to be buried at sea. I felt sad looking at them. Most of the aircraft were very disheveled-looking—one without wings, another one with stripped or deskinned wings, damaged airframes, stripped cockpits, and some with stabilizers and wingtips missing. It certainly didn't look like a fitting memorial to their years of service. Not only were the Dakotas stripped to the bone, but also the transport and unloading had clearly done further damage to the wings and tails. Nobody really cared, however, since it was all useless scrap soon to be dumped into the sea. The helicopters were in an even sorrier state and I wondered why they had transported the derelict Sikorskys over such a distance and at such expense just to deliver what was no more than an empty aluminum garbage container.

Looking at this death row of Dakotas, I instantly realized that either I had been

In my desperate attempts to save a couple of wingtips, I finally managed to remove one single specimen after days of hassle and tension between the parties involved.

The Dakota Hunter sitting here on a wingtip. This prey, however, also escaped at the last minute into the deep, despite the agreement I had with the Thai Diving Association.

misinformed by the TDA or the transport company had wrongly informed them. After a quick count, I could see only four wingtips on the wings of the Dakotas. The rest were missing and the score available to me was less than half of what I had hoped for. Worse still, most of the wingtips were also damaged. That was not a good sign and there were still more surprises in store for me. This was only the beginning of a whole lot of misery.

Before anything could be done, however, we first had to see the TDA president, who was a good friend of Rainer. The man spoke only Thai, so with Rainer as our interpreter we started to discuss my proposition. It quickly became clear to all of us that the ex-officer had most probably tried to make his own deal with me, keeping it all out of sight of the other board members. When that fell apart, due to Rainer's telephone call, he obviously saw no alternative other than to cancel the deal with me. Then, when the truth surfaced, the TDA had no choice but to suspend him from his function. An investigation had started into his activities based, as it turned out, on more suspicions of corruption.

From the outset, the man had played a crucial role in the ongoing dealings between the RTAF and the Divers Club to acquire, transport, and sink the aircraft. So it was regarded as very embarrassing to have to suspend the man right in the middle of an operation that had not yet been completed and that still needed a lot of funding for the final leg, the sinking of the planes. My plan was interesting to them because it could add much-needed revenue to their budget.

But the most important question had not yet been asked. Now was the time and, frankly, I knew upfront that this was going to annoy him: "When I pay for the wingtips, who is going to collect my money? And who will issue me an official invoice for the export documents?"

My questions triggered a very embarrassing silence and instantly wiped the oriental smile off Mr. President's face. A deep furrow crossed his brow and the

Some of the C-47 wings were in pretty bad shape. I wondered who on earth had been behind the idea of randomly shearing off the wing skin and wingtips. Some of the damage might have been inflicted during the long transport, more likely it was caused by cannibalization for keeping the final C-47's in operations.

Some USAF C-47's in Vietnam were converted into AC-47 Gunships/Dragon ships or Spooky ships with sideways firing machine guns. With the aircraft flying in tight circles and sharply banking over the port wing, they could concentrate their fire on small areas to devastating effect. Vietcong soldiers were ordered not to shoot at the Spooky's for fear of attracting their attention and then watching all hell break loose.

conversation stalled. This is Thai lingo for "Holy shit, why do you have to bother me with such awkward questions?"

It was a very sensitive issue, no doubt, and one that no one dared to address since it was not clear who held the deeds of the aircraft. Was it the RTAF or the TDA, or maybe another party? The President did not want to burn his fingers on such a tricky deal and preferred to contact his military friends in Bangkok first. They were the presumed owners of the aircraft and you do not want to play games with those guys.

MEETING WITH THE GENERAL

A day later, I was suddenly invited to Bangkok for a meeting with a general at the military air force base right next to Bangkok International Airport. Although I had some qualms about the very rapid response of the general, the prospects were too good for me to reject such an invitation. I flew there, with Rainer as my guide and interpreter, to meet the general at the RTAF museum on the air force base. The man was waiting for me with his warrant officer and they first showed me around the museum. There were lots of interesting fighter and training planes on display and, outside, the inevitable Dakota in RTAF colors.

It was clear that the collection needed some maintenance, not to mention an overhead roof for the aircraft parked outside to protect the legendary planes against the scorching sun and torrential rainfall. It was déjà vu, very similar to that which we had encountered in Honduras. The military were friendlier and more open-minded here, but the staging was more Madagascar style—like a big mousetrap under construction.

The basic mini-guns mounted in the Spooky were 3 Gatling-type GAU-2As—a six-barrel, air-cooled and electrically driven 7.62 x 51 mm caliber rotary machine gun with extremely high firepower. Their rate of fire was a theoretical 3,000-plus rounds per minute per gun, which resulted in a shotgun effect or "perforation pattern".

The general invited us for lunch. A couple of beers later, he suddenly suggested that I donate a sum of dollars as a symbolic contribution to the new museum roof in exchange for all of their C-47 wingtips, not only from the Phuket Dakotas but also from all the other RTAF C-47s stored at Lop Buri Air Force Base. Impressed by the simplicity and transparency of this proposal, we all agreed that this was the perfect and legal solution in order to avoid all kinds of potential nuisance.

The mood was ecstatic at this win-win situation and, as the icing on the cake, he invited me to accompany him on a visit to the RTAF base north of Bangkok. To my utter amazement, he told me they had another sixteen Dakotas parked out there. All reserved for future sinking operations in an effort to save the country's diving-related tourist industry.

The low and slow flying helicopters and C-47s attracted enemy fire that easily penetrated the non-armored aircraft, making them vulnerable when the aircraft slowed for landing. Here they could depend on the repellent power of the Spooky flying overhead. Its 18 rapid-fire spitting barrels must have been a welcome source of comfort to the crews.

There were hangars full of spare parts, too, and wingtips and other components that I could acquire in exchange for my donation to the RTAF museum.

Elated by so much generosity, we had yet another glass of beer. After my third glass or so, he told me about another general, a colleague in the army, who was interested in acquiring a similar donation for his army museum. Unbelievably, in exchange for a financial gift, I could have a look into his toyshop, too, a depot full of Willys Jeeps also shipped from Vietnam in 1975 and soon to be put up for sale.

My mind was in a whirl. Had I had too much beer? Was it all a fantasy? Were we uncovering a treasure trove here or were we sitting on a cloud that would soon turn out into a torrential hailstorm?

By the time we had gotten back to the airport for our return flight to Phuket, the alcohol had worn off and reality had slipped back into my head. Their proposals were simply too good to be true. I racked my brain to find the snag in their story.

The snag was big—very big—but it remained invisible to me for the moment. I was also worried about the number of parties now involved in the whole deal. Had the smell of money spread so fast? It was like in Madagascar, but different. For sure, they all knew how to make their story sound interesting enough, but the follow-up was often very tricky, up to the point of that one suspected a scam or an illegal deal.

The military here were more sympathetic than those I had met on other expeditions. They did not force us to wait for hours to see them and they offered us very good Thai food and a beer or two.

With the general's invitation sitting snugly in my pocket, I decided to return later to visit the air force base at Lop Buri with him. The plan now was to start with the sinking operation in Phuket and, given a successful outcome, the RTAF would then make the decision whether to extend the deal to the remaining Dakotas and helicopters that they had stored, with me involved as the "official sponsor" of their museum.

We returned to the island to commence the sinking operation but were stalled by adverse weather conditions. In fact, the start of the monsoon season arrived much earlier than normal so all preparations for the sinking of the Dakotas had to be postponed until the season was over.

In my opinion, the monsoon delay was the perfect excuse for a string of mishaps and intrigues, all of which were aimed at stalling the sinking operation. Rainer and his German colleagues seemed honest enough and were serious about a deal with me. But listening to their hectic phone calls in Thai, I gathered that things were not going as smoothly as they would have liked or wanted to tell me. Did it have something to with the dismissal of the ex-colonel? In any case, the operation was to be suspended until the next season, so I was to fly back to Holland and wait for further news from Rainer.

THE WINGTIP SEPARATION

His call came some seven months later. I decided to go back and this time to take Axel with me in order to film the spectacular action to come. By November 2008 we were back in town just in time for the pre-tourist season before Christmas.

All of the Dakotas in Phuket Port were in the process of being firmly attached to their concrete support frames or cradles: two in front under each of the engine nacelles and one at the rear under the fuselage tail. The cradles added weight to the aircraft and would position them some five feet off the sea bottom. These structures were to be firmly anchored to the seabed straight after the sinking operation.

Having accepted the fact that I wouldn't be getting my hands on any wingtips, I still had another job to do: the sinking of the aircraft in a rapid and even manner. Without the necessary precautions, an empty aircraft will not sink quickly but float for as long as 24 hours instead. And that was definitely not the desired outcome, with all the guests, TV crews and press milling around for a spectacular sinking act.

As I watched the Dakotas being hoisted onto their frames on the quayside at the port, I sensed that this was the perfect time to start removing the wingtips from the wings.

There was a lot of work going on now on the platform, with dozens of workers, from subcontractors and a diver crew, all very active under the guidance of a younger and energetic Thai diver. He rode around on a Harley look-alike motorcycle, a good-looking dude in his early thirties who was obviously popular with his team, not to mention the ladies. I noticed that this Thai Easy Rider had watched my arrival with more than normal interest. He was very eager to shake hands with me when Rainer introduced me to him. But the atmosphere at the port was markedly different from the first time I had been there some seven months earlier.

The simple fact that I was prepared to offer good money for the wingtips initially seemed more than enough to get the deal done. But now I was confronted with a new round of questions from Rainer and the TDA regarding the wingtip removal. This unexpected critical attitude became clearer to me as I felt the tension rising on the work floor here at the port facility. It was a totally different situation, and one in which it seemed Rainer was no longer the Big Boss. It actually seemed now that their intention or willingness to facilitate the removal of the wingtips had evaporated completely. I got the nasty feeling that the ex-colonel had something to do with this, as if taking revenge for his dismissal by TDA.

Facing a suffocating conflict of interests, I decided, in a final attempt to resolve the matter, to deal with the problem directly myself. After all, I knew how to perform the separation of a wingtip. I found an electric drill, but the screws attaching the wingtip to the main wing turned out to be so completely corroded that the drill bit just ticked over without any effect whatsoever. The next option was to use a grinding disc, but that machine turned out to be too small and too weak for the job. So I ended up having to resort to the only other but very radical solution: the cutting torch.

The cutting torch is normally a very destructive tool when it comes to removing parts because it tends to melt the fragile skin. But all of the other options had failed, so I went looking for a man with a torch who under our goggled eyes then proceeded to do a very neat job without causing any damage to the wingtip edges. Fifteen minutes later, the wingtip came off from the first wing and I finally had my first trophy in my hands. This was what I had come for.

The TDA president and council officials were there to watch and to perform a kind of unofficial handover to me, albeit with no help from the technical crew.

I had explained to the president the environmental rationale behind removing the wingtip. The removal opened up the main wing at its end, which enabled better entry into the "safe house" of the wing chambers and therefore a faster-growing small fish population. This would significantly help restore the colorful reef and marine life and hence the reputation of the attraction for tourists. The president asked me to give the same explanation to his team. In simple lingo, and using lots of sign language (they didn't speak any English), I asked for their attention: "Gentlemen, please look here, I have removed the wingtip and you can now see seven holes in main wing where wingtip was located, okay?" Everybody nodded and smiled with oriental politeness, while following my lecture with interest.

"Wingtip taken away, small fish can enter through the holes now opened in main wing, okay?" My hand made a swimming movement into the fist-sized openings. Everybody nodded and I continued: "Small fish inside but big fish cannot come in, too fat, okay?" The show became more intimate now and the entertainment factor rose.

"Small fish can breed safely inside, no stress of looking over their shoulder for big hungry predator fish. More relaxed breeding gives better and more offspring and bigger families. Just like you have at home." Smiles all round.

I acted out the expression of a fish looking over its shoulder by turning my head

The first C-47 goes overboard, ready to be buried in its final resting place. Or maybe not?

backward, but the gestures for "relaxed breeding" were of a more banal kind. Nevertheless, they seemed to understand it all and had a hilarious time copying my "breeding" gestures over and over again. One of them even had the guts to repeat my final phrase in a loud voice: "Yes, ha ha, just like at home!" They all obviously now understood and, more importantly, agreed with my lecture. The wingtips should be removed immediately for the sake of those poor little fishes' relaxed breeding!

The top brass, of course, welcomed the sale of the wingtips for more practical reasons, because they would be taking all the profits. The local divers, however, had a somewhat different view on the matter. Their interests had been neglected for too long and their frustration would finally boil over the following day.

I was walking along the quayside when I saw Rainer approaching with a very angry look on his face. He had just heard the bad news that had been hanging in the air ever since my return.

"We have a revolt going on here; the whole country is screwed up with these stupid demonstrations. Bangkok has been in turmoil for weeks and now the Thai divers here are protesting too," he yelled.

He was furious and continued in an upset voice, "They don't want any more wingtips to be cut off. They all have to stay on the aircraft and that is how they will be sunk."

During my absence, a long and hot discussion had taken place over who had to pay what share of the outrageous transportation budget for the aircraft. The parties involved—the TDA, the Island councils, and the communities—had all paid their share of the excessively expensive operation, which had been fiddled by the ex-colonel and his friends.

Now that the scandal had surfaced, all of the contributors were very upset and, given that they also now knew that funds were coming in from abroad, they were demanding their fair share. The fact that the TDA had claimed exclusive rights to this income had generated serious opposition.

The massive public protests in Bangkok were the spark needed to ignite the war of the wings (control over the funding) that had broken out as a result of the rake-offs by the ex-colonel and his mates.

Surmising this new situation, it suddenly dawned on me who the leader of this protest was: the Thai Easy Rider, of course, who else?

He was an ex-Navy seal, a master diver, and instructor with a high status. He had worked for years in a German diving school on the island and was in charge of all diving operations for the sinking of this so-called Dakota Reef Squad. He was the real boss around here and all of the Thai workers treated him with respect. Without his approval, nothing was going to happen and no more wingtips would be cut off.

In a final attempt to save the situation, Rainer placed a call on his cell phone, hoping to turn the tide by getting some support from the TDA president.

In the meantime, the Thai divers took over control of the operation and the Easy Rider ordered that the hoisting of the Dakotas on board the barge could start. One airframe after another went off from the quayside to be neatly placed on the pontoon deck, while in the background both Rainer's voice and the batteries in this cell phone slowly faded away.

The three disputed wingtips were all still in place and no one from TDA could or would do anything to change the situation.

The sea was dead calm, and so were the Thai divers onboard. They were in charge here now and they knew it. As the last helicopter frame was being loaded, a long blast of the ship's horn indicated that they were on their way to their final destination.

SHOWTIME

The next morning, the barge had been anchored in place for the cemetery ceremony and we came onboard with a whole bunch of press people and television crews from a variety of networks. The town mayor was also there with his dignitaries, including the state governor, the military, and a number of religious leaders from both the Buddhist temple and the Islamic mosque. They were all seated in rows on the barge's deck, the religious groups of monks and imams well separated from each other, with the military representatives and the mayor in the center.

Ironically, according to the operations plan, I had to cooperate with the Easy Rider

The ceremony with the Buddhist priest. We threw flowers over the aircraft as a blessing before their final flight to eternity.

in overseeing the perforation job on the Dakotas before the actual sinking took place. Our initial contact was somewhat embarrassing in light of what had happened the previous day, but we displayed no animosity toward each other. I understood from him that the sinking operation had presented the divers with an ideal opportunity to acquire more control over their waters, their funding, and their income. His refusal to help with the wingtip removal was a symbolic act against the rulers of the old diving club's structure and organization represented here by the TDA and the military. The public protests that were sweeping the country at the time probably helped them gather the critical mass and the required spirit for their own uprising against the establishment. I had no argument against this new movement of freedom.

In the end, we were talking about a mere three wingtips, not worth the hassle of trying to fight against "the perfect storm" as he called it.

I resigned myself to the fact that I was not going to get my wingtips. Instead, as the self-appointed "expert" in airplane sinking, I decided to concentrate on the consultancy side of my job. Under the watchful eye of their boss, the Thai divers were being instructed on how to make the holes in the airframes. They clambered over all the planes and perforated the fuselages and wing chambers with hundreds of thumb-sized holes using spike hammers. It was crucial that the number of holes in the left and right wings was more or less equal, so as to ensure a balanced sinking of the airframe and to avoid any rolling or banking.

The final stage of the plan involved anchoring the frames to the sea bottom after their correct positioning in a U-shape pattern, so as to avoid the possibility of the underwater currents causing any drift or swiveling of the aircraft.

With all of the officials and guests now onboard, it was time for the official ceremony to start. It was show time and hundreds of spectators in luxury yachts and dozens of other smaller boats had gathered to watch the sinking of the first Dakota. The first C-47 was lowered over the side to the sound of a trumpet playing the "Last Post."

With the Dak resting flat on the surface, the monks stepped forward and threw flowers into the water, as in a Buddhist burial ceremony, to bless the "dead" before their eternal trip to the infinite beyond. The television cameras whirred and hundreds of camera flashes lit up the scene.

For me, it was an emotional moment seeing that old war bird go down over the side to disappear forever into its watery grave surrounded by thousands of flowers drifting around in the calm sea. The ship's horns blew as a final salute and the Dakota was slowly lowered further into the water. The airframe rapidly took on the water that came rushing through the holes that the divers had made. She went down slowly, perfectly balanced, no rolling. I dove from the barge platform into the water to join the scuba divers. They were filming the burial as it progressed underwater and we accompanied the Dakota on its very last "flight" to a depth of twenty-five meters, where it finally settled in its final resting place on the seabed.

I was surprised by the limited underwater visibility; this was not the crystal-clear water everyone had seen in the James Bond film, probably because of the monsoon that had just passed. The remaining ten aircraft followed one by one until they were all gone. Including all of the wingtips, except for one, which were also gone, submerged forever.

After fifty years of reliable military service, followed by fifteen years of redundancy and neglect, their eventful lives ended here. They went overboard like dead sailors do when buried at sea. Not covered with a flag, however, but still proudly wearing their authentic camouflage colors. Remarkably, with all the uniforms present, there was not one representative from the US embassy or US military. For them, these war veteran planes had died long ago back in 1975 during the sudden and dishonorable retreat from the Vietnam War theater when they had left via the backdoor with no speeches, no flowers, and no decent homecoming ceremony.

They were the stragglers left over from a controversial conflict, but was that reason enough to bury the memory of these aircraft forever? Was there no respect left for these derelict war birds despite their participation in three military conflicts defending the interests of the United States with pride and stoic reliability?

It would soon become apparent, however, that the long arm of the US military had not entirely forgotten about these planes.

When I got back on dry land, I stood watching the diver's team scramble up onto the beach in their cool black inflatable boats. They were the proud winners in this game and I had to admit to myself that their arguments were more than justified.

The Thai Easy Rider came over to me to say goodbye. He smiled, with an intense look of relief on his face, and shook hands with me, saying, "Sorry, Hans, you lost

Show time. The military, the governor, council members, dignitaries and the press were all there to watch this fascinating moment: the burial of the aircraft and the foundation of the Phuket Reef Squadron.

your wingtips but they lost face. You understand our case here. Coming Monday we will all go to Bangkok to join the revolution and we will win there too, just like we won here."

I wished him luck and never saw him again.

SURPRISES IN THE WAKE OF A FAILURE

Was this the end of my adventure in Thailand, with only one wingtip to show for two long journeys? Not quite; things were about to get even worse.

The rightful owner of the C-47 wingtip we had saved had not shown his face once in the entire process, but he now made his presence felt from far away, suddenly claiming the rights of ownership.

The lone wingtip stood in the TDA office in Phuket like a forlorn trophy waiting for me to pay for it in cash and take it back home. Before I could do so, however, I received an astonishing telephone call—one that would see this already poor scenario go from bad to very bad.

While I was making arrangements for the export of my single wingtip to Holland, I got a call from Rainer. He had been talking to the military at the US embassy and a colonel wanted to speak with me over the telephone. A day later, I phoned the colonel and he told me that he worked for the organization JUSMAG THAI—Joint United States Military Advisory Group. They look after all US bilateral military materials, exercises, and operations in Thailand and other allied nations.

The very amiable US colonel told me about the Military Aid Program (MAP) under which the C-47s had been handed over to RTAF in the mid-1970s in a kind of a gift/loan contract that strictly forbade the re-export of military goods under MAP jurisdiction. And with good reason, I guess. In fact, it turned out that JUSMAG still had a decisive say over what happened with military goods here, including the Dakotas that had arrived thirty-three years earlier. Very strict rules apply, even to military hardware that has no value other than as scrap, and all re-export is forbidden without prior consent.

So now I was facing a fight over a null and void deal involving a wingtip taken from a derelict aircraft that had just been buried at sea. Unbelievable. The colonel advised me to contact yet another colonel to request dispensation from Washington. I said okay and he gave me a telephone number at the Pentagon.

At the what?! I asked him twice if he was serious about this. Talking to someone at the Pentagon is not a daily occurrence for me, but the colonel was not fooling around. I rang the number and I got a female colonel on the line. Unfortunately, she was not at all amused by my antics with that single "MAP rule" wingtip. For a moment she suspected me of trying to smuggle the wingtip out of the country and threatened me with prosecution. This lady was meaner in her attitude than the meanest of mean colonels I had ever met on any of my many expeditions. In despair, I hung up and gave up all my efforts to save the deal for one lousy damaged wingtip.

In the end, it was not worth drawing the wrath of the Pentagon down upon myself, as they are not in any way like the MINDEF in Madagascar, where you can stir things up a little and still walk away unscathed.

I had spent a huge amount of time and effort on a deal that, ultimately, not one party at the poker table was ever in a position to deliver on, despite appearing to be deadly serious about it all. The wingtip that had escaped burial at sea is likely to stay at the TDA main office forever. A nice souvenir and symbol from a game that they ultimately had lost.

There were two more interesting developments in the wake of the Dakota Reef Squadron sinking operation. The first one concerned the ex-officer who was a board member of TDA before I arrived on the scene. Just before or during my first trip, he had been suspended pending an investigation against him. It turned out that he had set up a foundation for the environmental protection of the Thai seas and had collected donations and council subsidies from all over the island in order to finance

As a last measure, with the planes lying on the water, we had to check the water influx into the hull and wings. In order to prevent the aircraft from floating or rolling over on one side, all of the trapped air first had to be allowed to escape through multiple perforations made in the upper skin panels.

The Thai divers had done a perfect preparation job; the C-47s began to sink quickly and evenly. There was one final snag, however, but one for which they could not be blamed: the planned anchoring of the airframes to the sea bottom was never carried out. It would turn out to be a tragic omission.

the project. The outrageous transportation expenses took the lion's share of the project's budget. It soon emerged that the company that was assigned the hauling job was way more expensive than the other competing transport companies that had been kept out of the tender. Rumors of corruption and bribery began to circulate in the national press.

A scandal broke out around the man and his "sticky fingers" foundation with his old boy's network. He was accused of self-enrichment using public funds. I have no idea if he was ever indicted for his dealings. As an ex-colonel, he probably had plenty of influential connections. Ironically, one of the main reasons for the mass demonstrations in Bangkok that broke out at that time was the public outrage against widespread corruption and self-enrichment that had ingrained itself like a cancer in the main Thai political parties and beyond into governmental organizations. The tidal wave turned against him and the mighty army was no longer willing or able to keep him out of court, but could it be that they have managed somehow to keep him out of jail?

Whenever the military get involved in my dealings with Dakotas, things tend to get very complicated, sometimes involving endless delays and mountains of red tape or, worse still, rake-ups and scams. I had lost the game with the military three times in a row now: in Honduras, Madagascar, and Phuket. However, they had all yielded extremely interesting expeditions in which I had encountered bizarre situations and fantastic people, both heroes and villains, and I had always managed to find my beloved Dakotas, albeit sometimes in the dreadful ending of their lives and, in all cases, with poor commercial results for our Avionart company.

As I was heading home via Bangkok, the uprising was gradually developing into a street revolt. Antigovernment demonstrators barred the entrance to Bangkok International Airport and all overseas flights had been cancelled. The proposed visit to the air force base Lop Buri was nullified. Evidently, the JUSMAG veto had voided all my dealings with the military and the generals now suddenly had more important things to do. They had to save the kingdom from an outright revolution. The country was in turmoil and their multimillion-dollar source of income, the tourist influx from abroad, stalled overnight due to the Bangkok airport blockade.

INTO THE ABYSS OF THE OCEAN

The second unexpected development came six months later when, back in Holland, I heard a sad story from Rainer. After more tropical storms, the unthinkable had happened. Four of the five sunken Dakotas had disappeared from their sea grave.

Had they drifted away on the strong currents? Or gotten stuck in the nets of

The near perfect picture of an underwater museum as shown here in Bodrum, Turkey. But in Phuket, the expensively produced underwater display of 5 C-47's would not last long. Entirely of their own accord, without any anchoring mounted, these ex-Vietnam veterans were able to slip off into the abyss of the vast Indian Ocean, never to be seen again. (Photograph: Rico Besserdich)

fishermen's boats and then torn asunder? Or maybe buried under the sand in the storms that devastated the coasts? Nobody knew the answer, it seemed, but it eventually turned out that the concrete cradles on which the Dakotas had been bolted had not been anchored to the seabed, as had been stipulated in the original plan.

The project's budget had long been exceeded and there was no money left to execute that final precaution, which would have prevented the possible dislocation of the Dakotas. Thanks to the greedy rakings of our ex-colonel with his excessive bills for the foundation of the Dakota Reef Squadron, the final installment of what was basically a marvelous plan had not been properly executed.

The man had since fallen from grace but, as if in a final act of revenge, his crime had caused the complete failure of the plan's original mission: to restore the coral reef of Phuket Island and reaffirm its attraction for scuba divers.

The most likely scenario is that the Dakotas, with their wings still in place, had been dislocated by the strong sea currents. The wings can act underwater as lift-generating foils. Water is much denser than air, so it needs less flow speed to create lift or upward pressure. It is therefore feasible that the combined effect of the lack of anchoring and the strong currents created by the tropical storms caused the aircraft to start "walking" over the sea bottom to an unknown destination far away from their original drop zone.

It was an amazing end to the story. We had fought tooth and nail with the TDA over four lousy scrap wingtips, while they did not actually own them at all. And they weren't even the property of the RTAF or the museum general either, despite all their claims. Every protest had been nullified by the claim to rightful ownership by the US military, backed up by JUSMAG as the defender of the law of the Pentagon.

But even they could not have foreseen such an ending.

The grave at the bottom of the Andaman Sea, planned as an attractive underwater coral reef and aviation museum for tourists, did not turn out to be the aircrafts' final resting place. In a convergence of bizarre circumstances, the vintage aircraft had managed to slip out of everybody's grasp, including mine, the TDA's, the RTAF's, and even the US military's.

The four Dakotas have since "flown off" on stealthy missions to secret destinations. The spirits and derelict bodies of the old war veterans are now possibly soaring restlessly over the infinite ocean bottom in search of eternal peace after a military career that spanned half a century.

As they say, "Old soldiers never die, they simply fade away."

And that is exactly what happened with the derelict Dakotas of the Phuket Reef Squadron. There are gone forever, somewhere in the eerie depths of the Indian Ocean. Probably the best grave they could have wished for. They slipped quietly away into the abyss where no human claim nor quarrel can ever touch them again.

I could not have dreamt up a better ending for these brave warriors.

Vaya con Dios, my friends.

CHAPTER 9

Alaska and the Yukon

L'adventure se prolonge

The breathtaking scenery and the prospect of bush aviation in Alaska, both abundantly available in that vast state, had attracted me for years. I first visited Anchorage way back in July 1965, en route to live with my parents in Japan. In broad sunlight, I had enjoyed a stunning flight from Amsterdam over the North Pole. That trip was a most exciting event for me. After seven harsh years in Jesuit college, I was free and could finally fly out over the world again. It was also my first ever flight in a jet airliner, a KLM DC-8, and as an added bonus we made a fuel stop at Anchorage.

Now, forty-two years later, here I was planning my second visit to the Last Frontier State. My long-time friend Michael Prophet got me in touch with a renowned Canadian specialty airline operator, Buffalo Airways, a company that operated in the north and west of Canada with a remarkable fleet of vintage propeller aircraft. The company used to be known only to locals and aficionados but has recently been introduced to a wider audience around the world thanks to their participation in the Discovery Channel series "Ice Pilots."

I was told that I should go see them and a number of other Alaskan piston prop operators, all of whom were still flying the Dakota in active service. Armed with this information, the time seemed ripe to set out on a new hunt.

Just as I finished my preparations, I got a call from a French journalist named Julie who I knew from when I worked in Paris in the early 1990s. Back in 1994 she had been selected as one of the journalists to accompany us on our second Catalina Odyssey. Already a promising young reporter, her coverage of that epic trip in the Amphibian PBY-5A over the Caribbean was chosen as the winning report from the forty-eight contestants that made the trip around the Atlantic. Thereafter she had decided to follow her passion and had become a full-time journalist. We had kept in touch after that trip, but the contact had faded out over the years. She was now looking for something out of the ordinary and had a commission from a French men's magazine to find and write up a good story.

In her research she had stumbled across my Avionart website, where she had read about my exploits as the Dakota Hunter. She decided to call me and ask if she could come along on my next trip with the intention of writing an article for the magazine. I agreed to her request and drew up an itinerary for a trip to Canada and Alaska, starting in the Yukon, that remote state of gold-rush fame in the northwest of Canada.

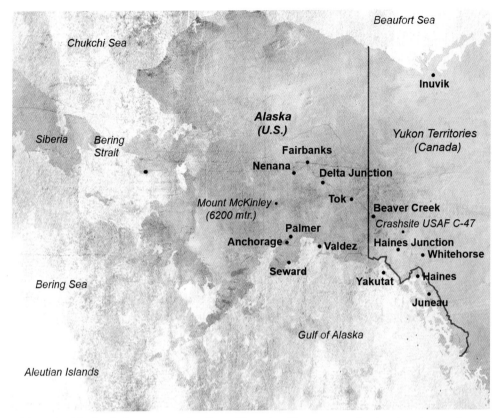

Although Alaska is known as the Last Frontier State, as a destination it was by no means as hostile as South America's frontier states of Colombia, Honduras, and Venezuela. And so, with fewer extremities in terms of discomfort and risk, I figured that a woman of Julie's caliber would be well able to handle such a demanding expedition.

I planned to start in Whitehorse, YT (Yukon Territories), and then to drive west along the famous Alaska Highway 1. This road runs from Dawson Creek, British Columbia, all the way up to Delta Junction, Alaska, 100 miles southeast of Fairbanks—a journey of almost 1,250 miles along one of the most scenic routes in North America that may not have the reputation but is way more authentic than the mucked up "no-riginal" Route 66.

The plan was to travel from Whitehorse all the way west to Tok, Alaska, just over the Yukon border, and to drive from there on a clockwise loop via Anchorage and Fairbanks back to Whitehorse. As a bonus, I planned to squeeze in a visit to the Buffalo Airways facilities at Red Deer Airport in Alberta. And all of this in just nine hectic days. We flew to Canada at the end of August 2007, with Julie arriving from Paris and me flying in from Amsterdam, and met up in Edmonton for the start of our strenuous trip.

We flew together to Whitehorse, and upon landing my eyes were immediately drawn to the largest wind vane in the world in the shape of an immaculate DC-3. The aircraft was mounted on a seven-foot pylon, its nose turned into the wind just like an iron rooster on a church tower. What better welcome could you wish for as a Dakota Hunter than to see a tribute to the aircraft that had helped to open up this vast and barren land?

The Yukon village of Whitehorse set the scene for the next six days, with its low timber buildings in pleasant pastel colors, its fast-flowing river, and, as a monument to the past, a Mississippi-style river boat that served as the town's museum. The famous gold rush region of Klondike lay next door and the town had an amazingly laid-back atmosphere, with only the occasional tourist passing through. The huge mountains in the background, the wide-open spaces, and the clear-blue sky bode well for the start of our tour. Though it was the end of August, the sun was still hot, and nature still blossomed in abundance.

Alaska in wartime. A C-47 flying patrols along the chain of Aleutian Islands. Right after the Pearl Harbor attack in December 1941, the Japanese occupied two tiny American Islands, which lead to widespread fear that they would try to invade Alaska by "hopping" the string of Aleutian Islands from Siberia to Alaska. In an attempt to reinforce the military installations on the mainland, it was decided to build the Alaska Highway No.1 that runs from Dawson Creek, BC to central Alaska. A year later the road was finished, but in the meantime the Japanese had suffered their first naval defeats in the SE Pacific. The threat of an overseas invasion in the north now receded but the lonesome and scenic Alaska Highway remained, a true gift from God for travelers to the Gates of the Arctic.

In Whitehorse, Yukon Territories, we were welcomed by the largest wind vane in the world: a Canadian Pacific DC-3 on a pylon at the local airport, erected as a tribute to the plane that had contributed so much to opening up Yukon Territories (YT) after the war.

After lunch we drove west to Haines Junction, a typical junction settlement with only fifty houses and a small airport where you can hire a helicopter for a sightseeing tour over the nearby Kluane National Park. And a chopper was exactly what I needed to travel up north into the Ruby Mountains in search of a lost USAF C-47B that had crash-landed somewhere out there in January 1950.

From the moment I saw the first photos of that stricken aircraft, I was mesmerized by the site and the story behind that spectacular crash. Julie saw the potential for a scoop, too, and was more than eager to accompany me to that godforsaken place high up in the mountains. I met up with the pilot and discussed the flight plan with him. He did not know the exact location of the wreck but he was sure he could find out. However, it would not be possible to fly up there for the next few days as it was too foggy in the mountains, even though the weather was stable and sunny down in the valley. So we decided to continue on to Alaska and to stop off again five days later on our return trip to Whitehorse.

Although it was already evening, the sun was still shining brightly and we were treated to a spectacular, long, drawn-out sunset, close to "the Gates of the Arctic." We drove further west over the Alaska Highway and were soon enjoying the experience of being completely alone in a kind of lost world.

The scenery changed rapidly around us: lakes, snow-capped mountains, glaciers, endless forests, and tundra. And, needless to say, the very pleasant company of a curious and cute French journalist didn't hurt either. We had traveled together before on the Catalina trip and were now repeating the experience driving through the Yukon landscape. Julie continuously asked me to slow down or stop for the countless photo opportunities presented by all these marvels around us. Every time we pulled over and she stepped out, the first thing she asked me was to keep an eye out for bears. In an attempt to make her feel more relaxed out here in the wild I had told her about my own close encounter with a black bear. She wasn't entirely convinced, however.

MEETING THE BLACK BEAR

I had my first encounter with a black bear at Sproat Lake on Vancouver Island. My friend Fritz and I were on a Harley tour in the western United States and Canada searching for the dinosaurs of the piston-prop aircraft world, two fire bomber hydroplanes of the Martin Mars type. We had the good fortune to arrive at the lake just when one of those monster planes was being pulled out of the water onto the

Palmer Airport: legendary relics of the past, the DC-3 and C-119, standing side by side on the airport ramp. Very scenic surroundings but the place appeared completely abandoned with an eerie silence.

ramp for an engine change. The plane and its hangar were now a museum that, alongside films and photos, gave the visitor first-hand insight into the fire-fighting operations of the aircraft on that lake. After being shown around the hangar and inside the aircraft, we were walking back to our motorcycles in the parking lot next to the hangar when I noticed a crude cardboard sign saying "Beware of Bears" next to our Harleys. We smiled, thinking it was some kid's idea of a joke, and walked on into the forest behind the parking for a quick pee. As we stood there hosing in the dense woods, we suddenly heard the noise of branches cracking high above us.

Fritz looked up and said, "Holy shit Hans, look! Up there!" Right overhead, about fifteen feet up a rather thin tree, we saw a huge black bear munching berries like they were going out of style. To make things worse, two cubs then appeared from the bushes looking for their mum. All three bears were now eyeballing us and we just stood there frozen to the ground with our mouths and zippers open, peeing in their backyard. Mama Bear was really pissed off at us and growled deeply; she clearly intended to dish out some stern treatment to these two intruders whom she had caught in the act of trying to mark and claim her territory with their confronting behavior.

Suddenly, she retracted her impressive nails and half a ton of muscle and fur sank straight down the tree trunk, cracking each and every branch on the way. For a moment we stood there petrified, simultaneously glued to the ground and watering our shoes out of pure fear at this startling pole-dancing act. We quickly regained our senses, however, and ran in a mad panic back to the parking lot, sparing not even a thought for the decency of reeling up our hoses.

A passing car stopped and the family inside saw us running toward them. The driver shouted to me, "Look out, there's a bear behind you!" For a second I thought of replying, "A bear? What bear?" but this was no time for jests.

While they rolled up their windows in a panic, we realized we didn't have the same option with our motorbikes, so we took refuge behind their car. Fortunately, the bear seemed to have a good sense of territorial division. She stopped at the forest's edge and looked at us with a clear message in her eyes: "You stay out of my forest and I'll stay out of your parking lot, got that?" We got that for sure; this was the law of the land around here and a good old-fashioned lesson in the pecking order of the wild— if you enter a forest, never forget that you are entering bear country.

THE ALASKAN SEARCH

We crossed the border between the United States and Canada and arrived at the town of Tok, where we decided to stop for the night. We found a little motel and retired to the bar, where we soon met the townsfolk. Julie got chatting to the local Indian women, who wore their hair in long braids down their backs and were happy to let her take their picture. Pool tables and booze are the medicine against loneliness here, but they provide only temporary respite from the crushing lonesome feeling that often leads to widespread alcoholism in places as remote as this town.

The locals were very nice to us but were a little too eager to have us join them in their heavy drinking. We soon found ourselves participating, or rather competing, in the Great Alaskan Beer and Booze Contest while still jet-lagged and in dire need of some rest. It turned into a long, long night.

The next day, we struggled out of bed early to set off for Palmer. At the local airport we found a fine collection of vintage piston props, including five Dakotas and a couple of Fairchild C-119s—a Canadian-built twin-boom cargo plane with a huge clamshell rear door. For years they had been the leading player in the air transport business in Alaska, but their numbers have dwindled rapidly, and the ones here had clearly been standing idle for quite some time. There was hardly a soul around—the place had the appearance of an abandoned freight station—and after taking some photos of the airplanes against the staggeringly beautiful scenic backdrop we headed for Anchorage International Airport, the biggie compared to all the other airports out here.

Anchorage International Airport was a beehive of aviation activities: on the cargo ramp we saw B-747's that dwarfed the DC-3 on the runway. Though both operate in totally different worlds, they meet occasionally here at this crossroad.

There we witnessed the weird spectacle of a huge Boeing 747, ready for take off, with a dwarfed Dakota in its wake maintaining a respectful distance so as to avoid the vortex blast of the jumbo's jet engines. These planes operate in totally different worlds but they still meet here like this every day on the runway junction. In Anchorage, we found a huge number of aircraft of all types and ages, all of which were commercially operational and covered a time span of four generations. Planes from the World War II era like the C-47 and its contemporary, the Curtiss Commando C-46; from the postwar era the DC-6 four-engine prop liners of the Evert's Air Cargo company; the older jets of the 1980s; and lastly, the modern jumbo

Evert's Air Cargo DC-6 starting up its four powerful radial engines: the pulsing of the exhaust stacks literally knocks the breath out of your chest. It made the mechanic dance around, like he was standing in front of a speaker tower at a rock concert.(All Alaska photographs: Julie le Bolzer)

jets used by the international carriers.

However, we had not come to check out the international end of air cargo but rather the local freight area on the far northern end of Anchorage International Airport, where Julie's jaw dropped at the sight of five Dakotas lined up together far away from the big passenger jet liners. There was quite a lot of activity here—open-air tinkering on the perpetually oil-dripping engines with their cowlings removed, oil pans placed on the tarmac, and overhauled radial engines placed on dollies under the wings waiting to be changed.

The hunt for wingtips could start right here where all these DC-3s were gathered. The local wrench jockey, Dave, wasn't able to tell us much about the availability of surplus parts and he advised us to go see the bigger operators. Julie, though, found plenty of material for her photos. We then went to visit the facilities at Evert's Air Cargo, a legendary name in the Alaskan aviation world. They have an impressive pair of pristine Curtiss Commando C-46s, complete with WWII-style nose art, and the much bigger Douglas 4-engine DC-6.

We met the owner, Robert Evert, in his office and told him about Julie's article on the sky trucks of the North. Julie's good looks and French accent charmed everyone wherever we went. I was lucky to have her around, not only because she was intelligent and entertaining company but also because she turned out to be excellent at opening doors. The people at Evert's granted us access to their workshop and cargo platform, where we were able to watch the loading and start-up operations of one of their DC-6s.

Julie had never experienced anything like this before and was mesmerized by the show and the sound of rolling thunder when the plane revved up its four engines for the ride out to the runway. What most people would experience as an immensely deafening noise was like music to our ears. The beat of big bore pistons is absolutely

Everywhere in Alaska and the Yukon we encountered impressive scenery complete with snow-capped mountains, lakes and, as here in this photo, fantastic glaciers that dwarfed any vehicle that drove along the road in the foreground.

enthralling, and when the aircraft turns its exhaust pipes to you, you can feel the pressure on your chest generated by the hefty pulses of hot air. It is like standing right in front of the speakers at a Rolling Stones concert.

Robert eventually brought me to see their scrap yard, where I found a pair of forgotten and damaged Dakota wingtips on top of a container. Given that they did not fly with the Dakota anymore, I figured that these parts must have been lying there for quite a while. I was in the right place at the right time; they wanted to get rid of that old scrap from their yard and I was happy to make my first score of wingtips in Alaska.

We had made a catch and were soon on our way to Fairbanks, heading north over George Parks Highway 3 on a long scenic drive. Again, we took in endlessly fabulous views as we traveled along Denali National Park, which features the highest mountain peak in North America, Mount McKinley, protruding proudly above the warm late-afternoon haze. With an elevation of over 20,000 feet, this majestic mountain can be seen for tens of miles around, and I remembered flying over that very same peak in full sunlight way back in 1965.

We stopped for the night in a small town, Nenana, on a big river fork where the Tanana and Nenana Rivers come together. The scene there could have come straight from a Jack Kerouac novel: a long freight train crossing Front Street and trailing an endless row of wagons; a huge old riveted steel bridge over a stony river; and a little bar in the shadow of a railway station building. The sun seemed reluctant to go down and the streaks of yellow light burst from behind the bridge giving its steel girders the appearance of the blackened carcass of a dinosaur.

It was all very laid back in that little town and our quaint hotel on the main street only accentuated our sense of having entered a time warp. The train departed with a lonesome whistle and the railroad men in their overalls retired to the bar for a couple of beers. When we joined them, Julie got all the attention. It only took a few pints of beer before she had become the pin-up girl from the workshop calendar with her long blonde hair, cute looks, and slim-fitting jeans; not an everyday sight around these parts. Her sultry French accent was the clincher and soon the booze was flowing at an ever-faster pace. They plied us with drink and started asking us the same questions we had heard everywhere else: Where are you from? What brings you here? Are you a couple?

And before we could answer they pressed another full pint of beer into our hands, which we had to drain as quickly as possible. Slow drinking was frowned upon around here. It was all hail-fellow-well-met stuff and it reminded me of my time living in Australia with my parents and in South Africa with friends, where the consumption per hour of liquids was of a tempo not unlike that of a gas-guzzling radial aero engine!

We were definitely not your usual tourist couple; we looked different and we had an even more unusual story. We were in Alaska looking for an airplane. That sometimes provoked interesting reactions since Alaska has a long relationship with aviation, so our story invited a lot of good-natured discussion. With a limited road

Crashed DC-4 at Nenana airfield: the pilots barely escaped a fatal accident when one of its engines caught fire. They managed to land the stricken aircraft right here and survive their predicament before the nightmare of a folding wing could materialize.

At Fairbanks Airport on the premises of Brooks Air Cargo. The legendary Roger Brooks showing me the burnt-out engine of the DC-4 that had made that lucky crash landing near Nenana.

infrastructure and remote settlements, the state was an early adaptor of specialty aircraft like bush planes that can land on water and ice or snow. Fortunately, in Nenana we were spared the kind of heavy booze-slurping contest we had had to endure in Tok. Nevertheless, by the end of the evening the locals were convinced that Julie was the reincarnation of Marilyn Monroe and the thought surely left some of them twisting and turning in their beds later on that night.

We had heard about a DC-4 that had crashed nearby and been salvaged and stored at the local airport. So the next morning I wanted to go and see that wreck before we drove on to Fairbanks. When we arrived at the airstrip I spotted a white fuselage sporting a big Douglas DC-4 logo. The plane looked fairly intact, although the wings had been separated from the airframe either during or after the crash. I stepped out of the car and walked up to the plane. Right at the front of the cockpit, where the pedals were, I saw a huge gaping hole where the front wheel had been ripped off and slammed back into the aircraft. The pilots had obviously been very lucky to survive such a harrowing emergency landing.

We took some pictures and continued our trip to Fairbanks, thirty-five miles further north. We headed straight for the airport, more than eager to see my "main man," Roger Brooks, the boss of Brooks Air Fuel and another legendary aircraft operator in Alaska. I walked into what could best be described as the perfect aircraft demolition yard, even though it was still primarily an airline that operated tanker airplanes from all of this junk. I met Roger, the somewhat taciturn owner. We walked around his yard and Julie took pictures of our interesting encounter in the most beautiful of weather. There were a few Dakota airframes lying around but these silver birds were partly fragmented and all had had their wings removed. The company now only flew with the Dakota's younger and bigger cousin, the DC-4.

The four-engine DC-4 can handle the fairly flat and open terrain in this part of Alaska and can even land on the hard tundra soil when there is no paved airstrip. I have not seen any other operator anywhere do that with a DC-4, a plane that has a payload three times that of the DC-3. As we roamed around his vast yard, I told Roger about our trip to see the crashed DC-4 in Nenana. He took me across the yard and showed me a blackened radial engine lying there like a big charred animal corpse. It was in bad shape, with some of the cylinders melted and the metal deformed. Roger

With the derelict Air North hulk next to us, Roger and I discussed the purchase of instruments and propeller blades from his company. Parts galore out here but no wing tips. It was a joy to finally meet the man in his "Yard of Passions."

told me that this engine had caused the crash of the Nenana DC-4 that we had seen earlier that morning.

Wow, right here before my very eyes lay evidence of the kind of havoc an engine fire can cause when flying at 200 miles per hour. The windblast at that speed can turn a fire into a blast furnace. Unlike jet engines, which are slung in pods under the wings, the radial engines on prop-liners are mounted right on the leading edge of the wing. This higher position was necessary to keep the large propellers clear of the ground. Consequently, a blasting engine fire undermines the wing's structural strength as soon as the exiting flames start licking along the wing's skin behind the nacelle. When exposed to a high-speed windblast, a fuel fire can quickly reach very high temperatures and cause the aluminum skin panels of the wing to weaken rapidly or even melt. That creates a soft spot in the wing structure that then starts to behave like a hinge. The weakened airfoil will eventually collapse and fold under the high wing load, pressing the wing upward. The result is almost always fatal. The aircraft immediately stalls or spins out of control and simply drops out of the sky.

This worst possible scenario with an avgas-fed fire is exactly what the DC-4 pilots had feared and faced on their ill-fated flight. When they departed Fairbanks, they were on their way to a mining camp carrying a cargo of 3,000 gallons of heating fuel. Over Nenana, an engine exploded and caught on fire. The fire extinguisher was not effective and the flames from the crippled engine were able to go about their devastating work unhindered. The crew made the one and only wise decision they could make—land immediately! This had surely saved their lives. They were lucky enough to be flying low over flat tundra near the Nenana airfield, so they were able to start descending right away. With the help of a guardian angel sitting on their shoulders, they managed to get down and get out before the wing could snap.

The whole story reminded me of a nightmare incident that I had survived as a kid when flying back to Holland from Indonesia in late December 1956 on board a KLM Lockheed Super Constellation L-1049, a journey that took three days to complete in the days before the advent of jet airliners. We departed from Bangkok in this four-engine beauty, nicknamed "the queen of the skies." With her majestic lines and very distinctive triple fins, this was the fastest airliner of the early 1950s. But she also had a darker side to her character. Engine failures and fires that could flare up out the blue. Many a Constellation had gone down in the past and quite a number of them had disappeared forever in the abyss of the vast ocean, possibly as a result of sudden engine fire or explosion. Our flight suffered the same dreaded mishap shortly after takeoff. We were only a few minutes airborne and climbing out when I heard a formidable bang, one that shook the whole aircraft.

I looked outside and in the darkening sky I saw flames coming from the outer port engine. My mum fainted on the spot. With three kids onboard, the sudden tension coupled with the plane's reputation for exploding engines was more than she could handle.

Port of Haines, Alaska. In the Lutak inlet, we found this stranded fishing boat and an old military camp now in use as exposition space for native crafts like totem poles and canoes.

The Wright Turbo Compound R-3350 engine had suddenly failed, but the flight mechanic was alert to the danger and immediately activated the fire extinguisher. Mercifully, it worked and the powder cloud suffocated the flame just in the nick of time before the flames started licking over the wing.

However, our ordeal was not yet fully over, as with our full tanks and a full load of passengers we were way too heavy to land. And there was no way of assessing the wing damage. In the pitch dark, we had to circle for three hours over the ocean in order to dump fuel from the tanks before we could return to the airport and make a safe landing. When we finally landed, many of the passengers were so relieved that they sank down on their knees to kiss terra firma. The next morning, we returned to the airport after a restless night in a nearby hotel. We saw the stricken aircraft and its damaged engine for the first time in broad daylight. With its nacelles removed, we watched while the mechanics disassembled the burnt-out radial engine, which was missing a few cylinders.

Now, fifty years later, here I was looking at the same kind of radial aero engine, also burnt out, and this one told an even more horrifying story, but luckily one that the pilots had lived to tell their families. I told Roger about my Super Constellation experience and we reflected on how hazardous flying with piston prop planes was compared to modern jet airliners. We had a fascinating conversation about his flying

museum fleet of DC-4 tankers and cargo planes. He was a bit of a lone ranger and extremely devoted to his vintage collection, but as a commercial operation it all seemed doomed.

I admire characters like Roger who try to preserve our heritage and make a living against all the odds. I have met a number of them on my travels and they all share the same determination and sometimes even outright obsession as they continue to struggle to survive in a time warp; one in which their vintage operational aircraft will gradually and inevitably turn into flying fossils.

Roger was not able to help me with any wingtips in spite of the impressive store of surplus components in that huge heap of junk of his. But what a day it had been; another magic visit to an ancient aircraft temple. However, I also felt sure that this would be the last time I would see this man and his yard because I knew that his company was balancing on the verge of collapse in its current setup.

HELICOPTER FLIGHT TO HEAVEN

With the Alaskan leg of our trip now behind us, we headed back east in the direction of Tok and the Yukon border. After a long drive through the endless Alaskan pine forests, we arrived back in Yukon and stopped for the night in Beaver Creek. The next morning we drove on to Haines Junction over an awe-inspiring scenic route with Kluane Lake on our left and the peaks of the impressive mountain ridge on our right. When we arrived, visibility in the mountains was very poor so we had to sit it out again before making our long-awaited helicopter trip into the Ruby Mountains. We decided

Driving along the shore of Lutak, we entered a natural zoo with seals, black bear fishing for salmon, bald eagles and one of the most beautiful lakes of the north, Lake Chilkoot.

to drive down to a small ocean port called Haines, a 125-mile drive to the coast that took us once again into US territory, 75 miles north of Juneau on the same sea inlet.

We went for a stroll along the majestic waterfront of this little town. We passed a stranded fishing boat lying like a dead whale on the rocky shoreline and an abandoned army camp—possibly a leftover from the wartime military effort to reinforce the Alaskan shore defenses but now being used for all kinds of local artistic activities, including the carving of totem poles and canoes. Later, we drove north along the bay and came to the Lutak inlet. It was there that Julie found what she had been longing to see: wildlife galore.

We spotted a few seals in the bay, and as we followed the winding road a man came up to us and pointed out a bear that was fishing for salmon. Fortunately for Julie, the animal was on the other side of the river and minding its own business and therefore did not pose any threat.

Everything I had promised her was here in abundance, in the wild, and clearly visible for public enjoyment. We saw a bald eagle and thousands of salmon trying to swim upriver. When we took the final turn on the road from the Lutak inlet we were astonished by the view that opened up before us: a deep turquoise mountain lake surrounded by very steep and immense ridges with snow-capped mountains in the background.

The search for the forlorn C-47 that crashed in January 1950. With our helicopter and GPS we were able to find the wreck in the Ruby Mountains north of Haines Junction, YT just before the mists descended and covered everything again.

They say that God created the world in six days. Well, on the evidence before us, by the seventh day he had obviously acquired some skill with all that landscaping and had decided to use his day off to create a masterpiece for himself—Alaska, his own private backyard with Chilkoot Lake as a garden pond.

I have seen many impressive lakes and coastlines in my life. From South Africa's Cape route to Maui's Hana Highway; from Albania to Vancouver Island; from Montana's Glacier Park to the High Andes in Bolivia and Peru. But the view in this part of Alaska and Yukon definitely ranks in my top ten of awesome, hair-raising visual experiences, the kind that can bring the world to a temporary standstill in your head.

The next day would be our last chance to take the helicopter flight into the mountains, so I deemed it wise to make it an early night and avoid joining the locals in their nightly pursuit of oblivion.

When we woke up the next morning the situation looked rather grim. The mountains were completely hidden in foggy clouds; there was no way we could fly up there. We waited in the hotel, had lunch, and in the early afternoon I spotted the first patches of blue starting to appear between the clouds. Time to head for the airport. I got so excited that I kept shouting at Julie to hurry up, much to her annoyance, as she tried to gather all of her camera equipment together. On the way, my thoughts were consumed by one question only: can we fly today?

The helicopter pilot, Andrew, had been phoning around and checking the weather forecast on his computer. He was the picture of calm—almost too relaxed—when we rushed into his office. After five minutes he stood up and casually said, "We can fly now if you like, though there is still some haze and clouds up there in the mountains."

I, of course, couldn't wait to go. Every minute that we spent lingering down here was pure torment to me. Finally, we stepped outside and saw that the sun was shining brightly in the valley but that there was still some fog around the mountaintops. Fifteen minutes later we climbed into the helicopter. I sat next to Andrew, and Julie, laden down with cameras and lenses, sat in the back. The rotor blades started to spin around faster and faster. A brief jerk and we were off.

Through my headphones I heard Julie shout in exaltation, "*Allez! Hans, on plane.*" We were off! We had been looking forward so much to this flight and up to only an hour ago had feared that it would be denied to us yet again on our very last day out here. Now, at the last minute, we were airborne and on our way to what I hoped would turn out to be the ultimate in Dakota Hunting.

We had to fly some 30 miles to the north over a mountainous area covered with pine forest and small lakes. As we gained height, the mountains became barer and soon we were above the timberline. At 6,000 feet we spotted a flock of white mountain goats. We followed them for a few minutes while they tried to flee from the chop-chop of the helicopter. The leader of the flock then stopped all of a sudden and

Close-up of the damaged aircraft that made a very lucky crash landing. The hillside was snow-covered and, after a powerless near-to-stalling glide, the aircraft finally must have settled on this hill. Miraculously, all 10 crew survived the crash, but their ordeal was far from over.

looked up at us, all aggression and proud anger and willing to defend his family against this monster bird in the sky. A golden moment for Julie and she snapped away taking the pictures that I had promised her in a setting more enchanting than anything I ever could have dreamed up for her.

We went higher and further over the Ruby Mountains and the pilot started to look around for what we had come for: a crashed aircraft. We were now flying at well over 7,500 feet and there was only tundra-like vegetation below us on the wide open flats between the ridges, displaying a most amazing variety of colors from yellow to ruby red to purple. Suddenly, we were engulfed by mist, but it faded away quickly thanks to the wind at this height. As the sun began to make increasingly bigger holes in the carpet of clouds, our confidence that we were going to find the wreck grew.

Andrew and I scoured the landscape below us. After checking his GPS again he suddenly pulled the chopper to the left, and there right in front of me and in full glorious sunshine lay the wrecked airplane! I felt the hairs rise on the back of my neck—this was our target!

"Julie, look, there she is!"

As excited as she had been about the goats, this would prove to be the highlight of the tour for her in terms of photos. Her reaction was loud and clear: "*Oh, Mon Dieu, c'est fantastique.*"

The bare-metal polished skin acted like a reflector and you couldn't miss the shiny Dakota lying there glittering on the rocky ground, the airframe almost fully intact. However, as suddenly as she had loomed into view, the aircraft disappeared again, lost in the flurry of mist and we worried about losing our bearings. But Andrew kept everything under control and pulled the helicopter gently up over the clouds.

When we circled down again the crashed aircraft came back into view. We were now even closer to the C-47 and I was able to assess the condition and position of the stricken aircraft on the hill. The fuselage was lying at a 20-degree angle with her nose pointing uphill. We circled around her and Andrew prepared to make a landing nearby on a higher mountain plateau, 200 meters away from the wreck. When he landed I stepped out with Julie and we looked around for the best route down to the wreck. Miraculously, the sky had now cleared completely, like a sign of welcome from the mountain gods. We had a staggering view over the surrounding mountains, which stretched out colorfully before us all the way to the horizon.

I approached the stricken Dakota with care and respect, as if I had just found the secret tomb of an Inca mummy. It was a magical meeting with that plane, the absolute pinnacle of my adventures as the Dakota Hunter.

The first thing I noticed was that the highly polished skin seemed to be in remarkably good condition despite fifty-seven years of exposure to the elements. The engines and nosecone were gone and the propellers broken off and lying to one side. For the most part, however, it looked like it was all in one piece. It was not as fragmented as most other crashed aircraft I had seen over the years, so the question

Inspecting the wreck I noted that the engines and most of the instruments were gone, but otherwise the aircraft was structurally intact and its aluminum skin still had its polished finish, looking almost "like new."

began to bubble up in my mind: how did they manage to land like this in such a mountainous area with huge boulders strewn around everywhere? How had the aircraft suffered so little damage? Something of a miracle by all accounts, as the story of this Douglas C-47B Reg.nr. 45-1037 (17040/34306) relates.

It all started back in January 1950 when a four-engine USAF C-54 Skymaster (military version of the DC-4) en route from Anchorage to Montana, and carrying forty-four passengers, vanished near Whitehorse. A huge search was organized that lasted for twenty-three days without any trace of the C-54 being found. On the very last day of the rescue operation, this USAF C-47B (military version of the DC-3) had been flying in the area searching for the lost C-54.

However, this search plane also ran into trouble, probably due to fuel starvation after the crew got lost in bad weather. That may have resulted in both engines quitting and an ensuing powerless glide over the Ruby Mountains. They must have had the incredible luck of being able to make a wheels-up landing on the gently sloping side of this mountain ridge. The mountain was covered in snow at the time of the incident and this had probably flattened out the uneven terrain and softened the impact when the aircraft hit the ground.

It is likely that the aircraft went gliding down at near stall speed. The captain, faced with the slope right ahead of him, would have pulled the yoke, and in a final attempt to avoid ground collision he probably tried to pull the aircraft's nose up and maybe even managed to maneuver the aircraft into a 25-degree angle, more or less equal to the slope of the hillside. A dream crash scenario, if there could be such a thing, in which the aircraft stalled at exactly the right moment just above the ground and dropped out of the air over one wing onto a soft snow bed, which would explain the neat separation of the left wing from the fuselage.

I am no crash expert, but it seems safe to conclude that the plane didn't make a long ground slide, as planes often do when they crash land, leaving a trail of sheared off wings and components. Another feasible scenario is that the thick layer of snow allowed the aircraft to slide a short distance without causing too much damage.

In any case, thanks to this miraculous emergency landing the plane remained more or less intact and all ten occupants onboard were able step from the wreckage alive. It must have been bitterly cold, however, in the middle of January on that windy, snow-covered ridge at high altitude. Thankfully, the fact that their fuselage had not broken up on impact also gave them much-needed refuge from the elements.

Their misery was not yet over, however. Sitting there in their cocoon having survived the crash, they still had a tough battle for survival ahead of them. It had been some time since their last radio contact and their position was unknown. With that in mind, and the fact that the DC-4 they had been looking for had not been found despite three weeks of intensive searching, the pilot decided against sitting it out and waiting for a rescue that might never come. Another factor behind his decision was that he knew that intense snowfall could cover the crashed airplane in less than an hour, making detection by search and rescue aircraft almost impossible. So the captain made the very brave decision to leave the shelter of the crashed Dakota and to start walking, armed only with a pair of snowshoes, a compass, and all the courage and determination he could muster.

He walked thirteen kilometers through the barren snow-covered mountains that we had just flown over on our way up here. Even in summertime, that terrain is a challenge, due to the many obstacles on these steep hills but in wintertime, the problems only aggravate with walking and orientation in that all-white, snow-covered landscape. The pilot eventually made it to the nearest road (the Alaska Highway, probably) where he was found, exhausted and half-frozen in the snow, by a truck that picked him up and took him to the town of Whitehorse. Without that incredible stroke of luck he might have ended up covered with snow and eventually frozen to death.

The next day, recovered from his ordeal, he led a rescue party in a helicopter to the crash site and the other crew members were brought to safety. The search for the original missing plane, the USAF C-54, and its forty-four passengers was called off and no trace of it was ever found.

The rescue team that arrived the next day on the snow-covered hillside must have been a very welcome sight for the 9-man crew, in a situation similar to what we see in this photo.

Later on, I heard that the actual landing spot of the crippled C-47 had probably been higher up on the slope and that the airframe must have slipped down along with the melting snow and eventually settled in its current position. The most valuable parts of the plane had been removed or stolen—the cockpit had been picked clean and most of the instruments were gone. The engines had probably been airlifted by helicopter in order to salvage their parts. The plane's nose cone, elevators, and rudder were all missing and one wingtip was also gone. The other one, on the left-hand wing, was still there and in good condition.

I stepped inside the cabin and found that, even fifty-seven years on, it was still very slippery due to the hydraulic oil that had leaked out over the floor. The first thing to look for in any crashed aircraft is the manufacturer's tag, but it was gone, possibly taken by the crew right after the crash. Despite the plundering by previous souvenir hunters, I found a USAF military canvas boot under the cockpit floor and an instruction notebook, both in good condition. I tried to pry them out and noticed that my fingers were nearly frozen; even at the end of August it was still very cold up here. A thin rim of snow had formed under the fuselage that obviously never saw the sun and therefore never melted. The severe cold of near permanent subzero temperatures, along with the fiercely blowing wind and frequent snowstorms, also must have helped preserve the skin in such pristine condition. Normally, the aluminum of a crashed plane loses its luster after a few years. Decay sets in quite quickly, eventually reducing the aluminum to a brittle metal that crumbles into a white powder-like substance in your hands. This wreck, however, exhibited no signs of corrosion, and it will probably survive in the same state for another fifty years or more, as long as visitors show it the respect it deserves, of course.

Julie called to me to come back out so that she could take a few pictures with the aircraft and mountains in the background. We walked around together taking in and enjoying everything around us and quickly arrived at the same conclusion: removing the wingtip would be a crime in this picturesque environment. The crashed plane and its location are like a small Titanic wreck site; not situated in the eerie deep of the oceans, however, but way up in hostile mountain territory. The place is a monument to all the crews and planes that have ever flown in search of the victims of plane crashes. Any further fragmentation of the remains of this plane would only diminish that tribute.

As we were taking in the view, we both suddenly sensed that the wind was picking up and that the clouds were moving back in. We had had our sixty minutes of glory, but now the gods, who had been so generous to us, had decided that the show was over; it was time to go. Our pilot had already returned to the helicopter; he was getting nervous with all the clouds moving in so fast and wanted to get the hell out of there. I walked slowly back up the hill but Julie was struggling to keep up with me. She kept turning around again and again to take one last picture of the desolate but magical sight below us. The light was fading quickly and a sinister-looking bank of fog was rolling in.

I suddenly realized the tremendous impact that this whole experience had had on both of us. It was like some kind of hallucination, possibly triggered by the memory of our epic Catalina voyage some twelve years earlier or by the fatigue and lack of oxygen.

The pilot was on edge and I called to Julie to hurry up. Completely caught up in her reminiscing, she barely reacted. Eventually, I had to go back down and retrieve her and I could hear her sobbing and breathing heavily in the thin air. When we finally got to the helicopter she turned around once again and begged us exhaustedly, "*Encore une fois.*" Just one more glimpse, please.

Clearly, we had both been through an emotional and mind-blowing episode at this magic shrine, a place that in our eyes at least was on a par with Stonehenge or Machu Picchu. One of those rare places where you can experience an instant disassociation from reality, as if your spirit is briefly allowed to soar away from your body, as if the whole world has come to a standstill for a short moment.

When we were back in the chopper we could feel the wind gaining strength and the majestic mountain bowl began to fill up with ghostly rags of mist. Andrew pulled the craft quickly up into the air. He seemed a little upset, possibly because of the turbulence, but gave a thumbs-up sign of huge relief as we climbed out of the clouds.

Despite the unbearable tension, I also felt ecstatic. The uniqueness of our encounter suddenly hit me. Our arrival had exactly coincided with the moment when the sun came out and the clouds lifted for a while.

In contrast, Julie was out cold, having fallen into a deep sleep on the rear bench of the helicopter.

ENCOUNTER WITH BUFFALO AIRWAYS' JOE MCBRYAN

Back in Haines Junction we packed our gear into the car and thanked Andrew for what had been a most memorable Dakota-hunting trip. We drove off and headed for Yellowknife. It had been another trip of a lifetime. Julie had a fabulous story and equally stunning photos, and I felt sure that I would return here again someday.

The next day, we flew back to Edmonton, Alberta, for the final leg of our journey through the wonderful world of classic aviation in Alaska and Canada. Edmonton is an attractive city with fantastic bridges spanning its river, splendid parks, and a quaint old city center. We settled in and treated ourselves to a drink or two after our strenuous efforts in the wilderness of the north.

The next day, Sunday, we had an appointment with the McBryan family, the owners of Buffalo Airways. They operate one of the largest vintage aircraft fleets in the world, transporting passengers and cargo to the remote Northern Territories of Canada. Yellowknife and Hay River are their operational hubs, while Red Deer, in Alberta, is their summer HQ.

We hopped into the car and drove 100 miles south over the flat and fertile Alberta plains. Again, it was fantastic weather, and when we got to Red Deer we went in search of the regional airport. Driving in through the gate, I immediately saw a fine array of vintage aircraft, including a yellow Douglas A-26 Invader, an ex-Air Force light bomber/attack aircraft. I got the feeling that this was going to be an exciting day.

Red Deer, Alberta, Canada was the location for our meeting with Buffalo Airways. A dozen vintage aircraft were at the small airport: many of the DC-3's were in a derelict state but the place had the smell of a large and imminent catch of desperately wanted parts.

Everything was closed up and quiet, but on one of the hangars we spotted what we were looking for: the green and white Buffalo Airways sign. We knocked on the door for a few minutes but there was no answer. Then, suddenly, we heard noise from inside and a grumpy-looking man opened the door. It appeared we had woken him up and, worse still, that we were not very welcome.

In a rather vexed voice, he asked us what the hell we were doing there on a Sunday morning. I reminded him that we had an appointment, which I had arranged weeks before with his son Mickey. He had obviously either not been informed or had simply forgotten.

I had told them in advance of my trip to Yukon in the company of a journalist who was interested in capturing the life of a vagabond cargo pilot. I had made no specific mention of wingtips or the name Avionart; that was all "undercover." This was the legendary Joe McBryan we were dealing with here, after all, and I was not yet fully abreast of his reputation. He had started his company in 1970 with the fleet parked here at this airport and another fleet of planes that was stationed up north.

Joe disappeared crustily back inside to his apartment on the first floor to freshen up just as one of his sons, Mickey, drove in through the gate in a big black pickup truck. In stark contrast to Joe, he was very friendly and confirmed our appointment when Joe reappeared, now dressed and shaven. We got to talking about Julie's magazine article and I gradually moved the conversation around to buying some surplus parts for aviation museums in Holland. He did not show the slightest bit of interest in my proposal; he wasn't even willing to let me look inside the big hangar next to the office. It seemed he hadn't fully woken up yet, but I knew that I had a good remedy for that: Julie. Charming Julie was the only thing that might help spark his interest. So while I went for a walk with Mickey around their premises, Joe and Julie chatted, which did wonders for Joe's foul mood.

In the meantime, Mickey showed me their collection of stuff, which included a DC-4 cockpit and a PBY-5A Catalina retractable wing float, all piled up outdoors, with more precious instruments stored by the hundreds in a number of containers. It was a scrap yard different from any I had ever seen in my travels as a Dakota Hunter. Maybe this had something to do with the fact that they fly a large variety of aircraft and, as a company, was much larger than any other bush plane operator I had encountered so far. The Buffalo Airways company offers a lot more than just bush planes, however. Over time they have expanded to provide a wide range of services. Their fleet now contains the DC-3, the DC-4, the Curtiss Commando C-46 and, until recently, the Lockheed L-188 Electra as cargo and tanker transport planes, and an array of amphibian planes, such as the Catalina PBY-5A and the Canadair CL-215 for fighting forest fires. They also own a fleet of smaller aircraft for passenger services and parcel deliveries, including the Baron, King Air, Travel Air, Cessna 185, and a Noorduyn Norseman, the rugged Canadian bush plane that is the pride and joy of every owner.

When we got back to the office, I saw that Joe had been defrosted by the combination of Julie's charm and lots of coffee. Julie had done so well in her role as pretty girl from Paris that Joe finally agreed to show us around inside his hangar. This was what we had come for. I was burning with curiosity; would we finally find the holy grail of surplus aviation parts here on our very last day in Canada?

The huge hangar was dimly lit and Joe kept the large sliding doors closed. As soon as my eyes had grown accustomed to the dark, I spotted the silhouette of a dusty Dakota at the far end of the hangar. Toward the front there was a workshop for their operational planes where I saw another Dakota and a Cessna. Again, a mountain of spare parts, including propeller blades, cargo doors, and engine parts, and shelves full of instruments and components.

I didn't miss a trick despite the lack of light inside the hangar. I peeked into corners, scanning the place like an owl, and all of a sudden there they were: a long row of wingtips stacked neatly upright high up in the garret of the building. I counted sixteen of them. Sixteen! This was a treasure trove of fairytale proportions.

I had to hide my excitement and, careful not to show any emotion, I let Joe do the talking. I followed him as he took us on a tour of his workshop-come-private

Weird aviation and automotive components from the past were scattered all around the premises. Catalina floats, DC-6 cockpits, cars, containers full of instruments and DC-3 parts galore.

museum and expressed my sincere admiration at everything he had collected over the years. The place was a kind of shrine to the 1940s and 1950s and was full to the brim with aviation objects and automobiles from that period. It looked like the film set of a wartime movie. Spielberg would have drooled at the sight. My obvious delight at seeing his unique collection fed his pride and made him show us a lot more than he had probably intended. We ended up in his private apartment above the office where he showed us his collection of memorabilia from bygone days: knives and buckles and lots more. There was even a Harley Davidson motorbike parked in the room right next to his bed.

"Do you still ride the bike, Joe?" I asked.

"Well, not that much anymore," he grumbled, probably not very pleased at being reminded of his inability these days to ride off when he liked. I stood there wondering how he had managed to get the bike up into this highly uncommon "Knucklehead Garage" in the first place.

I persisted with my line of questioning. "Well, why don't we go for a ride out together some day from here up north to Hay River? Then you can take me on a flight to Yellowknife and I can check out your hangars up there. We'd really appreciate that, and Julie would love to come along too, I'm sure."

The ride from Red Deer to Hay River is more than 800 miles and it would take us fifteen hours or two days to get there. Joe, however, clearly had a better plan, so he said dryly, "Know what? You ride; I'll fly, if you don't mind, and Julie can fly with me. More comfortable and better company."

Bingo. In the Buffalo Airways hangar we finally found what we were looking for—DC-3 wingtips hidden in the garrets, which Joe helped us to haul out into the daylight. The hangar is like a museum and is filled with vintage cars, DC-3's and many other aircraft plus tons of spares.

Joe, who has a reputation for a rant and rage attitude, was now really warmed up and with no shortage of jests and good humor he dominated the rest of the conversation.

These days he is a well-known television personality in a successful documentary series that is broadcast in many countries around the world. Acting is not in his nature, however, and in the series he is simply who he is: a moody man who also happens to be a dedicated entrepreneur and collector.

Eventually, Joe and I sat down to do business. It was time I revealed the real reason behind my visit so I told him about the work I did for museums back in Europe and my interest in wingtips. He didn't seem to care one way or the other, however. He obviously needed the money. I offered him a very good price for twelve Dakota wingtips and some horizontal stabilizers that he was willing to part with. He accepted my offer for the lot straight away and didn't even try to haggle.

It was a stiff enough price, double what I paid in South America, but here I was getting a dozen wingtips in one single deal in a hassle-free country with a perfect and cheap transportation system. No extra trips required, no export problems, and no military offering "protection"—that alone justified the higher price per unit.

It was the near ideal atmosphere for doing business with a man totally committed to his prized collection, and all done against the backdrop of a hangar full of relics from the past. Julie's charm had also played an unexpected but crucial role in the deal. She had turned matchmaker when I had found it difficult to establish any meaningful initial contact with Joe.

All in all, it had been a successful Dakota-hunting trip. I had found only two wingtips in Alaska but had reaped an impressive harvest here in Alberta on the very last day of our trip. Nothing short of a miracle really.

I also had the promise of a visit to the Yellowknife and Hay River facilities of Buffalo Airways at some point in the future. As an added bonus, Julie had had the time of her life and had ended up with a story and photos the likes of which she could only have dreamed of a week earlier.

Julie's charm offensive helped nudge Joe McBryan in the right direction with regards to my business proposals. We struck a deal in the end and everyone was happy that we had been able to round off our Alaska and Yukon trip in such a satisfying manner.

Before we parted, she said to me, "*L'aventure se prolonge bientot, Hans?*" Though I couldn't give her an immediate answer, not knowing yet what adventures lay in store for me, her question brought to mind a song that my parents used to play on lazy Sunday afternoons back in Borneo. A song sung by the legendary Doris Day, half in English, half in French:

Que sera, sera, whatever will be, will be.

The future's not ours to see.

Que sera, sera.

CHAPTER 10

Colombia II

Bats out of Hell

After Axel and I returned from our trips to Madagascar and Phuket we had shot miles of footage for the production of a documentary film of our expeditions, but in all honesty it showed more failures than anything else. We didn't have one single inch of film showing the score of a trophy in the shape of a Dakota wingtip. Not necessarily detrimental to the film but definitely bad for business, as all the time and money we had spent on those trips had been more or less in vain from a commercial point of view.

Therefore, we decided that the time was ripe for another visit to Colombia in order to compensate, hopefully, for the poor score of wingtips from our previous trips.

Early in 2009 Axel and I flew to Bogota, Colombia, from where we would travel on to Villavicencio. This was my third time visiting "DC-3 Heaven." I had first come here in 2006, and later in early 2008. During that second visit, I found that the war-ridden country had normalized somewhat and I was able to find six wingtips that I bought from my local "parts locator," John Montoya, who had stored them at his Air Colombia depot at Villavicencio's La Vanguardia airport.

Realizing that the transportation of only six wingtips in a 20-foot sea container would be an extremely expensive affair, I needed to find more wingtips on this third visit before even considering arranging container transport to Europe. With the country's bad reputation for drug smuggling, any kind of export from this narco-infested country is a most complicated affair, one that involves lengthy procedures for permits and stringent checks at customs.

In my search for more wingtips, I was prepared to look further than the Villavicencio area alone, as that region had already been scoured by my locator. I had been given a tip about a derelict Dakota in a jungle town called Leticia, a romantic name for a Wild West–like outpost in the southernmost point of the Colombian Amazon region. Soon I was onboard a flight to this busy little town located on the humongous Amazon River, right where the Peruvian, Brazilian, and Colombian borders meet. The neighboring Brazilian town is Tabatinga, with an open border between the two villages, and Peru is on the other side of the river. Hundreds of small boats and canoes crisscross that vast stretch of water every day and one can only imagine the amount of illegal border crossing that goes on out there.

The big American lorry and the Dakota side-by-side battling for the same freight to transport. In many places, the Dakota lost out due to improved road infrastructure but here in Southern Colombia the conditions are more difficult and the distances immense, meaning that the DC-3 can survive and even thrive.

On the waterfront, there was a hectic floating fish market boasting everything from the common pike to savage-looking piranhas, rays, sharks, and other monsters, all of which were still alive and flapping fiercely about with their fins.

Smuggler's Paradise was the appropriate name for the local bar at the border where I ended up for a coffee. It was full of locals who plied their trade in luxury goods, which included everything from flat screens to washing machines, all brought in by canoe. In the bar I met up with the man who would be my guide in this hornet's nest. I can usually handle Wild West scenarios on my own, but crossing a border into Brazil was more complicated here because of the Portuguese language. After having settled on a fee, we rode out by taxi to Tabatinga airport in a torrential downpour so heavy that the cars had to stop regularly, their windshield wipers useless in the face of the deluge. It was as if the river had suddenly decided to flow above us and tons of water washed over our taxi. "It rains fishes," was my guide's dry remark, while we were stuck in the meanest carwash I had ever seen, free of charge.

At the airport we met the director, who allowed us to enter the ramp of this

Tabatinga/Leticia airport. We found a derelict Dakota bearing a suspicious Ecuadorian registration number. The American pilots had landed here on one engine and said they would be back to do the repairs, but they never showed up again. Most probably an aborted smuggling flight destined for a FARC camp.

outpost airfield. With the thunderstorm now fading away, I suddenly spotted a forlorn Dakota standing there in the rising damp in a far corner of the airfield, painted in a retro burgundy red and with the word *Carga* written in sun-bleached letters on the fuselage. She looked fairly intact; only the canvas of the rudder, elevators, and ailerons was torn and partly gone. No wonder given the kind of pounding they got from the rain around here.

The director told us a weird story involving a group of North American aviation enthusiasts who had bought the plane in Paraguay with the plan of ferrying their trophy to the United States for refurbishment. However, one of the engines quit en route and they had landed here for the necessary repairs. I would have believed his story had it not been for the fact that the registration numbers on the airplane were obviously from Ecuador, a country far from here and certainly not on the route to the United States. So how had it ended up here?

The owners had said they would return for an engine overhaul and then continue their flight. But they never showed up again. Later on I found out how and why, and it most probably had nothing to do with a leisure trip being made by a few aficionados but more to do with a drug flight that had suffered the inconvenience of an engine mishap at the wrong time and place. They had been lucky to find a nearby Brazilian airfield where they could land and were able to slip away from the stricken plane with a good alibi. In any case, neither this Dakota nor any of its parts were for sale. Some years later the aircraft was confiscated and taken to the local wild life park for use as a gate guard and kid's playground.

The next day, the weather cleared and I decided to take a look at the river and the jungle around Leticia. A fast motorboat took me and my guide to an Indian village on a tributary of the Amazon River, where I saw the same pink dolphins that I had seen in the Orinoco River in Venezuela. In the village I met the chief and his wife, while half of the tribe stood around us staring at the foreigner with the curly blonde hair. The village reminded me of the more civilized Dayak tribal villages in the jungles of Borneo that I had visited with my father.

A man walked up to us sporting a huge snake curled around his neck—a boa constrictor or anaconda—that stunk to high heaven. Boas have a couple of bad habits, one of them being that they never brush their teeth after their favorite dinner of capybara, the local monster rat that can weigh anything up to ninety pounds. I can tell you that after a boa has consumed such a rodent, the ensuing foul odor escaping from both ends smells worse than a Dhaka sewer pipe.

Another bad habit of the anaconda is that they can grow up to nine meters in length (thirty farting feet!) and, to complicate matters, they get very aggressive when hungry. The female anaconda can grow twice the size of an adult male—a long, lean, and mean sex machine. Sometimes, after the deed, Mama Boa gets so hungry that she swallows the exhausted mating male straight after thanking him for the offspring; the masculine but midget-sized 'conda (a mere four meters long) goes from semen

The Amazon riverbank in Leticia. This huge river is a living space, transport route, sewage system and water and food supplier for the population. It is also home to countless and weird sorts of fish, eels, rays, caimans, piranha and water snakes.

On a tour of the Amazon, I met the "Snakeman" in a small tribal settlement. He was determined to hang his creepy pet around my shoulders. I was not really amused with that strangulation champ, as she started a bout with the master and almost won. Fortunately, the locals had more to offer, a young Jaguar and friendly smiles.

supplier to fast food in a matter of minutes.

In order to keep the monster snake under control, the man had one hand behind its head in a sort of permanent strangulation grip. The grip had the effect of a brake lever on a motorbike—the more you squeeze it, the less movement it makes.

Ever since my childhood in Borneo, I have not been particularly fond of snakes, and with good reason. Those vicious creatures have bitten me quite a few times, and now this man, who had spotted an opportunity to make some money, asked me to put the twisty and smelly snake over my shoulders for a photo! Not my idea of fun. Suddenly, as if able to smell my aversion—she was obviously not amused by not getting a hug from this tourist—the lengthy lady freaked out. In one swift motion, the predator's formidable head escaped from the master's tormenting hand and started to thrash about wildly, like a thick fire hose broken loose from its high-pressure coupling. The serpent was now able to breathe freely and it started to do what it was born to do: strangle the subject that it embraces, regardless of who or what that is— owner, rat, or mating buddy—and just squeeze it like a lemon!

It must have been a terrifying experience for the man seeing his hosepipe pet go wild, and the force of many more hands had to be applied to eventually bring the megalomaniacal worm under control again. In the ensuing wrestling bout, the snake charmer was bitten in the neck but he came away without too much damage, if a little shaken. Holy shit, I'd rather die in an airplane crash than have a creature like Mrs. Deep Throat here around my neck trying to strangle and swallow me.

VILLAVICENCIO REVISITED

Axel accompanied me on my third visit to Colombia for the filming job. It was his first visit the country and he was very excited about the prospect of diving into the

Taraira airstrip, a typical stretch of felled trees, flattened with sand from the nearby river. The construction of the airstrip is the start of a new colony, that in this case develops around a remote goldmine.

Amazon jungle. However, due to his American background and New York address he felt a bit uneasy at first, especially when he heard my stories about the serious risk of kidnapping in Colombia.

For reasons of security and in order to gain more insight into the intricate situation in Colombia, I had invited a well-known Colombian aviation photographer and friend of mine from Bogota, Javier Franco "Topper," to join us as our interpreter and guide.

When you arrive for the first time in Bogota, you immediately notice that Colombia is different from most other South American nations. It is not a poor country in the same league as Bolivia, Peru, or Venezuela. The economic growth rate of the country is impressive and the city centers display a certain level of wealth. In addition, it is well organized with regard to services and their road and air transport systems are efficient, too.

The biggest drawback is in the area of public security, which was and continues to be directly related to the widespread criminal drug trade and the activities of FARC. Over the years, this

Taraira, the remote gold mining camp near the Brazilian border, is nicknamed "Ciudad DC-3." Every single part of their houses, machines, generator, cow, pig, scooter, video, food and crate of beer has been brought in here by Dakota.

From Taraira, foodstuffs such as eggs, beer and milk are taken deeper into the wilderness of the Rio Negro on large canoes. The colonization spreads wider with the use of river canoes, now equipped with outboard engines.

organization has shifted from being a politically motivated club of idealists to a drug- and kidnapping-related mob of racketeers. They still see themselves as the inheritors of the greater leftist Latino movement that started with the Cuban revolution in 1958/1959. Positioning themselves as the new Che Guevaras of Colombia, they soon turned out, however, to have more in common with the likes of Pablo Escobar.

During my visit in 2006, the military regarded my presence as a nuisance that would only attract the attention of FARC or the drug lords, both of whom were always on the lookout for a kidnapping target. But the war on drugs had made some progress with regard to public security. I felt a marked difference in the attitude to foreigners outside Bogota. The military presence in and around Villavicencio and the Amazon region also seemed less intimidating.

Most of the military roadblocks around the cities and airports were gone. For years, Villavicencio had intermittently been FARC controlled and, subsequently, many of the Dakotas that flew there were engaged in the business end of drug and arms trafficking that funded the ongoing illegal activities of the guerrillas. The plane acquired a bad boy image in the eyes of the military and DEA officers in Bogota as the gangster's primary means of transport. As a result, there were frequent confiscations of Dakotas. In time-honored South American tradition, these seizures were often a bit too random and sometimes carried out without much evidence. Some companies lost their Dakotas to the national police and the military for no apparent reason, only to find out later that those same governmental organizations had sold their so-called drug-runner planes to other parties or had confiscated the planes simply for their own use, even before a fair trial in court could be held.

In recent years, a number of remarkable developments had compensated for the waning influence of FARC in this region. Aside from the massive influx of assault helicopters, crop dusters, and Agent Orange, which I had noticed during my previous visits, it seemed that a new era had begun at Villavicencio Airport. As a result, the poor reputation of the Dakota had improved dramatically and the aircraft was no longer the proverbial "usual suspect" when it came to drug trafficking. Moreover, it is still the only means of transport capable of flying in an out of the jungle with a decent payload of passengers and freight, so its rehabilitation also had a practical side.

Over the years, Colombian armed forces and pilots have slowly regained control of the remote jungle airfields. They now fly their patrols with more bravado and with less fear of being photographed. Unlike the situation only three years earlier, they were now willing to pose proudly with their choppers and guns.

But the war was not yet over and, up to the present day, all aircraft involved in flying in and out of the jungle are still subject to meticulous scrutiny by heavily armed soldiers and their sniffer dogs.

We had come to Villavicencio looking for the "DC-*tres*," as the Dakota is known here, and there was no shortage of them. It was good to see that with the demise of FARC operations and other drug-related activities, the entire province had opened up. Increased economic activity had led to a larger number of flights from Villavicencio into the endless backcountry of southeast Colombia.

The almost defunct Aliansa Company, whose owner I had had met in 2006, had since made a remarkable recovery with a fleet of three Dakotas. A woman named Johanna had taken over the management of the firm from the sister of the deceased former owner. And she was keen to do business with me.

On our first day at the airport, I introduced Axel to my friend John Montoya, the director of Air Colombia, a firm that had three very cool-looking Dakotas in their fleet, just like Aliansa. Two of the aircraft looked to be in good shape, two were in overhaul, and one was being used for spare parts or for a future project. In a further sweep over the small airport, we met another three Dakota operators, all running similar operations with two or three aircraft in flying condition. I noticed that all of them were working hard on overhauling their Dakotas and they obviously had an optimistic outlook with regard to the future of air transport to the *llanos* (plains) and the *selva* (jungle). Unlike what was happening in Bolivia with the improvement of the road network, this vast region was almost impossible to open up as the distances are simply way too immense and the conditions too difficult in the swampy rainforest.

Overall, the airport of Villavicencio is very well equipped to keep the local Dakota fleets in the air, and with remarkable results. The aircraft are all well maintained, by far the best I have ever seen in South and Central America. Almost all of them have a splendid mirror-polish finish in order to save on weight. A full layer of paint on a Dakota weighs around 200 to 250 kilograms, so if you skip or strip the paint and polish the aluminum skin instead you can carry that weight as extra payload. Smart thinking that generates extra income.

The airport also has an excellent repair facility for the radial aero engines, a workshop that has been delivering top quality work for decades now.

In this sound mechanical setting with high safety standards and adequate pilot training, the future looks bright for this seventy-year-old flying war relic. With the

San Jose del Guaviare Airport: not in the picture on the left is a huge military helicopter base that is supplied by trucks and DC-3's from Villavicencio.

anticipated boom in aerial transport into the jungle, the Dakota is likely to remain the dominant transport here for at least another decade, or maybe even much longer, since the turbo-converted DC-3 made its first appearance at Villavicencio airport in May 2014.

In terms of my own business, the yield so far of surplus or for-sale wingtips was meager. John Montoya had found six wingtips for me over a period of one year. Some of them came from remote jungle sites, usually taken from derelict or seized aircraft. In our desperate search for more sources we contacted all of the operators and their suppliers, offering good prices in US dollars, the magic note. It worked wonders.

One day, when we were back at Aliansa and talking to Johanna, she invited us to have a look at their surplus stockpile. They actually had piles with parts divided over three depots near their hangars. They took me to the nearest barn and I walked inside the oven-like storage space and looked around me, bursting with excitement. The place was literally jam-packed with instruments, radios, dashboards, overhead switch panels, and lots of other goodies, all stacked and piled up to the ceiling under a thick layer of dust and rubbish.

When we had finally culled my selections and brought them out for an assessment, I was covered from head to toe myself in a layer of dust that crusted in the sweat on my forehead. But I could not care less, as we had finally hit the jackpot after our two previous letdowns in Madagascar and Thailand.

Just as we were about to relax, one of the men suddenly remembered that there was another surplus storage area in the attic of the office building. We went back and scrambled upstairs to the top floor. The chief mechanic opened a little door that gave entry into the garret of the roof. There was no light inside but, despite the heat and the stench of our sweat-soaked bodies, I quickly caught the sweet smell of "precious" metal.

Helicopter pilot Rambo proudly posing for my camera while telling me the fascinating story of the nightly hunts for FARC rebels in their choppers equipped with FLIR (Forward Looking Infra Red) cameras. At night, when all the peace-loving folks are back in their villages, anyone they detect moving in the vast dark jungle below is marked down as a bad guy and becomes a legitimate target for the kill.

Three more wingtips emerged from that attic. Johanna decided to keep four of the best wingtips that we found for their own use and declared the rest surplus to requirements and thus available to us for purchase. Six more ticks on my scorecard.

It was a fantastic haul. Finally, I was now able to reap the rewards of my endless patience and persistence and the PR that I had built up here since 2006.

The improved security situation certainly contributed to the smoother circumstances for doing business. The locals, finally freed from the inhibition caused by the years of terror, were now more willing to deal with *extranjeros*.

So had all the danger simply evaporated into thin air?

Certainly not, but the new situation revealed itself when I decided to take a flight into the Amazon in an effort to compensate for the Dakota jungle flight I had been bumped off in 2006.

In Acaricuara, the rumor spread that "extranjeros" were on board the DC-3 and carrying a camera. Wow, it was like all of Hollywood had landed and everyone came out to watch the magic film machine equipped with instant replay. Fantastico entertainment for the curious population.

We were able to book a flight into the deep hinterland to previously no-go areas where, apparently, we might be able to track down a few more derelict Dakotas.

The DC-*tres* that we boarded was the Aero Vanguardia HK-3199 and this aircraft flew us around the Amazon region for a couple of days. On our first flight we had an amazing stopover in the small town of San José del Guaviare, which, weirdly enough, had a rather large airport. There were five Dakotas parked on the ramp, all busy with flight preparations, and one disabled plane with one engine dismantled.

After we landed we were directed to the military at a sort of *Control de Migracion* checkpoint at the airport. In a friendly enough manner, they asked us about our mission and what we were planning to do with our cameras. After scrutinizing our passports and equipment and getting us to fill out several documents, we were granted entry. Security was still at a very high level here and it would soon become clear to us exactly why.

Javier was a great help in breaking the ice and later they even allowed us to climb up into the small air traffic control tower. The elevated view quickly provided me with the answer to my question regarding security levels. In the distance, behind a huge white wall and out of sight of prying eyes, we saw several rows of black assault helicopters parked on the hidden military side of the airport. The dimensions of the setup were astounding and the message was clear: the aerial war on drugs in southern Colombia was now being fought from here, completely incognito and far away from the attention of the critical western media and the public.

By sheer coincidence, we had come here in a Dakota that was delivering food and domestic goods to the military camp. Not long after we arrived, another C-47 landed and parked on the ramp right in front of us. The cargo doors opened and at least a dozen soldiers surrounded the aircraft. They started unloading the food, ammo, and fuel onto flatbed hand-operated trailers. I grabbed my camera and walked over to the plane. When I was about ten meters from the men, I started taking a few snapshots. Much to my surprise, they let me carry on and even smiled; the fear of FARC was gone. These guys were now calling the shots around here and they didn't mind showing it.

I got talking to a friendly Colombian pilot wearing a military uniform and a black headscarf. He was small in stature by European standards but looked every inch the perfect Rambo. He was eager to talk to me and seemed both curious and proud. In Spanish-American lingo, he told me that he would be going into action later that evening. I asked him what his mission was and in a very open conversation he told me about his training in the United States as a helicopter pilot. They had recently acquired the latest night vision instruments and goggles for their combat missions, so from now on they would be engaging more often in nighttime operations against FARC rebel forces. Quite an amazing story unfolded over the next half hour. I was not aware of the presence of such advanced equipment in this war theater, including FLIR (Forward Looking Infrared) cameras coupled to guided weapons systems that were slung in side pods attached to their modified Blackhawk AH-60 Arpia III helicopters.

"We used to patrol and hunt them during the daytime with our helicopters," he told me, "but then they could see us and we couldn't see them. Only with satellite intelligence and a lot of luck were we able to discover a jungle camp or coca plantation every now and then. But now we fly at night with infrared goggles and cameras and we can see them but they can't see us. The tables are turned now. Anything that moves in the jungle outside the villages after 10:00 p.m. is a legitimate target and we shoot them all up like in a video game. Believe me. *Desde ahora, las Farc se han acabado aquí*"—FARC is finished out here.

It was a simple enough tale but very convincing. They got hi-tech weapons from the United States, and satellites, drones, and spy planes to cover the area and catch any cell phone or radio transmissions. They also took infrared photos of the coca plantations and the camps, and at night the FLIR cameras could detect any heat-radiating body that showed up in the jungle away from the villages.

Where is there left to hide when that smart detection system comes after you? Even in the dense jungle there are no safe places for a camp, a laboratory, or even a single human body. The US-supported missions became a very professional posse that never stopped hunting down its prey.

I asked Rambo what the outlook was for FARC in the future. Evidently, he hated their political ideology, but the worst thing was that when they lost the support of the public they turned into nothing more than a group of bandits. For over a decade they had pulled their country to the brink of civil war and had destroyed the nation's economy and any prospects of peace. However, they had become more and more

Flight to Acaricuara, with its rough airstrip where no bulldozer has ever been. Upon landing, we were all thrown back up in the air when the big wheels touched a huge mogul. Any other plane trying to land here would have crashed on that bumpy surface.

isolated and were doomed to trying to survive on the margins of the jungle. But even that refuge was now open to easy detection by the military.

What made enemy soldiers usually so hard to track down and neutralize in a guerrilla war was their ability to dissolve into the local communities, as had happened in Vietnam and Afghanistan. For years, FARC used the same tactics of hiding behind this combined role of partisan and peasant. But when FARC lost the support of the rural population, their option of playing the peaceful peasant evaporated. That, and the ensuing political alienation, was the first crucial turning point. From then on, FARC was forced to move out into the jungle for cover.

THE ADVENT OF ADVANCED WEAPONS SYSTEMS

For many more years, having to survive in the jungle did not present any real problems as it gave them the perfect hideout. In addition, they were able to generate income from the coca they harvested in that same jungle. But the second pivotal development came in or around 2006 with the advent of infrared cameras and advanced weapon systems. Their days (and nights) of glory in splendid and camouflaged isolation had come to a definite end.

I had one more question for Rambo. A year earlier, in March of 2008, the Colombian armed forces had launched an assault on a FARC jungle camp. The camp was not in Colombia but in Ecuador, where the rebels thought they had a safe haven hidden from the plague of helicopters and attack aircraft that hunted them down ruthlessly in their nightly missions.

They were badly mistaken, however, and fatally so. One night a small armada of aircraft and helicopters crossed into Ecuadorian territory, without knocking on their door. They homed in on the rebels' "holiday resort" just one mile over the border and caused havoc. Big time.

Taken completely by surprise, all twenty-five guerrillas in the camp were killed, including the organization's second-in-command, Raúl Reyes.

By coincidence, I was in Bogota at the time and saw the amazing television footage that showed the camp littered with a dozen or so naked dead bodies but not a trace of bloodshed or visible destruction from explosives or shells. So how did they do it? With no obvious blast or collateral damage, how had they killed the bandits? The press reports hinted at the use of an ultra secret weapon, which in turn suggested the involvement of the US military. After all, who else could deliver the intelligence, satellites, drones, and spy flights required for such an intricate operation?

And there was more. It quickly became clear that the Special Forces had come for more than just the kill; they also wanted the laptops of El Comandante. That meant that they could not just fire a Hellfire rocket into the camp. Though the use of such a weapon would guarantee a thorough killing job, you probably wouldn't recover even a single chip from the coveted memory sticks.

So I asked the pilot what trick they had used to avoid destroying the laptops. He only smiled at me, however, and said, "*Yo no se*"—I don't know.

Only very recently, on December 22, 2013, did the *Washington Post* confirm American involvement in this assault. One of their reporters, Dana Priest, wrote a fascinating article about the operation titled "Covert Action in Colombia, US intelligence, GPS bomb cripples Rebels." For more detailed background information and photographs (this article is a must-read) see www.washingtonpost.com/sf/investigative/2013/12/21/covert-action-in-colombia/.*

Apart from that GPS-guided bomb, about which I only heard much later, it eventually turned out that another weapon was frequently used in the night assaults on FARC camps. That was also a complete surprise to me, as we were not aware that a heavily modified WWII veteran had played a role in the conflict.

Half a dozen war-weary Dakotas, revamped as AC-47 Gunships, were put back into service here in an attack role (hence the "A" in AC-47). That Gunship was an invention first used in the Vietnam War, the war in which the Phantom F-4 jet had ruled the skies along with its compatriots the F-100 to F-105, F-5 and F-8. These aircraft were all extremely fast but employed bombing and forward-shooting techniques only when a big bang was needed. The jets' strafing power, though devastating, was not always adequate for close air support for ground troops in tight or awkward combat situations.

The idea was to have a slower aircraft next to the fast jets that could deliver precise and concentrated bursts of fire on one focal point. For that purpose, three Gatling machine guns were mounted in a DC-3 aft cabin. The guns, each one boasting six small-caliber (7.62 mm) rotating barrels, protruded from the side windows and cargo door and fired in a lateral direction.

During an attack, the aircraft rolls over the left wing and commences on a tight orbiting maneuver. The side-mounted guns are aimed by the captain over the wingtip sight and he activates the firing, while at the same time controlling the aircraft's banking and

Wherever you go now in Colombia, the well-equipped military are everywhere keeping the peace. They are steadily taking over the jungle with their helicopters, which enable them to undertake rapid deployment counter measures, all thanks to the help of some powerful amigos in the North.

turning. Pilot and gunner all in one. The result is an accurate cone-shaped firing field with the focal point on the ground target. With such a concentrated and deadly hailstorm, the aircraft can pump out a ton of ammo in controlled quantities into a very small enemy-infested area, such as a jungle camp. Moreover, the plane could provide continuous suppressing fire for hours on end, thereby preventing the enemy troops from repositioning or evacuating themselves from the scene.

This mode of firing could inflict a lot of lethal damage, especially in jungle settlements where the camps were built from bamboo and thatch. The bullets from these guns came with such spread that it was like they had been fired from a huge shotgun.

The small-caliber ammo inflicted relatively minor collateral damage. This advantage of performing only as a body-perforating tool was probably seen as perfect for the air assaults against FARC, where the missions were intended to achieve more than just the kill.

This legendary AC-47 Gunship (during the Vietnam conflict also called "Spooky" or "Puff the Magic Dragon") is operational here in Colombia in a hi-tech version based on the turbo conversion of the good old C-47. The Basler BT-67 is a successfully updated version of the Dakota with turbo props replacing the old piston engines, a stretched fuselage, and much better performance and payload than its older brethren.

And there was even more. In order to bring the old veteran aircraft back into shape for night combat, they upgraded the C-47 to an AC-47T (T for Turbo) and packed it with more goodies than ever before, including special infrared electronics and advanced avionics and armaments. The older Gatling guns were replaced with a modern three-barrel machine gun and a rapid-fire cannon with a long barrel. With this upgrade, the formidable "Fantasma" was born, the Spanish translation of Spooky.

The Colombians have six of these planes with a Forward Looking Infrared (FLIR) camera slung under the nose and the pilots equipped with sci-fi-like infrared goggles. The pilot's equipment and the cockpit interior bear all the hallmarks of a hefty jet fighter bomber, but in fact it is only a modified Dakota. One that is still flying combat missions at night at the ripe old age of 70!

This somewhat wrinkled but otherwise very fit "low-budget high-impact flying weapons platform" is much cheaper in terms of operational costs and purchase price than any other similar aircraft able to handle a payload of four tons of guns and ammo. This vintage design tail dragger aircraft also retains its big balloon wheels and low approach speed, meaning that it can land without trouble on an unpaved and short jungle strip; very handy when it comes to reloading and maintenance on forward-lying bases far from the nearest airport.

Every night, these legendary Gooney Birds go on combat missions carrying their horrific firepower. Flying low and slow over the dark jungle, they hunt down their targets using their night vision radar head. With their "blind" homing capability, they surprise their prey like a true bat out of hell.

Will this be the Dakota's last trick in war operations? Only time will tell, but for now it is filling the most deadly role that it has had in its legendary 80 years long history.

The air raid that destroyed the FARC camp in Ecuador was carried out in a joint operation. Both the Air Force (FAC) and the Army Aviation of Colombia participated in a complicated master plan, presumably involving the use of the AC-47T and also many other types of aircraft. These included the Embraer A-29B Super Tucano and another Vietnam veteran, the Cessna OA-37B Dragonfly. This observation/attack plane was allegedly the platform that launched the smart bomb—the Raytheon-manufactured Enhanced Paveway II—that inflicted most of the initial damage. Normally, the Blackhawk troop carrying helicopters from the Army Aviation would have had the job of dropping Special Forces for the mopping-up operation. Reading the official reports, however, there was no mention of any aircraft having penetrated Ecuadorian airspace. If that is true it means that the troops must have come over land for the cleanup and the search for the memory sticks.

This highly controversial raid over the border did the relations between Colombia and its neighboring states no good at all. However, the Colombian authorities were not particularly worried about the international criticism that followed their violation of the territorial integrity of Ecuador. They had a massive

AC-47T Fantasma (Spooky). This Bat Out of Hell is by far the most daunting model ever made of the Dakota and its variants. Seventy years after its birth, this old warrior now flies combat missions at night in hi-tech style. Note the FLIR camera under the nose and the Turbo Prop engines. The plane's most devastating component is not visible in this photo.

internal problem that needed solving, and if Ecuador could not keep FARC out of their backyard then Colombia was prepared to do the job themselves, with or without the permission of the Ecuadorian government.

President Uribe had driven this point home in an unprecedented military show of strength in order to let both Venezuela and Ecuador know that any sort of support or refuge for FARC from its neighbors would result in retaliation or a cross-border assault. Allegedly, both of these countries' presidents, Hugo Chavez (Venezuela, died March 2013) and Rafael Correa (Ecuador), secretly sympathized with FARC's political ideology, and they probably had full knowledge of their illegal activities. Although Uribe, under pressure, eventually backed down and apologized to Ecuador, his neighbors did not have many options when it came to counteraction. Their combined military strength was not even a shadow of the striking power of Colombia, whose friendship with the United States provided it with the necessary muscle to bully the bad boys in their backyard.

But the mission of delivering a real knockout blow to FARC's power and lifelines had actually only just begun with this particular assault. The memory sticks found in the camp were the jackpot and they were transported linea recta to the CIA and/or DEA headquarters in the United States, providing invaluable data on weapons deliveries, supplier names, bank accounts, and lots of other hot stuff. This data would unwrap the business end of a Mafia-like structure with ties to the underworld and the upper world, including the aforementioned leaders of Venezuela and Ecuador.

President Uribe was among the first to be informed and he made his famous "F..k you!" television speech based on the data acquired from the FARC computers. Announcing this incontrovertible evidence to the world, he accused his neighbors of acting as silent partisans in the FARC cause. In particular, President Hugo Chavez came out as the man who seemed willing to channel funds and advanced weapons to the neighboring guerilla force that challenged his foe, the United States and their puppet, President Uribe.

Journalist Ben Whitford wrote a most interesting report in The Guardian. Please view www.theguardian.com/commentisfree/2008/may/22/caughtredhanded

THE RUSSIAN JOKER CARD

Amazingly, only five days after the attack, the DEA was able to set up a sting operation in Bangkok in which they arrested a much-coveted target—the notorious Russian arms dealer Victor Bout, aka The Merchant of Death. He was said to be the biggest weapons dealer the world had known for decades and was involved in all sorts of uprisings against Western nations. A kind of one-man army, he had successfully taken on the role of global shit stirrer after the demise of the Russian KGB in 1991.

Bout was an ex-USSR Air Force pilot and ex-GRU (Military Intelligence Directorate) member. With such a background, he must have had excellent relations inside the Kremlin and he allegedly enjoyed the protection of his friend Putin. Armed with diplomatic status and superior intelligence information from his old GRU comrades, he seemed immune to arrest and was able to escape the clutches of every spy agency in the West. On the run for more than ten years, he had managed thus far to stay out of their hands. He had earned his nickname Lord of War with good reason and was proud of it, too. A Hollywood movie of the same name was made with Nicholas Cage playing the role of the legendary Viktor Bout.

However, the DEA was now in a position to spring a surprise on him. They had long suspected him of being the main weapons supplier to FARC, transporting tons of AK-47s and ammunition from the ex-USSR states of Kazakhstan and Ukraine over the years. Serious rumors had been circulating for a long time that arms were being shipped via West African nations into troubled African regions such as Angola, Rwanda, Congo, Liberia, and Sierra Leone, and also to Gaddafi, Charles Taylor, and Hezbollah. To supply FARC, shipping lines were used via Argentina, Venezuela, and Ecuador, and from there the weapons and ammo were flown or shipped directly to FARC forces in the jungles of Colombia, Venezuela, and Ecuador.

The question as to whether or not such a supply line really existed seems superfluous. How else could FARC get their hands on cartloads of Russian weapons and ammo for their massive military operations over decades in these remote jungle areas, far away from those weapons' country of origin?

The business end of the Fantasma is located in the rear compartment from where two hefty-looking barrels protrude—a machine gun with rotating barrels and a rapid-firing cannon.

The timing of the arrest of Viktor Bout is most interesting and unlikely to be a coincidence given what had happened on the other side of the globe. The war on drugs in Colombia had reached a pivotal point. The US supply of advanced weapons systems, training, and superior intelligence had led to the very efficient use of Colombian military air superiority, which enabled the dramatic extermination of FARC's armed forces and the ravaging of their camps and coca plantations.

By 2008 the guerrilla movement must have been on the verge of a total disintegration due to the massive morale-breaking air attacks that had killed their leaders and made many a survivor desert their cause. They were in dire need of a weapon that could keep the armada of night-flying spy and attack aircraft at bay. There was only one weapon that might shake off the "electronic" posse—the Russian-made SAM (surface-to-air missile)—and they must have tried desperately to acquire it.

The SAM was capable of clearing the killer bats from the jungle skies. As the FARC hunters started to fly at night with FLIR cameras, it became soon clear that the "shaking off" job could not be done anymore by the simple "short distance only" RPG-7 shoulder-launched rocket. While effective in Afghanistan's theatre of war in 'ambush' situations with attacks from close by, the Colombian conditions obviously required now a more advanced infrared homing weapon that could target helicopters and low-flying aircraft not just during the daytime but also at night in "blind" situations, as that had become the favorite playtime for the posse planes.

Viktor Bout, by now officially divorced from Russia, was acting as an 'independent' renegade gunslinger and was the only person in the world who could realistically purchase the extremely effective Man-Portable Air-Defense System (MANPADS) in numbers and make a delivery to the distant Colombian war theatre. With his political contacts, logistics network, and ability to bribe, he was the most serious if not the only contender for such a job.

Clearly, this scenario could become the United States' next and worst nightmare. Just as they were starting to dominate the skies over the jungle and the final countdown to FARC's annihilation could begin, a potential party pooper like SAM would have to be kept away from this scene, whatever the price. Big Fish Viktor had to be caught so that all the former Soviet Union's old supply lines, which threatened to screw up the United States and its allies in their South American backyard, could be blocked for good.

After his surprise arrest by DEA agents in a Bangkok Hotel, the battle to lock Bout up forever had only just begun. First, the man had to be handed over to the Thais, who then kept him in custody awaiting trial. Both Russia and the United States fought hard in the Thai courts for the extradition of this delicate trophy but, after massive political pressure, the United States finally won the battle and got their hands on Viktor. He was brought before a New York court in April 2012. After being found guilty, he was convicted based on the evidence of spy cameras and taps in which he had agreed to deliver SAMs to FARC. That delivery, which in the end never took place, could have killed many American pilots. This simple assumption was deemed sufficient as evidence by the court and he was promptly sentenced to twenty-five years in jail.

As it turned out, the DEA agents had gone undercover as FARC intermediaries and lured Bout from his safe haven in Moscow to Bangkok with a hundred-million-dollar deal. It was probably not greed for money but more likely the hunger for adventure after a couple of fat-cat years that eventually proved to be his undoing. In any case, he rose to the bait and was hooked immediately. The rather flimsy evidence against him would probably not have stood up in the courts of most Western countries, but in the United States it was enough to lock him up. The years of hunting him down had finally paid off, and just in the nick of time too.

For more detailed information read the stunning adventures and trial of this man, view www.newyorker.com/reporting/2012/03/05/120305fa_fact_schmidle?currentPage=all.

The Ecuadorian jungle raid was a huge success for Colombia, with Reyes killed and, subsequently, Bout out of action forever, both the executioner and the arms supplier were deactivated. That signaled the end of FARC's weapons supply and was surely a deathblow to most of their large-scale hostile rebel activities.

Uncle Sam's fear of that tiny rocket SAM as a potential threat to their air superiority was now gone.

A still from a sci-fi film? Guess again. This is the Fantasma cockpit interior with both pilots in combat mode, complete with goggles linked to the FLIR camera. They can circle around a rebel camp for hours and detect even the slightest enemy movement.

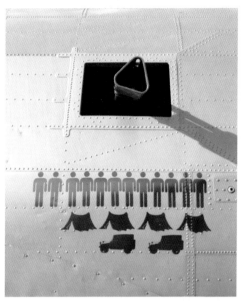

The scoreboard gives an impression of what they encounter on their nightly hunts. No fun having this ultimate posse killer on your tail, they see you wherever you go, no more place to hide.

KILLING THE TOP BRASS

The Dakota played a dual role in that awesome history of the war on drugs. The plane had been widely used for decades by the drug lords and later by FARC. Via Ecuador's sea harbors, such as Guayaquil, and possibly also via Venezuela's sea and river ports along the Orinoco border line, the Russian weapons came in by boat and were flown to the guerrilla jungle camps. On the flight up, arms, ammo, food, fuel, and chemicals were delivered by airdrop and, if an airstrip landing could be made, the aircraft picked up the rebels' narcotics and flew back to the coast. From there, the stuff could be forwarded to the user markets in speedboats, regular cargo ships, and later on even homemade submarines.

This cannon can pump out half a ton of ammo in minutes, while the C-47 banks and pivots over the target. The cone-shaped shooting pattern is controlled by the infra-red goggles worn by the captain.

But now the tables had been turned and that same Dakota had become part of the military supply system to remote camps for keeping up the war effort and controlling the countryside. Moreover, the highly modified Fantasma AC-47T was part of a phenomenal electronic manhunt system. The guerrillas' supply of new weapons quickly dried up, and with it went their ability to barter and transport their drugs. With no new weapons and no more jungle camp supply flights, FARC ran out of money and gradually lost their friends, their suppliers, their promoters, and the support of their international fan club.

No wonder, then, that they began peace talks with the government in 2012, first in Oslo and later in Havana. Before the eyes of the world press, they pushed a Dutch girl, Tanja, into the limelight, she being the pretty face of their idealistic group. After spending years in the jungle camps of the movement, she was presented as the new female Che Guevara in a charm offensive aimed at making the world believe that FARC only had sincere humane and political intentions.

However, our cutie Tanja has lots of blood on her hands, too, and her name is on a United States wanted list for terrorism, as she had been involved in the kidnapping of three US citizens. In a surprise night assault in 2007 on the camp she was in, her *comandante* Carlos Lozada was killed. She escaped alive, but her diary was found in the rubble after the attack. Blackhawk Arpias or AC-47 T Fantasmas had discovered their nightly hideouts and had let loose with their machine guns and rapid-firing cannons.

A similar scenario occurred in September 2010 when her boss Mono Jojoy was killed in a nightly Fantasma attack. The US policy of deliberately targeting the rebels' top brass must have meant that Tanja's life was in permanent danger. According to the local gossip magazines, her bed was a warm and welcoming place to sleep for many a *comandante*. But also an extremely perilous one.

In the heat of the night, when the Fantasma pilots were homing in on the faintly gleaming silhouettes displayed on their IR goggles, they suddenly came flying overhead: the funeral music instantly started to play. The fire-spitting organ pipes wreaked havoc and before he realized what was going on, *el comandante* Jojoy was lying in agony, slowly bleeding to death. Miraculously, his wicked guerrilla girl managed to get away unscathed every time, like a cat with nine lives. Some might have thought that she was better informed than others were?

It seems unlikely she will ever return to the scenes of bloodshed that she somehow managed to survive. It would be better for her to stay in Cuba, far away from the vengeful sentiment that one day will surely surface in Colombia against her and her comrades. Her "rebel-celeb" face has become the public face of FARC, as the real power brokers within the movement stay wisely out of the picture on TV reports. They let her put on the show. No wonder.

Many a Colombian will have wondered why the government has decided to engage in peace talks, when it was clear that such negotiations had only been made possible by the fact that FARC was now on the verge of extinction. They can still carry out small-scale attacks and kidnappings in remote areas, but their days of lording it over large parts of the country with more than 10,000 soldiers are long gone. So why talk now? Why not flush them out from their last hideouts and push them over the edge in one massive manhunt? It is a widely held opinion that such a

On the flight back to VVC: tons of river fish being transported in big bags, with the passengers sitting right on top of the smelly freight. The company had the foresight to provide us with a plastic tarp to keep our bums dry. The concept of a passenger complaints department hasn't reached these parts yet.

final shoot out would do more justice to the more than 150,000 victims of the past few decades than the puppet theater currently being played out in front of the media ever will. FARC is pretending that they still have the support of a large section of the Colombian population as a serious political alternative in a democratic system.

THE FLIGHTS INTO AMAZONIA

After our fascinating visit to the stealth helicopter base at San José airport, we boarded our Dakota again and flew south. For our next stopover, we landed in a small jungle settlement named Acaricuara in the southeast of the country near the Brazilian border. The landing we made on that bumpy grass strip was another demonstration of the astounding qualities of the DC-3.

When the wheels touched the ground, we went right over a huge bump that threw the plane straight back up into the air. Everyone onboard, whether sitting on the cabin floor or on foldable canvas benches without any safety belts, was thrown from their seat and then fell back down with heavy thumps and startled shrieks. Nevertheless, the plane landed quite safely.

The airfield was nothing more than an open meadow claimed from the forest with an axe or a chainsaw, and the landing was like something straight out of *The Jungle Book*. No bulldozer or grader had ever made it out here, and that simple fact only added to the profound feeling of having arrived at the real last frontier.

Tricky landings were a great source of entertainment for the Indian populace, but now with two tall dudes and a camera onboard it must have seemed like Hollywood itself had landed. The younger kids stared at us as if we had come from the moon. It was probably the first time they had ever seen white people and blonde hair. We shook hands with the chief and some other leaders; all of them were shy at first but later only too happy to pose for pictures.

It was only a short stopover and, like movie stars, we departed again in the same style as we had arrived with the plane bumping and jumping over the bulging *pista* ahead of us. The downward slope of the terrain helped to get the Dakota airborne in no time. The captain climbed higher and, as a special treat, he made a low fly pass over the airstrip for the spectators below us. They applauded and waved in delight as their weekly "Discovery live entertainment show" vanished in a soaring sweep over the "Green Hell."

Another flight with an Air Colombia Dakota took us to a gold mine settlement named Taraira. This was a nice little village on a river crossing with a small-scale gold prospecting business right next door. The pilots named it *Ciudad DC-tres*, as the Dakota had flown in literally all of the materials that had been used in the creation of that camp. After having flown in this mini Home Depot of construction materials, the furniture then followed suit. Later on, the mining equipment, the Jeeps, and the motorcycles were also delivered by the Dakota.

Any goods that were too big for the plane were simply disassembled and put together again after the flight, as was the case with the diesel electric generator for the settlement. Once the village was in operation as a mine and a domain for the laborers, it needed a constant supply of food, fuel, TVs, DVDs, and beer, and the frequent transport of passengers back and forth. Moreover, as the population grew there was also a need for small-scale agriculture and livestock.

Departing from Villavicencio, we were carrying a young bull as part of the cargo. But the bull was in no mood to board on a voluntary basis; I could see and smell his bad temper when he was being taken to the Air Colombia cargo ramp, squeezed into the back of a pickup truck. The vet came over and drugged the bull with a shot of a narcotic tranquilizer (widely available in Colombia). It did its job immediately; the bull was down and out for a while, though it kept on rolling its eyes. This created another problem, however. How do you get an immobilized bull into an aircraft when its legs are unwilling to cooperate?

They have a solution for that here called "push and pull the bull." It took fifteen minutes, four men, a long rope, and good teamwork, and they managed to do it without tearing the drugged bull apart. I was sure that the bull's tail would come off at any moment but it held against the pulling and dragging by the four riggers. Natural Kevlar tissue, no doubt.

Once inside the aircraft, the bull's legs were cuffed with a rope as a precaution. In the event that the beast woke up, it would not be able to stand up and stretch its

Another seized Dakota in which I found that orange wingtip on my very last day, with the added bonus of a yoke that eventually made its way to Normandy in France. The Merville Museum's C-47 SNAFU Special, an original D-Day veteran, was the deserving recipient of this gift (see next chapter).

legs. With a possible headache from the drugs and a throbbing pain in its tail, it would otherwise run amok and raise hell inside the plane. As an innocent passenger lacking the experience of a toreador, the last thing you would want is to end up in a bullfight inside the cramped cabin of a flying Dakota.

We stayed overnight in the camp and enjoyed a very tasty dinner and drinks at a local bar. Early the next morning we flew out again to yet another jungle settlement. The empty Dakota was now loaded with tons of fresh fish caught the previous night in the river. The smelly cargo—huge tuna-like fish up to four feet long—had been carried onboard by hand in big bags, straight from the sleek fishing canoes that lay in the river at the end of the landing strip.

The DC-3 takeoff was again a delight for me. Standing at the very end of the runway, the throttles were pushed to the front of the quadrant. Then the engines were let run at full speed against the brakes for a few seconds before the brakes were released and off we went. The airframe and engines rattled fiercely as if ready to explode and, slowly, the wheels started to roll. Quickly gaining speed, we hurtled toward the river over a knobbly, sandy airstrip just as the first rays of the sun were creeping over the treetops on the opposite side.

The pilots were very experienced, disciplined, and relaxed; they had meticulously carried out all the preflight checks and had kept two hands on the throttles from the minute we rolled out so as to avoid any accidental slip of the handles due to the hefty vibrations. The copilot counted the airspeed out loud—a critical factor in lifting the aircraft from the sandy strip before we reached the end of the runway.

The plane came loose from the sand long before the high edge of the riverbank. In a majestic curve, they rolled her sharply over the starboard wing, giving us a splendid view of the broad and muddy river. As soon as we were comfortably above tree level, they pulled the throttles back further and the sound of the engines became more relaxed. That is the Colombian style of flying the Dakota—very aware of the limitations of age, weight, and the critical full-throttle running time.

With these limitations in mind, they have managed to achieve a remarkable flight safety record with no burnt or exploded engines at takeoffs or any such related accidents in the last ten years or so. They seem to be well aware of the fact that these planes need to be kept flying for at least another decade or so. Therefore, the boundaries of mechanical overstress should not be exceeded during the average of three or four starts that these seventy-year-old machines make on a daily basis.

PREPARING THE TRANSPORT TO HOLLAND

Back in Villavicencio, I had to collect the wingtips and components I had bought and forward everything to Holland. The process of arranging transport from Colombia to Holland was a nightmare in itself and it took me more than two years to get it all done. The upside of all the endless delays was that I had to return to Colombia two times, during which time I managed to double my score of wingtips with the help of Aliansa and John Montoya. Finally, late one afternoon, we had it all loaded in a truck destined for Bogota. Again, I suddenly had the anxious feeling that I would never see the contents of the truck again. When I have put a huge amount of time, work, and sweat into collecting stuff like this, the paranoia of losing my treasure within sight of its final destination always seems to get the better of me. In countries like Colombia, you never have 100% control over everything that can happen, but that is an inherent part of any great adventure.

Once the truck arrived in Bogota, the thirteen wingtips and all the other parts I had collected were loaded into a container. It would take another three months before it was finally on its way to Holland.

On my very last day in Villavicencio in May 2009, one of the Dakota operators came to see me and we roamed around the airport making our last deals. He took me over to his premises where a derelict Dakota airframe was standing outside next to his hangar. No wings, only the fuselage and a load of parts stored inside that plane. When I took a glimpse inside I spotted one single orange-red wingtip in the hold.

In order to extract it from the chaotic mess inside, the man had to move a few parts out first. By sheer coincidence, these included an olive green yoke—the u-shaped push/pull bar that is positioned right in front of the pilots. Both of the steering wheels were still in place and it looked to be in good condition.

I bought the wingtip and asked for the yoke as a bonus. Actually, I was only really interested in it as a personal souvenir of my visit to the last frontier of Colombia, the

The current operations of the DC-3 fleet can only survive with a good safety record. It is largely down to the companies excellent maintenance of vintage aircraft and engines and disciplined pilots with adequate training. In addition, the local machine shop that is doing all the prop and piston engine overhauls has a good reputation when it comes to the quality and reliability of their work. All these efforts should help keep the Dakota in the air for at least another decade or so.

After 3 trips in 2 years, I finally rounded up my booty. Thirteen wingtips from VVC. It would take another year before they finally arrived in Holland. No wonder, documented "Scrap metal wings from Colombia " are clearly on the "usual suspects" list of any Customs Officer worldwide.

Amazon region. The parts were from an authentic drug trafficking Dakota that had been seized by the military and sold to this operator. I wanted to have the yoke to hang on my wall back home, as a trophy, but it ended up somewhere completely different instead, the story of which you can read in the final chapter.

Colombia will remain, for me, a very interesting hunting ground. With so many operational and derelict Dakotas around, it is clear that my future resources, for the greater part, will be found here, hopefully for many more years to come. I figure that when the last of the wingtips and other parts are exhausted in the rest of the world, this country will still yield up the precious metal that I continue to look for.

There are so many wrecks around in that jungle and hidden sites that I would love to trace and investigate, including derelict airframes on forgotten airfields and strips. Clues continue to come in from my friends, which they pick up from the local Indians, the operators, and the military. But the time needed for finding and transporting any wingtips found in these remote places is sure to become longer. More traveling will be required, while the odds on finding the grand slam of six wingtips or more are becoming very dim. Yet the challenge continues to work on me like a magnet and I hope to continue my searches for at least another five or six years.

That magic Gooney Bird has had me under its spell for more than sixty years now. One day, inevitably, it is going to be almost impossible to find any more wingtips or even a single cockpit door. But, to be quite honest, the quest to collect Dakota parts has become less important to me. The search for components was an interesting and useful alibi that allowed me to find and meet the plane many times over the past twenty years, but even though the end is now in sight it will not mean the end of my quest.

I look forward to flying again over the jungle with that iconic "Transport of the Century." It is precisely in such a primitive jungle setting that the Dakota engenders the intense feelings of bygone days, feelings that come very close to what I experienced so profoundly as a young child in Borneo.

Flying high with the DC-3. Amazonia remains the last genuine frontier in this world—a place where thousands of colonists are willing to try their luck. How the West was finally won with the railroad system and the steamboat in the 19th century, that role is taken here by the DC-3, the gate opener to faraway settlements, created by new opportunities in gold mining, fishing and farming. That surely makes an expanding market for Dakota's operations, as it seems not likely that the prevailing primitive conditions will soon change in favor of more modern aircraft. (Photograph: Javier Franco Topper)

CHAPTER 11

Museums and Projects
The Icons of Victory

In 2007 I received a request for the delivery of a Dakota airframe intended for display in a new aviation museum in Southern China. The buyer was a Chinese American businessman called M. Teng. He wanted to buy a Dakota C-47B that had flown over the Hump (Himalaya Mountains) in 1941 to supply the famed Flying Tigers of the American Volunteers Group that had supported the Chinese in the war against the invading Japanese forces. He was the founder and financer of that museum, he wanted to know if I could trace and purchase such a C-47.

Finding an airframe with a specific war history is purely a matter of luck. Tracing a C-47 stationed in Burma or India during World War II that had flown over the Himalayas is an almost impossible mission. If you did manage to track it down, you would have hit a real jackpot, the kind sought after by many museums around the world. Unfortunately, we were not always able to respond to every museum enquiry that came our way, as was the case here.

Through the extensive searches we had carried out over the years, we had built up a number of special museum connections. One such long-term relationship is the one we have with the Wings of Liberation Museum in Best near Eindhoven in the Netherlands. The focus of their expositions is on the liberation of Holland, and the province of Brabant in particular, in the summer of 1944.

By September of that year, the Allied air forces had made major progress and were in the process of preparing a massive paratrooper deployment for an assault on the Arnhem bridges. But the ensuing Operation Market Garden turned out to be a bridge too far in their efforts to invade Germany before winter set in.

Their war machine came to a sudden halt when the attempt to cross the big river and to conquer the bridges ended in a dramatic defeat. That battle was a serious setback for the Allied advance, as it took the pace out of their thrust and gave the Germans time to reinforce their positions. Three months later, in December 1944, the Germans surprised the surrounding Allied armies by launching a massive all-out counterattack known as the Ardennes Offensive. Desperately trying to prevent the Allies from entering the German homeland via Luxemburg and eastern Belgium, they orchestrated a breakout attack in an attempt to reach the port of Antwerp. In the end their efforts were all in vain, as the tank-led assault was crippled by fuel shortages and, within a fortnight, the German troops were on the retreat again.

As a worldwide traveling parts locator, many war/aviation museums contacted us for their special requests. It started with the search of wings, props and instruments and ended with the purchase of this derelict C-47 airframe which had suffered a tragic transport accident. As the torch man was coming closer, we could save this war bird for a better final destination.

Sometime in 2008 Dolph got a telephone call from a man who presented himself as the director of the war museum in Best. His name was Jan Driessen and he told us he was looking for an authentic wartime Dakota/C-47 cockpit interior for a new display in his museum. I asked him what he had in mind in terms of a price or trade-in. He had heard about our business from Dolph and knew what was on the top of our wish list. "Wingtips" was the keyword and that was exactly what he used to entice us to come see him in Eindhoven.

He claimed he had four wingtips that he was prepared to swap. So we drove down there and met Jan, an older man in his eighties but still very energetic and a smart negotiator. He proudly showed us around his museum, almost like it was his private toyshop, and we were impressed by its location out in the woods north of Eindhoven. Housed in abandoned military barracks, it was a fantastic spot for a war and aviation museum.

On display outside were two C-47s standing next to each other. One was from the Ardennes, courtesy of the Arlon Victory Museum, where it was used as the gate guard and billboard along the highway from Brussels to Luxemburg. After that museum had gone bankrupt, Jan had acquired the airframe. It was marked "L-4" in big white letters just aft of the cockpit and set against the olive green airframe with its black and white stripes—the "uniform" of all the aircraft that participated in the Normandy Invasion in June 1944.

At the end of Jan's tour we sat down to do business. I told him about my trips to Bolivia, where I had found exactly the kind of Dakota/C-47 wartime cockpit interiors that he was looking for. These were the original WWII cabinet racks with direction finders and bulky radios with lamps. In Bolivia, this stuff was usually removed form the aircraft and kept in a depot at the underworld site at El Alto Airport. One lucky day, we had walked smack into that jackpot of antique aviation communications equipment.

I saw Jan light up with excitement as he looked at the photos and, thanks to our mutual eagerness, we quickly came to a deal involving the trade of our antique cockpit interior against his four wingtips.

Sometime later, we received delivery of the long-anticipated sea container from Bolivia. Inside were our DC-3 cockpit and the refurbished cockpit interior parts destined for Jan's War and Aviation Museum. I phoned him to inform him that the instruments had arrived. He was delighted and we arranged a new meeting at the museum. This time we came with a van full of toys for boys. When we drove into the museum parking lot half a dozen members of the staff and mechanics from the museum quickly gathered round, more than eager to catch a glimpse of the bounty from Bolivia.

When we opened up our van and invited everyone to come in and have a look, there was no holding them back. Amid cries of admiration, they stared in awe at the collection of instruments, radio racks, handles, seats, yoke, pedals, pumps, and yoke. A near complete and unique wartime cockpit interior eventually emerged out into broad daylight.

The sun came out and the mood was joyous after sealing the perfect deal. Jan asked his chief mechanic whether the stuff was good enough for the museum. The man nodded his head with a big proud smile; it was better and more than he could ever have hoped for. They had acquired something much more exclusive than the four wingtips we got in exchange, but a deal is a deal, and the wingtips were in good shape and were exactly what we were in the business of looking for. We cannot actually sell instruments to our usual clients, only to museums and a few private collectors who then reconstruct the cockpits. We never charge money but rather trade for wingtips.

In the course of our business with Jan, we met another man from that museum, Roland Korst, and our dealings with him and the museum would continue for a long time to come and lead to many more good deals in the future. When Jan Driessen died, at the age of 89, Roland Korst took over as museum director. The museum transformed its fine collection into a more efficient organization, expanded the exhibition, and upgraded all of their war relics in a much-needed improvement scheme. It is worth mentioning that in such schemes there are always many volunteers involved who spend a great deal of their spare time on the maintenance of

Because of the prohibitive costs of transport, the museum in Best decided to purchase only the C-47 cockpit of this ex-Mosquito sprayer. The separation job took place in Florida under the guidance of expert mechanic, Kenny. With a hobby grinder and an electric saw he completed the job in less than an hour.

museum objects. I have met these dedicated people in the United States, the United Kingdom, South Africa, France, Belgium, and Holland, and they deserve our warm appreciation for their altruistic efforts to keep those wartime icons in excellent shape.

FLORIDA

In early 2009 my friend Bart sent me an email in which he outlined the possibility of a new search mission. He had received a message from an American friend of his indicating that there was a derelict C-47 airframe for sale in Florida. Its last operational role had been as a mosquito control sprayer stationed on the western coastline of Florida near Fort Myers. Through Bart, I was able to make direct contact with a man named Kenny, who appeared to be a trader and expert Dakota Douglas C-47 mechanic. He was the man in charge of the sale and was acting on the part of the plane's owners. Exactly what he had for sale became clearer when I spoke with him directly over the phone. He told me about an incomplete C-47 airframe with the registration number N-10005 that was located at the municipal airport.

Bart had also done some research on the history of that aircraft. A couple of days later he phoned me, and I could hear the excitement in his voice: "Hans, I think the Florida C-47 is a bingo plane. We have found some documented war history. It flew in Europe as a pathfinder aircraft over the Ardennes in 1944 and was involved in the Rhine campaign in early 1945."

Wow, what do you know: a Pathfinder Dakota! There were only two of its kind to be found anywhere in the world—one in a UK museum and another one in the United States. This one could be hidden number three. As with almost all of the Dakotas/C-47s I had come across in my life, we did some aviation archaeology in order to find out its date of birth, its service life during the war, and its commercial career after military life. The information we dug up came as a huge surprise.

The military kept precise records of all data, including date and place of manufacture, delivery to the services (US or foreign), and location of delivery. Later on, when most of the Dakotas left military service, they entered the commercial registers or went to foreign air forces, and many of those registers are still traceable. Evidently, some machines are more interesting than others due to their engagement in special, historically interesting operations.

Aircraft that were engaged in Operation Overlord (the invasion of Normandy on D-Day, June 6, 1944) are the most sought after because of the heroic emblem that these aircraft carried and will carry forever. Most war and aviation museums look for aircraft that have a documented military career, preferably complete with epic stories

Kenny's son Josh loaded the cockpit onto a forklift truck and placed it on a trailer bed for transport to their home.

The transport over the road attracted a crowd of spectators, who followed us in their cars to the next gas station: Showtime on the Highway. Kenny was also a teacher and gave free lectures in how to split an aircraft.

that can be linked to the greatest invasion in the history of mankind. Thorough wartime documentation lifts a Dakota from the anonymity of an unsung hero to the status of a movie star celebrity, and all the boundless admiration that goes with it. The cuddle factor kicks in and translates into increased publicity and more business for the museum or owner. The museum in Brabant, however, had its focus on a different aspect of the war—the liberation of the province of Brabant that began in the summer of 1944.

The C-47B N-10005 that we were looking at in Florida had possibly previously escaped the attention of war historians and museum directors because the aircraft had been operational until recently in public US service. We did a quick check of its past and that sounded interesting enough for me to contact the Wings of Liberation Museum in Best. I approached Roland Korst again in early 2009 to see if this ex-Mosquito Control Duster might be of interest to them. He conducted a more detailed search of the documented history and his findings were confirmed a few days later by intriguing background information from the United Kingdom. This aircraft had been built in July 1944 in Oklahoma City, delivered to the US Army Air Force (USAAF), and served during 1944 and 1945 in Europe as a Pathfinder and supply plane in the Bastogne airborne dropping operations.

Armed with this information, the museum certainly wanted to have that Douglas C-47B, but its budget did not stretch far enough to cover the transportation costs of the whole airframe. So it was agreed that that I would go to Florida to buy the

In Kenny's garden, the cockpit was dismantled further and hoisted from the trailer bed by an ivy-covered crane. Removal of plants was not deemed necessary, as they were all eaten by the crunching gears.

(extended) cockpit of the plane for the museum. In terms of shipping costs, that was a much more affordable alternative since we could dismantle it and fit everything into a single forty-foot sea container. The option of salvaging the whole aircraft for transport to Holland was cost prohibitive and unfortunately had to be abandoned.

Transporting our new find required slicing the extended cockpit (forward fuselage starting from the wing's leading edge) into five large fragments. The eight-foot cockpit section, from nose cone to just behind the cockpit door, was kept in one single piece and the aft piece was cut up like a pineapple into four equal pieces. Once in Holland, all five segments of the front end of the fuselage would be reassembled by riveting all of the panels back into place to produce a museum-grade cockpit display. That work was carried out with the help of museum volunteers and others—the only way we could get it done at a relatively low cost.

My task was clear and it was now merely a matter of working out a deal with the man who was acting on behalf of the owner, Kenny. Over the phone I explained my plan to him and made an offer that included the work to separate the cockpit from the rest of the airframe and the subsequent loading in a sea container. We agreed on a reasonable price in which Avionart would buy the main wings, wingtips, and horizontal stabilizers of the aircraft, with Roland looking after the deal for the cockpit on behalf of the museum.

I called my friend Axel, the documentary maker, who had previously joined me on my Madagascar and Thailand Dakota-hunting trips. Axel said he would fly in from New York and I would join him in Miami after flying over from Amsterdam.

The next morning we drove northwest to Tampa for our first meeting with Kenny. After some searching, we ended up in a typical Florida swamp setting. The man lived in an old single-floor timber house surrounded by a huge parcel of land. The front yard looked pretty big, too, and boasted a few palm trees, and when we walked around to the back we saw an enormous space filled with bulky Dakota parts, including two radial aero engines and a DC-3 propeller standing on a little truck. It all looked a bit like a surrealistic sculpture garden; a weird combination of shiny metal objects and big palm trees sprouting up from the lush green grass.

Kenny was an aero engine wrench jock by profession who also ran a trade in parts and worked as a locator, overhaul mechanic, and lots more. The man had avgas in his veins; he was much more than just a passionate Dakota lover. We met him in front of his house, where his driveway was partly blocked by a forty-foot container that had arrived the day before for the transportation of our goods.

He lived here with his wife and eight children, who ranged in age from an infant

The cockpit was custom cut to fit in this 40-foot container : along with the wings, horizontal stabilizers and other components, she was filled to the brim before being readied for transport to Holland.

to a 16-year-old son. Kenny had all we needed to do the job: the expertise, the tools, and plenty of sons to help out when required.

We drove out to the municipal airport, where we found a number of derelict Dakotas/C-47s standing in the scorching sun on the concrete ramp. A little bit further down the ramp I saw four more C-47s under corrugated roof plates and still operational as mosquito control sprayers. I found it almost unbelievable that these vintage transports were still flying missions to keep those critters at bay in an environment "where the mosquito grows so mean that their extermination requires a flying machine."

Florida had witnessed a population explosion of over 145% between 1950 and 1970. This miraculous growth can be credited to two important innovations: air-conditioning and mosquito control. Way back in 1964, Hillsborough County was the first to take the remarkable step of purchasing two military surplus C-47s for the aerial spraying of diesel oil and waste motor oil collected from garages over the swamps in order to kill mosquito larvae! Times and methods have changed for the better since then, but the rugged Dakota was kept in service and extended to form a whole fleet of converted aerial sprayers based at Lehigh Acres airfield in Lee County, Florida.

The Dakota is perfect for this role and relatively cheap to buy. With long periods of inactivity in wintertime, the standing still expenses are affordable, as it has low depreciation costs and can be stored outdoors. The county is still using them today, almost eighty years after the birth of the Dakota! The one we had come for was from the same service but had recently been phased out. The words "mosquito control" were painted on the fuselage and on the wings in a faded orange color. The airframe was incomplete, with its wings, wheels, and engines removed, and the plane's cabin interior was stripped to the bone.

Most remarkably, the cockpit featured the authentic black to green interior of wartime and it looked fairly complete. The layout of the instruments and dashboards was as near to authentic military standards as could be and had not been modernized all that much. I gazed around in amazement; this was exactly what we were looking for, and the cockpit interior was more complete than any I had ever seen before in derelict Dakotas. Cockpits are normally swiftly cannibalized by operators or looted by souvenir hunters when the aircraft is left to stand derelict at open airports or out in fields. Usually, because all of the instruments and hardware have been taken out, it takes years to collect all the missing bits and pieces that make up these old machines.

This one was a remarkable exception, but why? Maybe because the airport was well guarded and the aircraft had only recently been phased out of active service. I looked at Kenny and asked him why this one was so complete. Not a man of many words, he said something like, "Don't ask me why boy, just grab the opportunity and enjoy."

We drove from his home to the airport, carrying some tools in the back. Not the sort of heavy tools that you would expect for the job of splitting a bulky aircraft into

This cockpit interior might look dilapidated but it is quasi complete and boasts many vintage instruments. Never before during my previous expeditions had I seen such an intact cockpit for sale. Usually they have been ravaged by souvenir hunters or operators who cannibalize them to keep other DC-3's operational.

pieces, however. Instead he had brought along a simple electric grinder with a small circular disc and a reciprocating saw with a bent blade.

"Hey Kenny, are we going to pick up the heavy tools at the rental shop?"

"No, I can do it with what I have here. Done it a dozen times before."

Okay. I was now very curious to see how he was going to handle such a big job with his tiny tools. I would soon find out; the man was full of surprises.

He and his eldest son Josh were a terrific team and knew exactly what they were doing. Once on the platform, Josh drove up in a heavy forklift on loan from the airport facilities garage and lifted the tail of the immobilized airframe. They then placed empty oil drums under the rear end of the fuselage in order to level off the Dakota to a near horizontal position. Next, the forklift was maneuvered under the cockpit carrying a makeshift wooden cradle on its forks and Josh carefully raised it up against the lower skin panels. With Axel filming everything, Kenny went inside and started to attack the outer skin of the fuselage with the reciprocal saw. He worked on a cross-sectional cut just in front of the leading edge of the main wing. The aluminum skin plating on a Dakota is only 0.75 mm thick and the saw blade sliced through it as if it was made of cardboard.

However, the stringers and the reinforced parts are much thicker and the old electric saw ran red hot before eventually cutting out altogether. Kenny simply switched to the disc grinder and before we knew it he had done all of the cutting around the fuselage, scalping the front end from the rest of the airframe. Josh lifted the sawn-off front part up on the forks and drove it carefully away from the rest of the plane. The separation had taken less then forty-five minutes and had been done by two men armed only with a simple disc grinder and a broken saw. We gazed at it, seriously impressed by the dexterity of father and son in this ultra-low-budget Dakota cockpit amputation job. Bravo!

Next the cockpit was strapped tightly onto a trailer bed. Towing it behind Kenny's weary red truck, we drove over the highway back to Kenny's place in order to finish the job in his front garden. With that exotic and conspicuous-looking lump of aircraft behind us on our trailer, we had all the attention of the highway traffic around us. We pulled over at a gas station and half a dozen of cars followed suit to investigate our fairground attraction. It took almost an hour before Kenny had explained it all to the spectators who had stopped to see for themselves the magic of an old warrior cockpit.

We arrived at Kenny's home with our prominent cargo on the trailer and Kenny went off to prepare for the further fragmentation of the cockpit into smaller panels that would fit inside the container. This gave me some time to take a good look around in his sculpture garden. Standing among the many bulky components littered around was a wooden house, once intended for use as a guesthouse, which was now packed with smaller Dakota airframe and wing parts, engine cylinders, wheels, and stabilizers. It looked like a complete aircraft had been taken apart here and all of its components then laid out in an exploded view.

Clearly, this was Kenny's world. The wings and wingtips of the C-47 that they had decapitated earlier that week from the airframe had all been stored in here. They were all in good condition and I decided to buy them as part of the deal for my own Avionart business.

To get the front fuselage to fit into the container, Kenny made another cross-sectional cut halfway. This second cut separated the front part of the cockpit at the point where it tapers off to a smaller diameter. The wider C-47 fuselage section, starting after the cockpit door, has a diameter of more than eight feet, so it had to be sliced up to get it to fit inside the container. Kenny did a perfect job; he was a master slicer.

Meanwhile, his son Josh had started up an old rusty hoist on a trailer bed; I could hardly believe that it still worked as a crane. An old Chevy engine mounted on the trailer kicked into life after some lubrication, a battery change, and a serious hammer-wrenching job. At the first wheeze, white smoke blew out of the greasy exhaust pipe but then quickly faded away. Josh maneuvered the crane trailer into the space between

Upon arrival in Holland, the Geiger counter on the table went berserk. Totally flabbergasted, I watched the beeping gauge, not understanding what had caused this nuclear Chernobyl blip. The source turned out to be five instruments/switches made from those green light-emitting phosphorous parts.

the flatbed trailer and the sea container. The heavy front section of our cockpit, which was to be kept intact as one single piece, had to be hoisted by the rusty cable winch on the crane. There were weeds growing all over this homemade Mad Max–type machine, but prior removal of the lush ivy vegetation was deemed unnecessary. Most of it was simply ground up and eaten by the winch, clutch gears, and hoist cable as soon as the machine started running.

A sort of green juice started oozing out from under the winch; not to worry, Josh said, liquid weed is environment-friendly stuff. He was very experienced with the handles, and he maneuvered the cockpit, dangling precariously on the cable, in through the opening of the container. Kenny and I then pushed it deeper into the tunnel all the way down to the end, a distance of forty feet, with just two old skateboards carrying the weight of the cockpit. Amazingly, they both stayed intact. Throughout the job their motto remained simple: low budget, great skills, few tools, many hands.

The container's interior was hot and humid; with the Florida sun burning on it all day it was now as hot as the fires of hell inside. As we pushed the bulky cargo inside, trying to balance it on the tiny skateboard wheels, we became completely

With all hurdles finally taken, and escorted by my friends on their WWII Harley's and Jeeps, we arrived in Brabant at the Wings of Liberation Museum to deliver the cockpit to its final destination.

soaked in sweat and were in dire need of a drink or two. Ma and all the other kids duly attended to all our liquid needs. Everyone had a task in this operation; only the baby slept on, blissfully unaware.

Later, the wings and wingtips were added, and at 10:00 p.m. we were finally able to lock the doors of the container. We had worked all day long and into the evening without a break, even for dinner. We had managed to complete the fuselage separation at the airport, transport everything back to the yard, slice up the cockpit, and load the container all in one single day. Amazed, tired, thirsty, and hungry—and above all satisfied—Kenny threw a little celebration party in the house with the whole family. I paid the money due and thanked him and his family for the terrific work they had done for us. It had been a memorable day with a remarkable family. I had enjoyed being with them and appreciated the simple work methods used by Kenny, a genuinely inventive wrench man and extremely hard worker.

Back home in Holland, we anticipated the arrival of the Florida container some three weeks later. The unloading of the cockpit from the container onto a truck bed was executed with all of us standing around. A final routine check of customs was then carried out in order to acquire the documents needed to release the cargo from the depot.

However, as soon as the cockpit emerged from the rear end of the container a serious problem showed up on the Geiger counter. For some reason, the radiation levels were excessively high. Customs called in the help of the "Duke of the Nuke," a specialist armed with Geiger counters mounted on long rods. The "Duke" looked uncannily like the weird professor in the movie *Back to the Future.*

The minute he approached the container in which the cockpit was stowed, all his counters started buzzing and beeping like he was walking into the Fukushima power plant after the tsunami. Totally flabbergasted, the man looked at me with a typical nerd's expression in his eyes. I could read the question on his mind: "What the hell have you got in there that could upset my babies so much?"

The ensuing search revealed that a couple of the instruments contained a greenish phosphorous light-emitting material in their dials that were the source of the high rates of radiation. The whole cockpit dashboard had to be disassembled in order to isolate the guilty instruments. In the end, only five lousy vintage gauges were seized by customs and tagged as dangerous for public health; no joke. We watched in horror as the rare WWII artificial horizon instrument and a few other gauges were placed in special bags and sent off for controlled destruction, like nuclear waste.

The next time you sit in a Dakota cockpit with an original artificial horizon in front of you, you had better wear your radiation-proof lead vest if you want to protect your wing nuts against radiation damage.

With all that eventually cleared up, our newly christened "Chernobyl Cockpit" was finally ready to be transported to Eindhoven. In the company of the Classic Harley Davidson Club on their wartime Liberators and riding in an authentic 1943 Willys Jeep, we accompanied the trailer to Best for a short handover ceremony at the museum. The museum volunteers and staff, under the guidance of Roland Korst and Bart Nopper, then spent the next six months working on it. First, to put the fuselage parts (which had been separated in Florida) back together to make a solid cockpit and, second, to restore the whole piece to museum-grade quality, ready for public display.

On the weekend of April 3 and 4, 2010, the Pathfinder Cockpit was officially unveiled at the museum in Best. Bart and I attended the ceremony along with the usual local dignitaries. Most interesting was the encounter I had during this ceremony with a charming American woman from Florida. Her name was Mrs. Karen Bobilya and she turned out to be the daughter of the wartime navigator of this very same Douglas C-47B with the military registration number 43-48266, US 9th Air Force. The aircraft had been in service with the 4th Troop Carrier Pathfinder Squadron of the legendary 101st Airborne Division in December 1944.

Pathfinders were a special airborne group. With their own aircraft and a team of selected paratroopers, they flew ahead of the main force of paratroopers that followed

The cockpit restored to its original wartime configuration. During the ceremony, I had a memorable meeting with the daughter of the navigator of this Pathfinder C-47: Mrs. Karin Gerni-Bobilya. She had brought her father's leather wartime briefcase as a gift, which was finally reunited with the aircraft after 65 years!

an hour later. These pathfinders paved the way through precision drops over the preselected terrain in order to put in place navigation equipment for those following behind them. Transponders, called Eureka, were activated at the locations and the flying armada had receivers (Rebecca) on board that homed in on the transponder's radio signal. With this system, the number of errors in droppings could be reduced substantially, saving lives and equipment that in the case of a missed drop often ended up in hands of the enemy.

This C-47, with Karen's father Claude M. Bobilya on board as a navigator, flew a special mission in December 1944 over Bastogne in eastern Belgium. The 101st Airborne troops were isolated and beleaguered in this town during the Ardennes Offensive and in dire need of supplies of food, medication, fuel, and ammunition.

In one of the low passes flown by this aircraft back on December 23, 1944, a small-caliber shot from a rifle entered the fuselage and went through the radio compartment behind the pilots. Amazingly, we had been able to find the original battle damage report of this incident, which says, "Aircraft 3-48266; Small-caliber bullet through Para rack, belly of aircraft and into radio compartment. Very slight damage."

After reading this, the very first thing I did was to check for a (patched) bullet

Unfortunately, her father died one year before. This aircraft was found thanks to the help of my friend Bart Nopper, who had a leading role in both the finding and restoration of this unique war relic. This report published in the Journal Gazette contains full details of the Claude Bobilya story.

hole in the lower right-hand front side of the fuselage. Much to our delight, we found that little patch exactly where the radio rack had once been located; the bullet hole was still there! It could easily have hit the navigator or radio operator, who were seated only a foot or so from the rack.

Imagine: you are sitting in your navigator's seat behind the pilots on a secret night mission. The aircraft goes into a descent, preparing for a low-altitude supply-dropping mission. There is enemy flak all around the aircraft. Each crew member is extremely tense, and right in the middle of that low pass over enemy territory the radio suddenly fails. Must have been a mysterious incident for the radioman, but he was fortunate that it was only the radio that got the bullet.

The same aircraft soldiered on in the war effort and was later engaged in Operation Varsity, the crossing of the Rhine at Wesel in March 1945, just six weeks before the end of the war.

The official documents that emerged provided a rare and detailed insight into a typical paratrooper flight in those days. On these flights, the plane carried five crewmembers, sixteen paratroopers, and a ton of battle equipment that had to be dropped using special red-tagged parachutes in bundles, mostly containing mortars, machine guns, and ammo.

Mrs. Karen Bobilya had come over to Holland with her husband for the inauguration of the aircraft cockpit that her father had flown in some sixty-six years earlier. He had died in January 2009, but his daughter had been found and contacted, and she had brought with her a most remarkable present for the museum. Her father had kept a small leather navigator's case from his wartime days stored in the attic of his son's house. This fitting souvenir is now on display in the museum, just in front of the war relic cockpit.

A few things make this story very remarkable:

Her father died in the same year that the C-47 came to the end of its existence as an aircraft. They had fought and won a war together and he had gone on to pursue a career in the shoe business.

The aircraft had soldiered on in the RAF and after a commercial career ended its life as a Florida-based flying Rentokil exterminator. The number of authentic documents found with the help of people in the United Kingdom and United States regarding this particular aircraft is most amazing.

The Wings of Liberation Museum in Best is extremely proud of this well-documented war veteran. It is unlikely that the museum will ever again find an aircraft that has closer ties to the liberation of Brabant than this particular aircraft. It probably even flew over the museum's present location many times, as this complex is very close to Eindhoven airport, which was used by the Allies as an advanced military airfield in the late summer of 1944.

Museum visitors can sit in the pilot seat and view the memorabilia, the wartime documents, and Claude Bobilya's authentic case; a lucky twist of fate has reunited them again after sixty-six years. This combination, along with the WWII photos and footage shown on monitors, further enriches the total picture. It is a moving insight into what happened out there in the fields of Brabant in 1944 and 1945 in the *Grande Finale* of a heroic war effort fought by young men just out of their teens.

Their efforts deserve a fitting monument, and we feel proud to have made a small contribution to making this museum's collection more complete for all the visitors who come to try to comprehend the impact of the apocalyptic nightmare that engulfed the world all those years ago.

SAVING A WARBIRD

One day, back in 2010, the museum in Best received a remarkable request for the hiring of their "Arlon" Dakota (dubbed the L-4) for use in a musical show called "Soldier of Orange."

A role had been created for the Dakota in the musical, for which an authentic hangar was converted into a theater on the old Naval Air Base at Valkenburg, fifteen kilometers north of The Hague. Every day, 1,100 spectators take their seats in a huge 180-degree revolving auditorium, and in the final act the platform turns to face the hangar doors, which slide open during the final act. The stunned audience is given a wide view of the outdoor platform out front. The Dakota then comes taxiing in with its engines running and stops right in front of the open doors. The Dutch Queen Wilhelmina sets her feet on liberated soil for the first time in five years after the German capitulation. This magnificent reenactment of the return of the Royal Family is played out under the rumbling roar of the two aero engines. Or rather, the wheels and the props are driven by a hydraulic compressor pump, but with the theater's Sensurround audio system at full blast you can hardly see, feel, or hear the difference. The musical is now running in its fourth year and has broken all box records in the Netherlands, having already attracted well over one-and-half million visitors.

But behind the scenes, an incident took place that would eventually cost the L-4 its planned starring role in this ingenious and novel production. During the transport

My first very own C-47, here standing proudly on its pylons alongside the motorway from Brussels to Luxembourg. It was the gate guard/road sign for the "Ardennes Offensive" Victory Memorial Museum near Arlon. Though probably seen by millions of tourists over the years on their way to the south, the museum closed down in 1998. The plane remained on outdoor display and was finally bought by the "Wings of Liberation" Museum in Best, Holland.

of the plane by road from the Museum to the Theatre Hangar in September 2010, it was decided to leave the fuselage and central wing section of the aircraft assembled in one piece—a decision that would ultimately prove fatal.

The dimensions of the load surpassed six meters in width and so required special arrangements and supervised transport at night as an "exceptional convoy." The route from Eindhoven to Valkenburg, over 100 miles, was well researched and planned to ensure a safe passage under and over bridges, through tunnels, and over the four-lane highways.

After more than thirty years of flying in the rough and tough and then surviving exposure to the elements for another thirty years, an unfortunate accident brought an end to this airplane's dreams of a career as a musical star.

The C-47 L-4 was on its final approach over the highway to the airfield and about to negotiate the last fly-over bridge. Without realizing it, however, the convoy had driven itself into a kind of wedge that turned out to be a giant mousetrap. The bridge ahead over the two-lane stretch of highway was one meter narrower than was stated in the official road book (and anticipated by the convoy). Catastrophically, the left-hand engine nacelle, slung as an outrigger over the trailer's side, smashed into a concrete wall situated on the center line of the fly-over. Ironically, this was a WWII

German-made concrete obstacle of "*Atlantik Wal*" quality stubbornly unwilling to give one single inch of leeway to the approaching Dakota, as if in a final and futile act of revenge aimed at stopping the advancing Allied armies.

The driver, unaware of the imminent crash, must have felt a sudden braking force and, with his nose now pressed up to the windscreen, heard a terrible cracking sound as the truck shrieked to a halt. The valuable vintage cargo on the trailer behind his truck was mangled in a matter of seconds. The airframe's backbone was broken and damaged beyond repair.

But the show must go on, and an instant replacement was arranged for the musical by hiring another Dakota from the Aviodrome Museum in Lelystad.

Overnight, the L-4 had gone from expectant musical star to crippled orphan, as after this cruel twist of fate nobody wanted her anymore. So, for the time being, she was dumped on the grass of the parking lot adjacent to the musical's theater hangar and lay there in agony for three more years, silently awaiting her fate.

But, as the saying goes, old soldiers never die, and as the musical became a mega-success the hoards of visitors who arrived in cars and coaches were quick to spot this wreck as they approached the theater. It soon became the ultimate photo opportunity for selfies and family pictures. The L-4's soul was revived and signs were placed around the wreck with text referring to the history of this aircraft and its sad end.

In early 2013 the museum owner decided to sell the derelict Dakota, as the insurance money did not cover a full restoration job. The wreck was put up for sale and

The Arlon Dakota arrived in Best in 2002 and became their second C-47 on display. In 2010, the aircraft was rented out for the musical "Soldaat van Oranje" in which L-4 was pencilled in to star in this innovative musical extravaganza. The show attracted almost 1.5 million spectators in four years, the most successful theater production in Holland of all time.

(c) PF

Unfortunately, on the road to the Musical hangar, disaster struck at the very last flyover/viaduct. Center sections on the flyover were actually three feet narrower than had been recorded in the files. The ensuing crash sheared the central wing section from the fuselage when the outrigger port engine hit the wartime-era concrete separation, a WWII built obstacle of reputed "Atlantik Wal" quality.

I immediately decided to buy it. (For more information and photographs see Avionart's Newsletter: www.avionart.com/newsletters/062013-spring-update/index.html, and part II of that operation, www.avionart.com/newsletters/122013-saving%20a%20warbird%20part%202/.)

With no client or budget forthcoming for an expensive overhaul, we deemed it best to take the plane apart and split her up into pieces so that it could live on in better conditions rather than rotting away in a muddy field only half a mile from the North Sea. In September 2013 we decided to disassemble the wreck, as the salty air had started to seriously corrode the airframe's skin plating. During the "Dakota Doomsday Party," I invited all my friends to come over with their wartime Harleys, jeeps, command cars, and trucks for a farewell ceremony. This was to be the last time the L-4 would be reunited with its contemporary brothers in arms. It was all filmed and photographed for posterity by a crew under the direction of Suzanne van Leendert for her TV production "Broken Dreams" about the life of this L-4 Dakota from 1944 to 2014.

The next day we started with a team of eight aficionados on the tricky job of cutting this war bird apart into little bits and pieces. In the process, the cockpit was carefully separated from the fuselage and loaded for transport to the Flight Simulator

With my long-time friends Fritz and Bally, I drove out to see the C-47 L-4 that had been discarded in a remote corner of the parking lot near the Musical hangar after the accident. Her role as a musical star was taken over by a fresher-looking C-47. Deleted from any publicity in her silent agony, I decided to buy her in 2013 and grant her a better ending than the awful cutting torch.

manufacturer MPS in Utrecht (www.flymps.aero). This innovative builder of professional Airbus and Boeing flight simulators uses real cockpits, cut from written-off jetliners, with upgraded avionics and layouts to the latest standards. They have plans to build the world's first certified DC-3 flight trainer/simulator, incorporating our Dakota L-4 cockpit as the platform.

The commercial exploitation of that unique virtual flying machine DC-3T (T for Training) will be in the hands of the DDA (Dutch Dakota Association) for the initial training of new pilots who want to learn how to fly this legendary war relic. Certified DC-3 pilots will eventually be able to earn their flight hours on this flight simulator and the DDA will save fuel and precious vintage engine running time thanks to this simulator c.q. virtual flight instruction system.

For the purposes of certification, the cockpit interior will be an exact copy of the PH-PBA, with a similar instrument layout and realistic feel from the controls. The huge 270-degree hemispherical IMAX-like screen positioned three meters in front of the cockpit provides for an amazing flight experience with state-of-the-art projection

As the plane's new owners, we were approached by a production company that wanted to hire the fuselage for a film being shot in the Ardennes. The scene in question featured a crashed C-47 near Bastogne. This would prove to be the L-4's final act as a complete airframe.

In September 2013, I organized a Dakota Doomsday Party to be held one day before final disassembly of the aircraft. We invited all our friends and they all arrived in their WWII transports—Jeeps, trucks, Harleys etc. for a farewell ceremony.

With great care, we broke the C-47 up into several pieces, all of which had been earmarked for display elsewhere. Only the badly corroded fuselage had to be cut up into panels. The cockpit remained fully intact.

techniques. As a result, the pilots fly with an awesome sense of roll, yaw, and pitch, while the cockpit remains on a fixed base. This makes the cost of this unique flight instruction wonder far more economical than the classic motion-based flight simulators with their complex hydraulic actuators.

By 2015 they should be in a position to announce the genesis of the first DC-3T. Or should it be the first TC-47? In any event, our L-4 cockpit will ultimately contribute to the simpler and less expensive training and instruction of current and future pilots and help keep the DC-3 alive and flying for many more years to come.

The tail section of the L-4 has gone to an interior decoration company. The center fuselage was in poor shape with most of its skin panels badly corroded and ruptured. The worst corroded pieces were removed and sent to the smelting ovens, while the rest of the fuselage was cut up into smaller panels. These will eventually be used for our company's aviation collectibles and designer aviation lounge tables and aviator desks.

The leftover scrap from our L-4 went to the smelter and has been recycled for the manufacturing of a limited series of wrist watches: the Dakota Flight Watch will be featuring an aluminum clockwork housing made from this iconic 1944 Douglas C-47 L-4. The authentic war relic watch will go on sale sometime in the near future. It will be produced and marketed by the company Aeromeister and will come with a certification plate made from the skin of the same aircraft.

The tail section was taken apart for display as a shop window decoration object, with the whole process being filmed for a TV documentary "Broken Dreams" about the history of this aircraft from her birth in the war and her military career to her commercial operations and, finally, the end of this war bird in one piece.

Not quite the end of the story. The L-4 cockpit will live on for many more years in a new role. It has since been converted into the world's first certified DC-3 flight simulator for the training/instruction of DC-3 pilots. The cockpit will become a copy of the DDA's Dakota PH-PBA with similar instrumentation and flight control inputs and a huge IMAX-like hemispherical projection screen in front.

FRANCE

The Douglas C-47/Dakota was already a highly successful aircraft before World War II, but during that war its star rose to almost mythical proportions and its manufacturing volume exploded to well over 10,000 aircraft, all made in the United States. The same happened with two other vehicles: the Harley Davidson WL "Liberator" 750 cc motorcycle (over 65,000 made of the WLA [USA], the WLC [Canada], and the WLR [Russia]) and the Willys Jeep (360,000 built during World War II, also involving many other licensed manufacturers). All three

Every year, in the first week of June, our Harley Club visits Normandy for the D-Day festivities. With the "Atlantik Wal" bunkers still largely intact along the coastline, this region is the largest and most mesmerizing open air war museum in the world. A 60-mile stretch of "wow" experiences.

transports continued in military operations for many more years after 1945, but the massive surplus stocks of the Dakota, Harley Liberator, and Jeep also began a new career after World War II as civilian transports. They all merit the badge "Icon of Victory," and each one made a lasting impression on me.

My father drove a Willys Jeep for years and as a kid I spent many hours with him driving down the sparse jungle roads of eastern Borneo around our settlements to inspect the scattered oil wells, pipelines, and derricks. We flew out many times over the jungle and the archipelago in the Dakota. During one holiday in the early 1950s in Bandung (Eastern Java), I was standing in a busy street with my father when I heard a sound approaching from afar like rolling thunder. I saw a man in military uniform riding in my direction on an olive green motorcycle, a big machine on two wheels the likes of which I had never seen before. Its eccentric appearance and sound frightened me a little (after all I was only 6 at the time) but my dad reassured me and said, "Look at that! That's a Harley Davidson motorcycle."

Rajlovac Airfield in Bosnia. This derelict C-47 once housed the "Dakota Club," a bar for NATO military forces stationed in war-torn Yugoslavia in the late 1990's. It turned out to be the legendary SNAFU Special of D-Day fame. The Dakota Club had probably saved the aircraft from the scrapheap. Over 250 bullet holes were found in the fuselage when she was being dismantled and transported to France in 2008.

Original wartime photo of the same C-47/Dakota flying for the 9th USAAF with pilot James P. Harper in the cockpit, June 1944

Same aircraft, this time with the Dakota Hunter in the cockpit, June 2014. Seventy years later, the aircraft has been restored "as new" and is back where she flew herself into history. A true war hero that has participated in all major war operations until May 1945.

That ten-second encounter was to remain imprinted forever on my mind; the last one of my three "glorious transports" had just come into my life.

My dreams of and affection for that bike were born out there in that Borneo jungle and then carefully fostered for the next decade at the Jesuit High School in Holland. My passion materialized for the first time when I turned eighteen. While all my friends were busy buying cars, I went out and bought my first Harley Davidson WL750cc flathead in Rotterdam. The car would wait; the Harley came first.

Without a motorcycle license, I proudly drove my iron horse home straight after buying it. Leaving the Harley behind and waiting until I got my license was not an option; you do not mess around with serious passions.

And even at this early stage in my life, the strong bond I felt with those iconic military war machines and their histories was already starting to forge friendships that would last for a lifetime.

It was in 2004 that I made my first trip to the D-Day commemoration festivities in Normandy. It was the 60th anniversary of the Longest Day and I made an unforgettable journey with two friends on our Harleys around the five famous landing beaches on that awesome Channel shore. It was so impressive that we decided to go back every year on D-Day, as a kind of pilgrimage. This year, 2014, we rode out there again for the 70th anniversary of the mightiest military invasion operation in history with ten friends on our Harleys, a Willys Jeep, and a Dodge Command Car.

During the 2009 Normandy D-Day tour, we drove to a museum in Merville-Franceville, just east of Caen, called the Batterie de Merville Museum, that housed long-range guns installed by the Germans as part of the Atlantic Wall to ward off a possible naval invasion (with 4 x 100 mm guns the battery had a firing range of ten kilometers!).

The Allied forces were well aware of the deadly threat those guns posed to the fleet that was set to sail on June 6, 1944. In order to knock out the guns before they could do any harm, the British sent over a fleet of 40 Dakotas with 600 paratroopers from the 9th Battalion of the Parachute Regiment who were assigned the task of neutralizing the Merville guns. Only 150 paratroopers made it to the final assault, led by Lieutenant Colonel Terence Otway. The rest had been dropped too far away from the target. That airborne operation almost ended in disaster, but with a heroic surprise attack the British were able to prevent the batteries from playing havoc with the approaching fleet at Sword Beach during the first day of the invasion.

For more details view www.batterie-merville.com/the-museum/?lang=en

In the open field where the bunkers are still to be found, just outside the village, the director of the museum and mayor of the town, Olivier Paz, wanted to add a more intriguing war display to his museum's collection. They are in fierce and constant competition with over twenty other war museums in an area that stretches from Merville on the easternmost side to Sainte-Mere-Eglise, 100 kilometers away on the western border of the Normandy invasion theater.

This area is by far the largest open-air war museum in the world, with many of the Invasion and Atlantic Wall installations still intact and accessible to the public. The war scene varies from huge bunkers with rusty guns inside to the artificial harbor

We first visited the "Batteries de Merville" Museum in France in 2009, attracted by the newly featured C-47 Snafu Special, only to find out that the yoke was missing from the cockpit. Considering the determined looks of my friends, that was not be accepted for long, so we decided on the spot to do something about it.

In 2010, we came back in style, this time with a present for the mayor of Merville and his museum staff. We arrived with the Dakota yoke strapped to the front bumper of a Willys Jeep and handed this souvenir, from a Colombian DC-3, over to the SNAFU Team in a "ceremonie protocollaire," a la Francaise with Champagne.

installations (Mulberries) at Arromanches, which lie silently in a huge arc out in the sea. The famed landing beaches, the Pointe du Hoc (from the movie *The Longest Day*) and the military cemeteries all contribute to a most impressive commemoration of the military operation that heralded the end of the Third Reich.

Olivier Paz and his team came up with the idea of snaring a legendary Dakota that stood hidden in Sarajevo, Bosnia. In every aspect this aircraft was an outstanding catch, possibly the very last Dakota with a long European war history to be found anywhere in Europe. Its career started before the Normandy invasion in the United Kingdom with the

The D-Day festivities are a week-long re-enactment show, both for visitors from abroad and for the French population. Thousands of people walk around in full battle dress. In between all these uniforms, two men came riding in dressed as members of the Resistance—French civilians who joined the Allies in their fight against the retreating German forces.

9th US Army Air Force. The aircraft participated in the paratrooper droppings with the 101st Airborne Division on D-day, June 6, 1944, south of Sainte-Mere-Eglise. Over the following months she was engaged in Para operations over the Provence (in the southeast of France where a smaller scale invasion took place), Operation Market Garden at the Arnhem bridges, the Battle of Bastogne, and the Rhine drops in Germany, until the Reich collapsed in May 1945.

This forgotten aircraft stood at a NATO occupied military airport in Sarajevo as an unsung hero, was in use as a club for the Helicopter pilots and had been machine-gunned during the war that raged across the Balkans in the early 1990s. The purchase of the Dakota from that site in that war-torn country must have been a true wonder of patience, persistence, and sheer luck, and a little

Near Utah Beach one can find the famous Airborne Museum in Sainte-Mere-Eglise. They have C-47s on display inside and a "crashed" Dakota displayed outside. While walking around, I found a wing navigation light protruding from the soil right next to this wheel. After getting permission, we found a pair of shovels and it wasn't long before an intact wingtip emerged from under the ground. What a find.

power play from the higher (governmental or military) authorities. From the wartime documents and photos that emerged about this aircraft, a special name and painted logo stood out that had featured as nose art on the plane in the late WWII operations. The name was "SNAFU Special," which stands for "Situation Normal: All Fouled Up" (the F for "Fouled" being the decent version). It made this aircraft even more special. Such a name was simply perfect for a profiling job with that iconic SNAFU name and fabulous nose art.

Olivier Paz is an amiable Frenchman. He is the town's mayor, but he also owns a restaurant in town and is a good entrepreneur who took on the responsibility for snaring this amazing aircraft. The plane, the last of the coveted Normandy Icon Dakotas, was tracked down by his people and brought over from Bosnia to his museum. Maybe one day I should take him aside and ask him how he did it, because he did a better job in Bosnia than I did in Madagascar or Honduras in my dealings with the military. What his team did with regard to the disassembly of the plane, the transport over road on deep-loader trailers (with no accidents!), and the reassembly and restoration work (including the patching up of over 250 bullet holes!) was a small miracle in itself. The work was nearly completed when I rode into town in early June 2009 with my group of wartime Harley and Jeep riders, attracted by this newly acquired Dakota that had been dubbed the "Snafu Special."

I told Olivier about my work as the Dakota Hunter. He showed me around, proud yet very hospitable, and we ended up in the cockpit of that illustrious C-47. We noticed something that apparently had been worrying him for some time, almost to the point of irritation. The yoke was missing. Bad news, as this rendered the nearly immaculate aircraft incomplete. But, *quelle chance*, on my second Colombian trip in the Amazon jungle I had found a narcotics-trafficking Dakota. By sheer coincidence, the yoke had popped up among the rubbish and drawn my interest as a souvenir of my last trip to Colombia. I told Olivier about my adventures and said that I could reserve the yoke for his Dakota as soon as it arrived in Holland by sea container some time in the next twelve months or so.

My reward was champagne all round for the gang from Holland. Olivier was simply euphoric that, unexpectedly, the nasty little stone in his shoe had been removed by a cowboy who, out of the blue, had arrived in a convoy of Harleys and Jeeps to save the day.

After dis assembly of the crippled C-47 L-4 from Valkenburg. we had some scrap material left that was smelted and molded into ingots. From this 70 years old aluminium of the legendary Dakota, Aeromeister Company will make a high quality limited series of the 'Dakota Chrono' Watch with certificate on a genuine piece of the C-47 L-4 skin. The pre -production model can be seen here, soon available for ordering via my web shop at www.dc3-dakotahunter.com

Dressed in our worn-out military jackets, some of the dignitaries must have seriously doubted whether we were honest in our intentions or maybe even just selling crap for the sake of a free lunch: Was this a yoke or a joke? That was the question and I guess they all thought they knew the answer. But, much to their surprise, when we rode out to Normandy again the next year, we came bearing a little present: the promised Dakota yoke had arrived from Colombia just a few weeks prior to our trip.

We arranged to meet Olivier at the museum in the company of all the local dignitaries, who were now our best friends, of course. The yoke was strapped onto the front bumper of my friend's 1943 Willys Jeep and, in a parade with all the Harleys, we rode from Bayeux to Merville to make our delivery in style. Both yoke and Jeep came in exactly the same military olive green color. The mayor, his staff, and the local press were all there for another typical French *ceremonie protocollaire*.

The handover of the yoke had to be done with speeches and champagne, of course. That is the French way of doing things and we weren't complaining. We took

At the former Naval Air Base Valkenburg (NL) a spectacular musical show started in Sept. 2010. Now four years later, the show is a most successful theater production with over 1.5 million visitors so far.
Inside an old hangar, a huge rotating auditorium with 1100 seats switches back and forth to multiple stages.

In the final act, the auditorium is rotated towards the hangar doors that slide open, giving the spectators a wide view of the platform. The sound of piston engines is heard as a genuine DC-3 comes taxiing in to the open front doors, re-enacting the return of the Queen to Holland in 1945 in this RAF Dakota.

This ex-Air Atlantique aircraft G-AMCA (see page 49) was based in Coventry (UK). In 2000, the aircraft had its engines dismantled. ready for the scrapper, but in an amazing twist of fate, she made a come back as a musical star in her role as "Icon of Victory".

In Dec. 2013, a typhoon tore corrugated roof plating from the Theater Hangar. They slammed into the tail of the musical's Dakota that stood parked next to the hangar. With this sorry sight, the producer had no other choice than to cancel the show. They called us for help and by sheer coincidence we had a rudder and one LH elevator in our depot for direct replacement. The show must go on, and it did after two days!

In the summer of 2014, Jessy repaired all other flight control surfaces as rudder, elevators and aileron, now clad with aluminium sheets. All damaged parts have been replaced by authentic Douglas DC-3 components. The restoration should give the aircraft again the status of a major public war monument, featuring in a show attended by over two million spectators.

the yoke into the SNAFU cockpit and the mechanics could hardly wait to start mounting it, as all of them had experienced the absence of that crucial cockpit piece as a painful feeling of incompleteness. Meanwhile, Olivier invited me and the whole gang for lunch in his restaurant on the boulevard of that nice little coastal town of Merville. Having lunch in the sun with twenty people on a terrace overlooking the Normandy beach and drinking a (free) glass of champagne or two—I can think of worse places to be. For a brief moment the Dakota Hunter turned into a fat cat, far away from the Amazon, Alaska, and the Andes. But Olivier hasn't heard the last of me yet. In exchange for my present, he promised to dig around among his Balkan contacts and arrange the delivery of a pair of wingtips to me.

SAINTE-MÈRE-ÉGLISE

The next day, we rode out to another museum that had caught my eye: the Airborne Museum in Sainte-Mère-Église near Utah Beach on the westernmost side. This little town was one of the first French villages to be liberated by American troops in the early morning of June 6, 1944.

Massive C-47 operations with Para drops of the US 82nd Airborne Division had taken place here. One of the paratroopers, John Steele, had landed in the middle of town, with his parachute getting hooked on the church tower. While hanging there, he was shot at by German snipers and hit in the foot, but he managed to survive by pretending to be dead. The now famous church is still a hangout, but now for Veterans and other D-Day visitors that come from all over Europe, the United States, and Canada.

Right next to that church is the Airborne Museum, with an immaculate C-47 on display inside. In 2010 they added an open-air exhibit in the field behind the museum and dug in a Dakota airframe, reenacting the scene of a crash after an emergency landing. As I walked around that staged crash site, I spotted a piece of aluminum that

The D-Day invasion was an operation of humongous proportions, as never seen before in history. The photo at left gives a good impression of the awesome Military & Naval deployment on Omaha Beach at the end of 6 June 1944. More than 1000 C-47's dropped 13.100 American and British paratroops and towed 517 Gliders that transported another 4000 troops. The 'Dakota Air Bridge' transferred 17.000 airborne soldiers over the channel on that 'Longest Day' and had a more than instrumental role in the final Victory.

I would have recognized from miles away, half hidden in the ground. It was the navigation light mount of a wingtip. Wow, maybe junk to them but very precious metal to me. I figured it was time for a serious chat with the *responsable*.

I went to see the museum director, introduced myself, and asked him if that piece of "trash" was maybe available for a purpose better than rotting away in the boggy ground. He obviously saw that I had a higher mission in my noble effort to save this damaged piece of metal from its staged burial. To my surprise, I was allowed to dig up that piece of wingtip, which I imagined was probably two to three feet in length, max. I started with a friend on the job using only a hand shovel. It was like the proverbial iceberg: only the tip protruded as a visible part, the rest was hidden underground. It took us two hours to dig a hole six to seven feet deep, but we were rewarded with an almost complete wingtip with only minor skin damage. This was definitely my lucky day—digging up a free wingtip only 800 kilometers from home. It normally takes a lot more effort in much more remote parts of the world to get the same result.

THE MOST IMPRESSIVE SALUTE EVER SEEN

I have seen many war museums in many places all over the world. From the very impressive Pima Air Museum in Tucson, Arizona, to the awesome exhibit at the Imperial War Museum in Duxford, Cambridge. And, more recently, the dazzling displays at the National Museum of the US Air Force in Dayton, Ohio. They are engraved in my memory as the best aviation museums in the world, but I still have a long way to go before I have visited all of the hundreds of other museums. Big or small, I love them all, both to visit and occasionally, I hope, to do some business with.

Finally, on the evening of June 6, 2014, we were standing again, as we do every year, near the Normandy American Cemetery and Memorial in Colleville-sur-mer on

The Normandy American War Cemetery & Memorial in Colleville-sur-mer is under guidance of the American Battle Monuments Commission (ABMC). The fields just next to Omaha beach carry almost 10.000 crucifixes for those who did not make it back home. Together with the impressive Ranger Monument at the legendary Pointe-du-Hoc cliff (photo at right), 8 miles to the west, they are the ABMC's most visited monuments outside the USA, receiving over one million visitors each year.

the cliffs overlooking the endless Omaha Beach right below us. This year, with so many presidents and royals present, there were more people in attendance than ever before.

As in previous years, at exactly 8:00 p.m. there was a three-minute silence in honor of the almost 10,000 US servicemen buried there. The sun set slowly on the horizon over a mirror-like sea in glorious hues of yellow, red, and blue. With nature's best light show as our backdrop, we were gathered together with tens of thousands of other people for the ceremony, all in perfect and respectful silence. Suddenly, out of the sky from far away an airplane flew toward us over the sea, silhouetted by the huge mellow yellow sun. It was a Dakota. She flew majestically over the scene, low and slow, in full camouflage battle dress with white striping over the wings and fuselage. All you could hear was the typical drone of its two radial aero engines. It sounded like the Last Post and all eyes were on this lone flying monument as she flew right over the endless rows of white crucifixes. After her first north-south flyby, she came back to do a west-east pass, as if marking out a crucifix in the air, this time even lower and slower than before. We stood there nailed to the ground, watching her in awe, and as she came over the central memorial she gently wiggled her wings in a farewell to all the soldiers who had not made it home from here. That flight was definitely the most impressive salute I have ever seen.

The Dakota forever. There will never be a replacement for this iconic plane.

Hans Wiesman, June 16, 2014

Normandy D-Day commemorations, 6 June 2014. The 70 YEARS event saw the arrival of 11 Dakota's in Normandy. Cherbourg Airport had not seen this many Dakotas together since the war! I had a unique opportunity to bring my two lifetime passions together in one picture: the Dakota and the Harley Davidson motorcycle next to each other on the Holy Battle Grounds of Normandy. (Photograph: Onno Wieringa)

Acknowledgements

A large number of people contributed to the development and completion of this book, and I would like to express my sincere appreciation and gratitude for all their assistance.

I would especially like to thank my sister, Corine Quaterman-Wiesman, from Vermont, USA, who acted as my coach and editor for the first twenty-four months. It was thanks to her persistence that I managed to carry on with the work, especially at times when I had lost all perspective and motivation.

I would also like to thank my Dutch publisher, Jitske Kingma, who from our very first meeting expressed her confidence in the concept of this book. She also insisted that I pursue the translation of the manuscript into other languages.

For the English version I must give special credit and thanks to my friend, translator, and editor, Danny Guinan, who worked on the manuscript with all of his enthusiasm and linguistic talents.

I would like to express my appreciation to Erica Sluijters, who gave me full support and coffee during the long hours of writing and research.

Below is a list of photographers, outfitters, and data suppliers to whom I also owe gratitude for the use of their works . Most of them have become friends over the years we have worked together in often awkward situations:

Julie le Bolzer, France
Bart Nopper, The Netherlands
Michael Prophet, The Netherlands
Javier Franco Topper, Colombia
Rico Besserdich, Germany
Axel Ebermann, United States
Frans Lemmens, The Netherlands
Laurent Kerbrat, France
Ruud Duk, The Netherlands
Brendan Odell, South Africa
Thomas Roeher, Germany
Sebastian Correa, Colombia
Alex Waning, The Netherlands
Daniry, Madagascar
Dolph and Suzanne Bode, The Netherlands, owners of the Plesman photo collection
Ron Goossens, Frank Uyt den Boogaard, the PME photo collection

Hjarald Agnes, The Netherlands, for the front cover photo
Onno Wieringa, The Netherlands
Pablo Andres Ortega, Colombia
Ron & Chris Mak, The Netherlands
Dirk Septer, USA
www.pararesearchteam.com, The Netherlands

I received valuable creative input, relevant historical information, and technical support from:
Bart Nopper, The Netherlands
Michael Prophct, The Netherlands
Roland Korst and his team at the Wings of Liberation Museum, Best, The Netherlands
Hans Combee, Musée Batteries de Merville, Normandy, France
Paul Warren Wilson, The Catalina Society, Duxford, England
Brendan Odell, South Africa
Roy Blewett, England
Ruud Leeuw, The Netherlands
Kees Vos, Dutch Dakota Association, The Netherlands
Trev Morson, United States, DC-3 Hangar/douglasdc3.com
Dr. Luc Kwanten, China
David Moussou, the maps supplier

Dakota Blues?
I have seen so many Dakota's go down the drain over the past 25 years. Nevertheless, there are many new initiatives from private owners, foundations, museums and commercial companies that will make sure the DC-3 survives, be it as a Static Display or a Flying Monument. The type will definitely not go extinct within the next 30 years, i.e. there will be at least one left that will make a flight at 100 years of age. Dakota forever.